CHANGING CHANNELS

CHANGING CHANNELS

America in *TV Guide*

Glenn C. Altschuler
and
David I. Grossvogel

UNIVERSITY OF ILLINOIS PRESS
Urbana and Chicago

This book is printed on acid-free paper.

Library of Congress Cataloging-in-Publications Data

Altschuler, Glenn C.
  Changing channels : America in TV guide / Glenn C.
Altschuler and David I. Grossvogel.
    p. cm.
    Includes bibliographical references and index.
    ISBN 0-252-01779-X
    1. TV guide. 2. Television programs—United States—
Periodicals—History. 3. Television programs—United
States—Reviews—Periodicals—History. 4. Television
broadcasting—United States—History. 5. United States—
Popular culture. I. Grossvogel, David I., 1925– .
II. Title.
PN1992.3.U5A47 1992
791.45′75′097305—dc20   91-18095
                                                       CIP

Contents

Acknowledgments

This book draws on the thousands of articles published by *TV Guide* in the last four decades. Marie Gast and the staff of the Department of Maps, Microtexts, and Newspapers at Cornell University were helpful and courteous as they provided us with microfilm copies of the magazine and the magnifying tools needed to read them.

Although Roger Wood and Joe Robinowitz maintained that *TV Guide* "speaks for itself" and declined to allow us to examine editorial files, they graciously granted us permission to quote from the articles under the magazine's copyright. We are also grateful to them for allowing us to use the *TV Guide* logo in our cover design. We also thank Patrick Buchanan for permission to quote from his column in *TV Guide*.

We have benefited greatly from conversations and correspondence with dozens of the men and women who wrote and edited the magazine. Some are quoted in these pages; others preferred anonymity. Without their keen insights we would not have been able to understand how *TV Guide* was put together. Edith Efron, Dick Hobson, Dan Jenkins, Martin Lewis, Robert MacKenzie, William Marsano, Merrill Panitt, Leslie Raddatz, Carolyn See, David Sendler, Robert Smith, and Dwight Whitney were particularly helpful and gracious with their time, their memories, and their intelligence. Each of them, we fear, will be miffed by something in this book, but we know they share our sense that *TV Guide* deserves to be taken seriously as an artifact of American popular culture.

Three friends, Stuart Blumin, Anthony Caputi, and Joel Silbey, read the manuscript with the kind of useful malevolence that characterizes academics. If errors remain in the book, we invite them to share the blame. We also thank two friends, Todd Bernstein and Jim Lansing, who handled the logistics of several trips to Philadelphia.

Marilyn Hine processed our words with prompt efficiency and unfailing good humor, even though she was working for two bosses with different, but equally neurotic, temperaments.

Introduction

With work and sleep as its principal competitors, television takes the time of most Americans. The small screen now serves as the main source of entertainment and information about current events, displacing radio, movies, and newspapers. For better or worse, as a "tube of plenty" or as a "vast wasteland," television reinforces, challenges, and alters the attitudes of Americans who watch it (at an average six hours a day). It may be only a slight exaggeration to assert, as one writer recently has, that the United States is now "one nation under television."

In the last forty years, in thousands of articles and books, television has been defended and damned, or simply discussed. Virtually no attention has been paid, however, to an extraordinarily pervasive TV-related medium, the magazine simply and appropriately titled *TV Guide*. Launched in 1953, *TV Guide* has been a phenomenal success story. For decades it has had a greater circulation than any magazine in the United States, leading as well in advertising revenue. At its peak, with almost twenty million copies reaching the living rooms of North America each week, *TV Guide* was read by well over forty million Americans—truly the mass medium's mass medium voice.

In this book we attempt to take *TV Guide* seriously as a cultural mediator. As the writers in the magazine engaged and entertained readers, they also addressed values, events, and experiences that mattered to them. At the most basic level *TV Guide* helped Americans define the possibilities and limitations of television and understand the entertainment industry as a business and an art form. In doing so, inevitably it has provided information and analysis of political issues and cultural trends, assessing them as depicted on television and experienced in "the real world." *TV Guide* texts, we recognize, were by no means unambiguous, nor were they understood by every reader in the same way.

Nevertheless, although many possible readings of *TV Guide* may well exist, they are neither infinite nor arbitrary: *TV Guide,* we argue, had a voice. To better listen to that voice we supplemented our close reading of every article in the magazine with dozens of interviews with the people who wrote and edited it. We attempted, as well, to place the history of the magazine in the context of American history from the 1950s to the 1990s. Whether or not it is true, as one friendly critic claimed, that we know the magazine's content "better than anyone in all of Christendom," we are convinced that *TV Guide* was a medium with messages.

Most of our friends claim never to have soiled their hands or muddled their minds reading *TV Guide.* They know that the magazine provides up-to-date, comprehensive, accurate program listings in its utilitarian midsection, which is locally assembled, printed, and bound, and that it also covers television in a glossy national edition in "wraparound" form filled with articles and photographs—a magazine within a magazine. They intuit what Daniel Starch and Co. report to the executive staff of *TV Guide* year after year: that readers use the program listings, absorb the ads, and read the articles with regularity in percentages comparable to those who purchased more prestigious publications. (Staff members like to boast that *TV Guide* is read by more doctors than even the *Journal of the American Medical Association,* and analogous claims are made for lawyers, teachers, and other professionals.) Our friends acknowledge that *TV Guide* has a gigantic audience but dismiss it as a fan magazine because few of them really know its content. They have overlooked an important text of American popular culture.

Written by staff writers in bureaus based in New York, Hollywood, and Washington and by free-lancers around the country, *TV Guide* was the creation of two men, Walter Annenberg, founder and publisher until he sold the magazine in 1988, and Merrill Panitt, a man of many titles who was, in fact, editorial director, providing inspiration, direction, and continuity for more than a third of a century. Although the *TV Guide* empire was far-flung, final authority over every essay rested with the editors at *TV Guide* headquarters in Radnor, Pennsylvania, and with Annenberg and Panitt.

At the outset they made their magazine a booster for television, creating customers for themselves in the process (see chapter 1). Dependent on network programmers and publicity agents, the magazine did reach for the star-gazers. Annenberg and Panitt, however, wanted to be more than boosters. Fan magazines, they believed, usually peaked at a circulation of one or two million. Equally important, they were men with a mission, aspiring to authoritative coverage of the industry. While teaching readers/viewers that television was a business and reminding network executives that it was an art form, Annenberg and Panitt insisted that a medium for the masses did not have to be mediocre. "Dialsmanship" was their democratic theory: with the information provided by *TV Guide,* viewers would be free to choose, would make good choices, and would influence programming to the good. Determined not to dictate (to be "authoritative but not authoritarian"), *TV Guide*'s zeal often overwhelmed its caution in the early years of television, as the men in Radnor (all staff members there were men then) chafed at the chaff on TV and then distanced the magazine from the judgments they had made. In editorials Panitt pleaded with readers to give Shakespeare or the symphony a try and scolded them when they didn't, endorsed selectivity, and allowed *TV Guide*'s reviewers to massacre the mediocre (though he repudiated the review if the massacre had been too brutal). And he always found space for articles featuring National Educational Television programs (which later because the Public Broadcasting System, or PBS).

In the 1960s, *TV Guide* came into its own, with a substance and style self-consciously shaped in Radnor. In chapter 2 we examine a magazine that was more skeptical, cynical, and adversarial, yet ready to accept television for what it was, in retreat from its plan to empower viewers. *TV Guide* expected less of the medium and of those who watched it; editors and writers recognized that *readers* were amused by articles that denigrated the intelligence of *viewers.* (Indeed, in this way *TV Guide* assured readers that they were far above the average.) At the same time the magazine looked at celebrities with a jaundiced eye, seeking its journalistic spurs by exposing the dark side of Hollywood. To be authoritative and consistently interesting *TV Guide* turned critical. Puff pieces decreased, as did the number of staff members who had a predilection for them. *TV Guide* profiles strove to be serious. They contained no scandals. In a sense they were commentaries on the perils of success and the frailties of the human character.

Annenberg and Panitt never forgot that their magazine must have mass appeal, but they reached for a higher common denominator. If television could be dismissed as a "vast wasteland," readers needed reasons to respect the magazine that covered it. Without them, they might rely on the program listings in the newspapers. To raise the intellectual level of *TV Guide,* Panitt cut back the number of profiles of TV personalities. Instead, the magazine commissioned background articles on subjects such as Johann Sebastian Bach, *Huckleberry Finn,* and Theodore Roosevelt and enlisted a veritable Who's Who in American Letters to assess the medium, or anything with some connection to it. Alongside pieces on TV shows like "Hee Haw" and "Starsky and Hutch" appeared essays by William Saroyan, Lewis Mumford, Margaret Mead, Alfred Kazin, Arthur Schlesinger Jr., Louis Kronenberger, and John Updike, to name only a few. Among contributing politicians were John F. Kennedy and Ronald Reagan. And experts with less recognizable names were asked to write background articles as well.

Prestige pieces, it turned out, were widely read. Merrill Panitt had suspected all along that "quality" was good business: the more respectable the magazine, the easier it was to attract upscale advertisers. In any event, as long as circulation kept rising, no one questioned the presence of distinguished guest columnists or the literary quality present in the articles of free-lancer Richard Gehman or staff writers Dwight Whitney and Edith Efron, with their allusions to Shakespeare and Kafka and T. S. Eliot. In retrospect, the magazine does seem remarkable. Dick Hobson, a staff writer for *TV Guide* in the 1960s, now thinks: "This is . . . let-em-eat-cake. [Panitt] made 'em eat spinach whether they wanted to or not. He had the vast circulation and the vast success and he put in all this high-minded *Harper's* stuff because he wanted to. . . . So you have to hand it to the man; this [was] his achievement."

As far as we know, no one ever confused *TV Guide* with *Harper's*. With few exceptions, its articles were short and stayed close to the surface. But the magazine did analyze virtually all aspects of television, taking readers behind the scenes, interviewing executives as well as entertainers, assessing news and public affairs shows (while lobbying for more of them), and reviewing programs and delivering editorials on everything from loud commercials to violence during prime time. The editors tried to avoid the controversial or the unpopular but—significantly, in our view—did not always succeed. Moreover, in seeking the middle ground, *TV Guide* has revealed much about American society—and itself. Perhaps inevitably, the magazine became an arbiter of taste, defining a form of culture for millions of readers, discussing what language and how much cleavage were appropriate in the living room, and debating censorship. Frequently, of course, *TV Guide,* like all other forms of popular culture, ritualistically depicted and affirmed a view of the world held by most of its readers, creating a bond through shared belief. But articles did not simply reflect American values: even if they imagined they knew what most readers thought, editors and writers ordered and structured reality, consciously or less than consciously, as they saw it.

In chapter 3 we bring the magazine into the present, beginning with its prime in the 1970s and concluding with *TV Guide* under siege. With David Sendler, managing editor and editor in 1989, *TV Guide* increased coverage of news and cultural affairs. The magazine more frequently assessed the impact of television on American values. Sendler encouraged investigative journalism as well, from a look inside NBC's planning for the fall season to an exposé of bias in the CBS documentary "The Uncounted Enemy." When circulation peaked, however, and competitors appeared, *TV Guide* began to reach down to its readers with shorter, fluffier features. When Rupert Murdoch bought *TV Guide* in 1988, it had already taken a few steps back toward the fan magazine format. Murdoch sped *TV Guide* down this road, ending an interesting moment in mass circulation journalism.

In part 1, then, we try to catch *TV Guide* in the act of inventing itself as the mass medium's mass medium voice. In part 2, "America in *TV Guide*," we attempt to decode the political and cultural signals in the magazine. Embedded in articles on entertainment as well as news was a discernible point of view. Often dismissed as the mouthpiece for Walter Annenberg's conservative Republicanism, *TV Guide* actually was a complex, occasionally confused, and even self-contradictory publication.

Not surprisingly, *TV Guide* changed with the times, and the editors sometimes reversed field. With hundreds of men and women contributing articles, as well as big names whose bylines announced that they spoke only for themselves, *TV Guide* was bound to contain a spectrum of opinion. Indeed, the editors we interviewed denied that a consistent point of view can be gleaned from an examination of a magazine that was committed to vigorous and visible debate. Nonetheless, we believe that on many issues the magazine made a dominant perspective available to readers. For thirty-five years, a remarkably stable group of men reigned in Radnor. They selected the bureau chiefs and the staff writers; they approved every idea for a story and chose the writer who would cover it; and they evaluated and edited (or killed) every article. They wrote the editorial column "As We See It" week after week. And when they disagreed, Merrill Panitt decreed, confident that he knew the mind of Walter Annenberg. Writers knew, or learned, what was favored and what was forbidden—and what they could get away with. The editors, we hasten to add, were too principled, too truly journalistic, and too shrewd to tell writers what to write. But they didn't have to. If *TV Guide* contained a spectrum of opinion, it wasn't the whole spectrum, nor were articles evenly distributed along it. *TV Guide* was a medium with messages—and quite a few axioms to grind.

TV Guide's portrayal of blacks is the subject of chapter 4, where we attempt to explain why the magazine ignored racial themes and failed to publish profiles of black entertainers until the 1960s. When articles began to appear, they presented a remarkably consistent program for the achievement of equality. On this issue a consensus prevailed in the pages of *TV Guide*. Through the editors' choice of which black performers to criticize and which to praise, the magazine assessed the speed and direction of the civil rights movement, told readers what to think of Uncle Toms and black militants, and graded the television industry on its depiction of prejudice and its response to it.

Chapter 5 focuses on women in *TV Guide*. For decades the magazine printed profiles of successful, often aggressive, career women while trying to maintain that domesticity was the duty and destiny of the American female. We examine the contested terrain in these articles and trace *TV Guide*'s coverage of the women's movement. In this case, as in others, the mass magazine's caution came into conflict with the need to be topical and even trendy. As it had with race, *TV Guide* found a safe political stance by denouncing feminist extremists. *TV Guide* supported women's equality while denouncing women's liberation; while Merrill Panitt was relatively silent about civil rights in "As We See It," he was rabid about "red-hots" and "bra burners." We ask why, looking closely not only at *TV Guide*'s dominant voice but at the dissenters who were invited to contribute to the magazine. What did *TV Guide* deem essential to the women's movement? What was considered dangerous? And was there a time, as with civil rights, when victory could be declared?

In the final chapter, in search of the magazine's own politics, we examine *TV Guide*'s treatment of the news. The anomaly of quite a few liberal writers covering a notoriously liberal industry in a conservative magazine aimed at a mass audience produced some interesting and unexpected results on issues like McCarthyism and the war in Vietnam. The turmoil of the late sixties and early seventies, however, evoked a more overtly political response from *TV Guide*. Prodded by Richard Nixon's appeal to the "Silent Majority" and Spiro Agnew's assault on the media, the magazine slid to the right, for four years publishing "News Watch," a weekly conservative column tenuously connected to television. More important, *TV Guide* added its voice to those who charged that network news was not only distorted but biased, a tool of antiestablishment leftists. After the seventies *TV Guide* was never again quite the same, although its political outbursts became more episodic and more often ghettoized in a column labeled "Commentary," and the drumbeat against bias became more muffled.

If these chapters have not always found "America in *TV Guide*," they do locate a vision of it. Often consciously, sometimes in spite of itself, the magazine responded to the political and cultural concerns of the television age. As they structured reality for themselves, the editors and writers of *TV Guide,* seeking to persuade as well as inform and amuse, left their mark on millions of Americans and contributed an important chapter to the history of mass media.

Part 1

The Mass Medium's Mass Voice

1

The Founding, the Format, the Formula: 1953-60

On April 3, 1953, a small magazine, about 5 by 7½ inches, with Lucy and Desi's new baby on the cover, appeared on newsstands in ten cities across the United States. *TV Guide*, the publisher Walter Annenberg announced, would not only list every program to be aired locally each week but would aspire, through its national section, to increase viewers' enjoyment of the medium while "serving the entire television industry." The magazine, almost instantly, became an enormous success. Its first issue sold one and a half million copies. By 1960 its circulation exceeded seven million copies a week, with listings published in regional editions from coast to coast. By the late seventies it sat atop the TV set in twenty million homes, with ninety-four editions in the United States—the magazine with the largest circulation in publishing history and the highest return from advertising.

From the outset, in form, tone, and content *TV Guide* bore the stamp of Walter Hubert Annenberg, who had apparently inherited the business acumen of his father, Moses Annenberg, as well as his wealth and worldview. An immigrant Jew, Moses Annenberg fought his way to the top of the circulation department of William Randolph Hearst's publishing empire. In 1922 he came across a horse-racing tout sheet put together by a former sports editor of the *Chicago Tribune*. Spotting a sure thing, he bought *The Daily Racing Form* for the handsome price of $40,000 and set about to change it from a mom-and-pop operation to a national newspaper duplicated and distributed in New York, Chicago, Miami, Houston, Los Angeles, Seattle, and Toronto. Very soon the *Racing Form* became the indispensable aid to horseplayers, who paid a steep twenty-five cents for an authoritative list of the thoroughbreds in every race

at every track, the horses' previous placements, and an analysis of performances by trained observers who recorded track conditions and unusual circumstances during the race.

To speed up and expand publication and distribution, Moses Annenberg invested in the General News Bureau, a network of telephone
lines out of Chicago that relayed racing information to some thirty
thousand bookmakers throughout the land. By the early thirties, as he
fended off underworld figures and bought out competitors, Moses had
turned the General News Bureau into an empire stretching across the
United States, Canada, Mexico, and Cuba.

During these years Walter Annenberg was more playboy than publisher, shielded from the unsavory side of the business. He first attended
the Peddie School, a private academy in Hightstown, New Jersey, then
entered the Wharton School of the University of Pennsylvania. Walter
found the courses at Penn dull and left the school after only a year.
When he lost a small fortune in the stock market crash of 1929, Mo
took him into the business, giving him little more to do than countersign
checks. For a decade Walter was a young dandy with a passion for
clothes, cars, parties, and gambling who was often seen in the company
of Ethel Merman and Lillian Vernon, a Ziegfeld Follies beauty. In 1940,
however, Moses Annenberg was sentenced to prison for tax evasion.
Walter moved into his father's office in the *Philadelphia Inquirer* building
and assumed control of Triangle Publications, which included, besides
the *Inquirer,* the eminently lucrative *Racing Form* and a number of magazines. Two years later Moses died, and the playboy became a president.

Walter Annenberg proved adept at modernizing his holdings. Over
the years under his guidance, the *Racing Form* would become something
of a technological marvel as computers stored the avalanche of information on every thoroughbred and as new printing presses improved
the paper's productivity. This experience with the storage and retrieval
of large quantities of information inclined Annenberg to accept the
daunting logistical challenge of assembling program listings and plot
synopses for regional editions of *TV Guide* that would share a national
section "wraparound" stapled to each issue. The idea for *TV Guide*
came to Annenberg in 1952 when he read a magazine called *TV Digest,*
whose circulation in Philadelphia and its suburbs approached one
hundred thousand copies a week. Similar publications, he discovered,
existed in New York and Chicago. Annenberg envisioned a national
publication that would grow with the medium that was entering every
living room in America. He sketched his idea to his administrative aide
at Triangle, Merrill Panitt: "Staffs in each city. Emphasis on network
shows. Complicated publishing logistics that would have to be worked

out somehow. Advertising could be either national or local. We could sell magazine space the way radio and television sell time, with the advertiser buying as much coverage as he wanted."

In the next few weeks, according to Panitt, Annenberg personally spot-checked newsstands in New York, Chicago, and Philadelphia to confirm his notion that the plan for a national *TV Guide* was feasible. He buttonholed buyers of TV magazines and asked them to explain why they were paying for information that was available in the newspapers. Apparently the answers he heard satisfied him.

Although his staff at Triangle were skeptical at best, Annenberg gobbled up the New York *TV Guide,* the Philadelphia *TV Digest,* and the Chicago *TV Forecast* at rather high prices and without any attempt to bargain. He acquired the New York publication's ownership interest in a Washington-based magazine. In Boston, Minneapolis, and Iowa he contracted with publishers of TV magazines to buy the national section of *TV Guide* (Triangle soon purchased these franchised editions too). Very soon Annenberg had a virtual monopoly, and the operation was launched. Merrill Panitt was installed as national edition editor.

Of course, not even Walter Annenberg knew what he had wrought. Panitt never forgot the long hot summer of 1953 when circulation figures dropped and new editions in Rochester, Pittsburgh, Detroit, Cleveland, and San Francisco failed to arrest the slide. Advertising, too, was slow to come in, and the atmosphere was gloomy in the steamy offices atop a popcorn distributor on Philadelphia's South Broad Street.

But Annenberg's instincts had not failed him. In the fall, as viewers prepared for the premiere of a new season, *TV Guide*'s circulation began a steady climb. In 1957, when the magazine moved to what would be its permanent headquarters in Radnor, minutes away from Annenberg's Wynnewood, Pennsylvania, residence, Merrill Panitt ordered a factotum to roam the halls ringing a schoolyard bell with a resonant clapper to announce to the staff each jump in circulation of one hundred thousand. It did not take long for the bell to applaud itself into disrepair. For a quarter of a century, in numbers of readers and (more slowly) in advertising revenue, *TV Guide* grew and grew and grew.

Essentially two magazines rolled into one, the production of *TV Guide* was a complex, labor-intensive operation. In each region programmers worked with station managers who were eager to supply information about the weekly schedule of shows. Before computers came into use, a file card was kept with a plot summary of every film and every episode of a series to assist viewers during the summer season of reruns. Had they already seen an upcoming telecast? Only *TV Guide* customers could know for sure. For spectaculars or specials, programmers wrote lengthier descriptions. It was a thankless, exhausting job with a premium on accuracy, but, many staff members believe, the local "logs" sold the magazine.

The national edition, or "wraparound" (a term Merrill Panitt detested), was put together at headquarters in Radnor. Most story ideas originated there in a fifties-style modern industrial building that could have housed a corrugated box factory, complete with small ascetic cubicles, dentist-office decor, and, several staffers remember, "a horrible junior high school–like cafeteria." Panitt presided over editorial and assignment conferences, which resulted in orders to staff writers in the magazine's branch offices in New York and Hollywood (and later Washington, D.C.). Staff writers churned out articles and sent them to Radnor, where they were edited and given titles. In an early and comical foray into automation, Panitt used a sheet-metal board with magnets holding in place the layout for the current issue. At the touch of a switch, the board moved into place or out of sight. Unfortunately, one staffer recalled, "it made a deafening noise as it ground its way, until one day, it simply collapsed and was not used again." Everything else, however, worked well. After the national edition was printed at Triangle's Gravure Division Plant in Philadelphia, it was loaded on railroad cars, shipped around the country, and wrapped around the program logs. Because the process took about six weeks, articles could be neither timely nor topical. Annenberg and Panitt worked hard to reduce preparation time, but neither man worried; they had found their audience.

Anyone analyzing the phenomenal success of *TV Guide* must confront the question Merrill Panitt himself once asked: "Why do so many millions pay thirty cents each for TV listings when their daily newspapers carry free TV listings?" Panitt, not surprisingly, credits the national edition, which "covers—and criticizes—a medium that has become an important force in our lives. Because *TV Guide* concerns itself with whatever television touches, the magazine has not only broad and interesting subject matter, but subject matter that is vital to its readers." Readers often purchased the magazine on Wednesday, several days before the program listings started, a clear indication, Panitt believes, of a desire to read the feature articles.

Some staff members remained convinced that *TV Guide*'s size, format, and local logs ensured its success. It also attracted attention in its snug perch near the supermarket checkout counter. A secret to *TV Guide*'s circulation, according to the publisher James T. Quirk, was conformity to supermarket merchandising practices: "We offer food stores a 26-percent markup on a small-sized, fully returnable product that turns over fifty-two times a year. There's no price stamping, no use of shelf space. No one has to break open a case; our wholesalers service each store. We bill direct to chain headquarters." Housewives dug into their purses, the editors discovered, when they saw their favorite star on the cover. It was no accident, therefore, that throughout the fifties male performers graced the cover of *TV Guide* far more than their female counterparts did. On a wall in Radnor the editors charted single-copy sales to identify the most popular performers. A handy size to place atop the television set, the magazine was designed to withstand a week of household use. Unlike the newspaper, insists Dwight Whitney, long-time chief of the Hollywood Bureau, "it was unlikely that anyone in the house would use it to wrap the fish before throwing it out."

TV Guide benefited as well from the fear and scorn newspapers lavished on television, which was recognized as a serious competitor. More often than not, newspapers ignored the medium or gave it scant attention. By the time they started to provide more detailed information about TV programming, Panitt believes, millions of readers had acquired the *TV Guide* habit. And in the best tradition of *The Daily Racing Form*, the information was accurate and up-to-date, and the show summaries competent and complete. All in all, *TV Guide* provided a useful service in an attractive package.

Although the relative impact on circulation of the wraparound and the logs cannot be measured with precision, the editors were comforted by the knowledge that most articles were read by a high percentage of *TV Guide* customers. To be sure, the magazine did not generate a large mail response: in its heyday in the 1970s, Associate Editor William Marsano estimates, *TV Guide* never received more than a thousand letters a month (Ann Landers receives that number every single day). About the only thing that aroused the ire of readers was an error in the crossword puzzle. Nevertheless, those who bought the magazine read it (including the advertisements) in percentages that compared favorably with far more prestigious magazines, a fact confirmed year after year by the surveys of Daniel Starch and Co. In 1960, according to a study commissioned by the magazine, in 92 percent of *TV Guide* households, one or more adults regularly read articles in the national edition. Whether it attracted readers or retained them, the national edition was to become the jewel in *TV Guide*'s crown, the opportunity of Walter Annenberg and Merrill Panitt to amuse, inform, and instruct. For over a third of a century, *TV Guide* would try to understand and occasionally alter the values and tastes of Americans as it covered perhaps the most influential medium in the history of the world.

TV Guide settled quickly into a format that, with some changes in emphasis, would serve it well for decades. Most of the articles in the national edition were profiles of television stars. In the first issue, for example, readers learned about Lucille Ball (and her "Fifty-Million-Dollar Baby"), Walter Winchell, and Herb Shriner. A regular feature, "In the Cast," described a supporting player in a current series. Throughout the fifties experts described the technological innovations that were improving television: kinescope, videotape, color, and satellites. The magazine also regularly reviewed TV shows, and in "As We See It," Merrill Panitt, and occasionally Walter Annenberg himself, had an editorial platform from which to survey the medium, the television industry, and social and political trends related to them. Always aware that 60 percent of the its sales were at supermarkets, *TV Guide* reached out to "housewives" (the *TV Guide* staff could not imagine a woman at home who was not a housewife) with a food column of inexpensive, easy-to-prepare recipes that might be served in front of the set. Nor were the men ignored: in addition to a weekly sports column, *TV Guide* included what staffers came to call a P.G.P. (Pretty Girl Page) in virtually every issue, which featured a brief sketch and picture of a television starlet. For fifteen cents *TV Guide* offered something for everyone.

At first, *TV Guide*'s editors and staff writers relied heavily on network publicity offices for many of their story ideas and all their photos. In fact, throughout the 1950s articles and reviews appeared with initials but without bylines. In the West Coast office, which was located first in *The Daily Racing Form* building on Vermont Avenue, far down Sunset Boulevard, and then in the Taft Building at the corner of Hollywood and Vine, "it was pretty much amateur night," according to Dan Jenkins, who was bureau chief from 1953 to 1963. Jenkins had to please a penurious Panitt while ingratiating himself with press agents and performers. The results could be hilarious, as Jenkins's explanation of expenses incurred at a cocktail party given by Charles Wick in honor of the opera singer Mary Costa indicates. Florence Gruskin (a.k.a. Florence Halop), of the "Meet Millie" series, latched on to Jenkins

> like a leech and first thing I know, I am involved in a dinner group at the Interlude, a notorious clip joint and Florence is eating like death is due tomorrow, and I, the president of the Bank of England, am signing a Diner's Club tab to the tune of something like $23. And after retrieving my car from a parking lot which is operated like it's the hatcheck stand at the Stork Club and getting stuck for nightcaps at Frascatti's because old friend (not *my* old friend) Morty Jacobs is playing the piano there, I am in hock for the evening to the tune of $31.25. . . . Next time Mary Costa can goddam well go to Europe *without* my saying goodbye.

Although Jenkins signed his letter "Patsy," he understood, as did Panitt, that *TV Guide* depended on good will. Consequently, profile pieces puffed and fluffed. If stories had any point at all, they were in the form of simple parables or homilies. An Eddie Fisher "Close-Up" (Aug. 4, 1954) demonstrated that nice guys could finish first: As a young man, Eddie helped his father with a fruit and grocery wagon in South Philadelphia. A singer earning eighteen dollars a week, he was discovered at Grossinger's by Eddie Cantor. Unchanged by his millions, Fisher bought a home for his parents and apparently lived simply, despite his '54 Cadillac. Even in the fickle world of show business, *TV Guide* stories insisted, persistence paid off, as the story about John Guedel demonstrates. A toothpaste salesman in 1932, Guedel spent nights in cemeteries in a sleeping bag. His "116 rejection slips were followed by a long string of successes—two," a joke for which he was paid five dollars and a story that yielded fifteen dollars. After twelve no-thank-you's for more scripts, he decided studios would respect a newspaper columnist, so he wrote to syndicates in alphabetical order until he got a job, then sent his clippings to movie studios, and Hal Roach discovered him. Guedel wrote for "Our Gang" comedies and eventually struck it rich as the producer of the Groucho Marx quiz show, "You Bet Your Life" (July 21, 1956).

TV Guide deftly turned the defects of the stars into homilies as well. Flaws existed only in a transcended past, as a lesson to readers. Hugh O'Brian was no longer "overly aggressive in behalf of his career, disdainful of advice, single-minded or dogmatic." Aware that "Wyatt Earp" had an obligation to be dignified, O'Brian, as of September 1, 1956, no longer could be seen in the company of "innumerable starlets." Phil Silvers had also reformed. His haunts, *TV Guide* reported on August 17, 1957, had been "the track, the stage door, the all-night restaurants. Lovely women moved in and out of his life like commuters." He divorced his first wife, Jo Carroll Dennison, Miss America 1942, because she wanted a home and a home life: when she suggested a promenade in the park, he bolted for Belmont. But now with his new wife, Evelyn, and their baby, Tracey, the prodigal husband had come home to stay.

Only rarely, very rarely, did profiles probe or criticize. *TV Guide* in the fifties was reluctant to bite the hand of the industry that fed it. One exception came with the well-publicized war between Arthur Godfrey and Julius LaRosa. Although *TV Guide* did not break the story, the incident could not be ignored. A three-part article in the fall of 1956, "What Success Does to Stars," characterized the basic ingredients of success in show business as "ego, inferiority complex, and a feeling of insecurity" and asserted that stardom brought misery as well as money. The article then named a few names: LaRosa maneuvered the conversation with Godfrey so that he could announce his salary; Sinatra became so vain that he left his wife and children for Ava Gardner. The series concluded, somewhat contradictorily, that most performers adjusted "normally" to stardom. Like Gale Storm, they stayed married to the same person and remained active in their church (Oct. 27, Nov. 3, 10, 1956). More often than not, a *TV Guide* "exposé" righted a wronged performer. Jack Webb, "TV's Most Misunderstood Man," was not a hard-driving taskmaster who "shucked coat-tail riders" as he climbed to dictatorial control of his TV empire. Cameramen, soundmen, and actors attested to his loyalty and generosity. "Our business needs more" of these perfectionists, the March 23, 1957, article concluded. And the magazine must have delighted Liberace's agent when "Close-Up" (Sept. 18, 1954) denounced the "sharpshooters" who wondered why he wasn't married. Twice he's "come very close" the writer insisted, but the modest, accommodating piano prodigy would not tie the knot while his beloved mother, who clerked by day and scrubbed floors by night to help him, was still alive.

In a self-examination in 1960 (a book entitled *TV Guide: A Study in Depth*), the magazine explained the philosophy of its profiles. "Personality write-ups are factual, pleasant accounts which acquaint the reader with the stars without trying to disillusion him." Free of "gossip-column pickiness," *TV Guide*'s "mild" and "discreet" feature articles were not "mere press-agentry," but if they tried not to "rave," staff writers tried even harder (and more successfully) not to "attack" or even "peek." This "discretion," the magazine's managers maintained, convinced readers that *TV Guide* was an authentic, authoritative publication.

Although only an occasional presence in the editorial offices, Walter Annenberg kept a tight rein on the tone and content of *TV Guide*. He called Panitt with ideas for stories, complaints about typographical errors, or objections about a cover photograph. Wherever he is, Merrill Panitt once said, "Walter Annenberg is in charge. . . . Since he holds that an executive is on duty 24 hours a day, he feels free to call us at any time during those 24 hours. Well, not quite. He has never called me before 7:30 A.M. or after 12:30 A.M." Panitt always made sure the boss could reach him. Bill Marsano recalls a poignant image of the editor, with hat, coat, and gloves on, waiting at 5:29 in the office with his hand on the telephone for a last-minute call from the boss that never came.

Panitt had apparently learned from his days on the *Inquirer* that Annenberg publications reflected not only the conservative Republicanism of the owner but his pet projects and peeves as well. According to Walter Annenberg's biographer, John Cooney (*The Annenbergs*, 1982), Walter was a sensitive, thin-skinned man capable of ordering that

Walter was a sensitive, thin-skinned man capable of ordering that a prominent Philadelphia woman be referred to in the *Inquirer* society pages as "a Chestnut Hills housewife" or of banishing the Philadelphia Phillies for several weeks from his newspaper (except for scores and team standings) because the management refused to reschedule a game that conflicted with a charitable event. In *TV Guide* as well, Annenberg occasionally exercised an owner's prerogative. Panitt knew well what Annenberg "had said or felt on certain matters. When I ran across something he wouldn't like, I didn't run it." Although evidence is hard to come by, many staff members are convinced that he told Panitt to keep Imogene Coca, Sammy Davis, Jr., Zsa Zsa Gabor, and Dinah Shore out of his magazine. Annenberg's interventions, Panitt maintains, were few and far between. "I hope you'll put it in perspective," he told us. On other magazines, "it usually happens a lot more."

On at least one occasion, however, Annenberg intervened to kill a story. In December 1965, the Hollywood bureau chief, Dwight Whitney, informed Radnor that he would soon be ready with "a helluva piece" on the "interlocking companies, deals and business operations" of Sheldon Leonard and Danny Thomas, then atop the heap of TV production companies. When Leonard returned from a Christmas vacation in Mexico, Whitney promised to complete arrangements on a story that had been a top priority for months: "This is a real coup . . . unless they back down, which I do not expect Danny to do." To Whitney's astonishment, Radnor was not pleased; the story was aborted. Danny Thomas, Whitney later learned, lived near Annenberg's new estate in Palm Springs and had some claim on the Tamarisk Water Company, which Annenberg had recently acquired. Evidently the publisher did not want to risk antagonizing his neighbor. Whitney asked managing editor Alex Joseph to call and give him "the drift." Instead, Joseph sent a not very subtle memo: "There is nothing either awkward or embarrassing that we decide to kill the partnership story. In cases like this, we feel that someone in our management would look askance at the result. Generally, I, myself, don't know all the ramifications—often Merrill doesn't either."

Such cases were rare, and they were always mediated by Merrill Panitt. Fortunately Annenberg forgot even if he did not forgive, and feature articles could be published when his passion had cooled or his attention had been diverted. But Panitt never forgot who the boss was. Nevertheless, he was more than a good soldier. Beyond his ability to intuit Annenberg's orders, he shared the man's values—and his commitment to make *TV Guide* more than a fan magazine. If Annenberg gave birth to *TV Guide*, Panitt nursed it, raised it, brought it to maturity and power, and gave it a distinctive voice. Born in Hartford, Connecticut, in 1917, Panitt was a reporter for the United Press during the 1930s. During World War II, one staff writer told us, he came to Annenberg's attention with a column he wrote from the base at Fort Ord, signed Private Pan-ITT. In the late forties he worked for Triangle as radio-TV editor of the *Philadelphia Inquirer* and administrative aide for Annenberg, before he was tapped for the top post at *TV Guide*. Like most good editors, according to one staff member, he could be alternately "bluff with the presentation of the self-made man who knows what he's talking about and won't brook any disagreement" or resemble "a Norman Cousins look-alike . . . kind of tweedy and professorial." But no one disputed that "editorially, graphically, in every way . . . , *TV Guide* was his baby."

The Annenberg-Panitt baby grew to be an all-American child. According to Max Gunther, a veteran free-lancer, *TV Guide*'s kind of writer was solidly middle-class, with views

> you might hear expressed over backyard fences in any middle-income American suburb. We were middle-of-the-road conservatives. Not conservatives to the point of being stuffy [but conservatives in] an instinctive distrust of well-meaning liberalism, especially when it veered toward socialism. We didn't want big government intruding in our lives (including our TV screens) in pursuit of social goals, however laudable. We were also flag-waving patriots, often growing irritable when critics harped too long on the supposed inferiority of American vs. foreign TV. All typical middle-American views.

TV Guide rode the crest of the wave of optimism that spread over much of America in the fifties, with its affable golf-playing, Zane Grey–reading President Eisenhower, its praise of old-fashioned family values, and its vision of endlessly expanding prosperity. In its reviews and its editorials *TV Guide* endorsed the homilies of feature articles. "My Friend Flicka," the magazine fretted on April 14, 1956, tended too often "to be down-beat," as when some varmints nearly blinded the beautiful horse. Viewers "might be too young" for such themes. Fortunately the show's unfailingly happy resolutions and its sugarcoated morality ("You did what you thought was right, son, and that's the important thing"), reassured the reviewer. Similarly, "Tales of Wells Fargo" (May 4, 1957) was an old-fashioned western "with not a single psychological overtone, where killers did not suffer "some traumatic experience as children" but were simply "mean and ornery." "Maybe that is what makes it such a darn good series." At a time "when wise-cracking, brash and brassy blondes infect the air like locusts," wholesome Donna Reed, who acted like a mother should, was as welcome to *TV Guide* "as a late summer breeze through an Indiana hay field" (Feb. 14, 1959). The family that watched this show together might well stay together.

Violence, as we shall see, was a concern and a crusade for *TV Guide*. But in a good cause, the magazine was willing to countenance a little gunplay. "Hopalong Cassidy" (July 24, 1953) was clean and wholesome; it never used slang, and it avoided violence whenever possible. Even better, William Boyd borrowed the virtues of his character and lived frugally despite his millions. Best of all was "Dragnet" (Apr. 10, 1953), where Sgt. Joe Friday used "just the facts" to catch the crooks while teaching the public that "crime does not pay."

In one respect, however, Max Gunther was wrong: *TV Guide* was not only stuffy, it was downright prudish. In moral matters the magazine reflected the attitudes of the times. Sex, divorce, and alcoholism were not fit for public discussion. That the program notes of the fifties found enigmatic euphemisms for pregnant teenagers ("she has a problem with her high school graduation") is not surprising. *TV Guide* was scarcely the only magazine in the nation to capitalize on Lucy's baby without ever quite saying that America's favorite comedienne was "pregnant." But the persistence of *TV Guide* taboos well into the permissive sixties and seventies is testimony to the vigilance and vehemence of Messrs. Annenberg, Panitt and Co.

Booze was the bugaboo of Alex Joseph, a newspaperman turned curmudgeonly managing editor of *TV Guide*, second in command to Panitt. At lunch, Bill Marsano remembers, Joseph regaled "the innocent and transfixed editors" with terrible tales of demon rum, of the Best Reporter in the World undone by drink. Walter Annenberg, Joseph insisted, shared his view, and wanted not even an implied endorsement of alcohol. Imagine his response when the food columnist innocently decided to do a spread on summertime cocktails. The editors approved, and the piece was scheduled until Joseph "looked at his copy and gasped and turned purple and began fulminating—alcohol! Booze!" He killed the idea but compromised a bit because the photographs had already been paid for: "In the end the largest circulation magazine in the known universe spent three expensive pages telling the American public how to make a Shirley Temple."

According to Merrill Panitt, a mass circulation magazine must be conservative lest it offend some of its readers. *TV Guide* reached "a lot of churchgoers in Iowa and a lot of children"; it should err on the side of omission, always careful not to get ahead of the mores of the times— and perhaps to lag a bit behind. Panitt knew that in the 1950s a magazine could be banished from schools for a mild discussion of sex. *TV Guide*, in any event, wasn't "in the titillation business," and Panitt kept material out, he claims, even when it did not offend him personally. Panittt fought relentlessly against smut, real and imaginary. Virtually every writer, on staff or free-lance, ran afoul of him at one time or another. When Arnold Hano wrote a piece about Dinah Shore and suggested that she and Burt Reynolds might actually, on occasion, have slept together, he received a curt communication from Panitt: "Not in *TV Guide* does she." Apparently, Hano discovered, all anatomical references were excised from the magazine. When in 1973 Shirley Booth mentioned that she was so short "I am slowly sinking into my pelvis," Hano included the funny quote in his piece only to see it cut: "That one hurt." Dwight Whitney, the Hollywood bureau chief, should have known better when he tried in 1969 to slip in a quotation attributed to William Holden ("bring back the scrotum of an enemy to prove his manhood"). After the article made its way to Radnor, it seemed that Holden only wanted to "kill and mutilate an enemy." Whitney protested this "shameful bowdlerization," but, since he acknowledged the editor's power to decide whether language was "too strong for use in a family magazine," he was reduced to protesting that the quotation should have been killed rather than distorted.

Panitt's scrutiny of photos was as scrupulous as his concentration on copy. During the braless seventies, Marsano remembers, a certain scribbled injunction from Panitt appeared so frequently on photo proofs that a few wags at Radnor thought of having a rubber stamp made for it: "Airbrush nipples!" Panitt, though, it must be admitted, was an equal opportunity censor. Dwight Whitney remembers a last-minute frenzied effort to yank a cover photo of Fred Astaire because Panitt detected "a crotch problem." In the late seventies the staff approved a cover shot of Robert Blake, the macho star of "Baretta," when Panittt suddenly announced that it was offensive. The astonished editors, including Bill Marsano, "looked hard to see what was wrong. It was only a head/shoulder shot, so there was no crotch problem." Finally Panitt enlightened them: you could see the hair on Blake's forearm. For once the staff held firm, and the editor-in-chief looked for allies. The usually reliable head of the research department, a southern matron named Mrs. Roberts but known to everyone as Magnolia, this time saw nothing amiss. At last a young "most virginal secretary was persuaded and prompted to say that, yes, if he thought forearm hair was offensive, then she was offended." The photograph gave way to a drawing, and the problem was solved.

Merrill Panitt had a strong sense of what might offend his readers. And *TV Guide* must not offend if it was to inform them about television and help them become selective viewers. In 1953 network television was only six years old; although almost two-thirds of the nation's homes had sets, it was not the colossal force it is today. It had its critics; it needed a boost. It was the genius of *TV Guide*, of course, to recognize that to boost the medium was to boost itself. Celebrating commercial television, however, came naturally to the "flag-waving patriots" who ran *TV Guide*. In the United States, they editorialized (Sept. 25, 1953), the viewer sooner or later makes the choice by watching the show or buying the product: "it's called private enterprise." In contrast was state-run British TV, with an occasional gem for the elite, but little for the average viewer. The British, "so valiant in war, can't face up to some of the challenging vagaries of peacetime" ("As We See It," Apr. 16, 1955). If they didn't act, the British faced the prospect of a Sovietized television industry, with no networks, few sets, limited broadcast hours, and a lot of propaganda ("Your Move Comrade," Sept. 3, 1955). To tune in commercial television, then, was to vote for freedom and capitalism.

Judged on its own merits, the home product looked pretty good to the editors of *TV Guide* in the fifties. For one thing, it was helping to educate millions and bring culture to them. Didn't Ed Sullivan (June 19, 1953) bring ballet, opera, and excerpts from Broadway to the masses? Hadn't the president of NBC, Pat Weaver, opened up the airwaves to the intellectual giants Bertrand Russell and Robert Frost in his "Wise Men" series (Feb. 12, 1954)? Culture on TV, Annenberg and Panitt argued, had to have mass appeal. They constantly exhorted networks to tailor shows to a discerning but average viewer while pleading with their readers to try better and more challenging fare. A review of 'Comment' (July 12, 1958), a show "unashamedly" for grown-ups, with interviews of the likes of Arnold Toynbee and Aldous Huxley, was typical. The reviewer feared readers "might assume that 'Comment' is a show for eggheads. Stay that impulse to flip the dial, mister," he commanded, adding the assurance that the show had a fine flair for drama and humor.

Fortunately television had proven that it could entertain while it enlightened and uplifted. In the fifties, it is important to remember, the magazine was not alone in its enthusiasm for television's potential as a dramatic art form. Although *TV Guide*'s boosterism seems naive from the vantage point of the 1990s, it is best understood when compared to Paddy Chayefsky's assessment (shortly after the telecast in 1954 of "Marty" and long before the film "Network"): "the word for television is depth, the digging under the surface of life for the more profound truths of human relationships." Better equipped than films to depict "the marvelous world of the ordinary" and the drama of

introspection, television "may well be the basic theater of our century."
Next to Chayefsky, *TV Guide* seems restrained.

On November 6, 1953, *TV Guide* boasted that "Kraft Theater" alone
allowed viewers to see two-thirds as many hours of drama as were produced on Broadway in a year. In 1956 an opera boom on TV clinched
the argument for the new medium, which provided more money for
opera stars than they made at the Metropolitan. That same year, Laurence Olivier's *Richard III* was released simultaneously in theaters and
on TV, and *TV Guide* gushed as it identified a trend in the making (Mar.
31, 1956): "an audience of 40-50 million [is] certainly more than have
seen the play since Shakespeare wrote it." Even when ratings were not
high, *TV Guide* remained bullish ("Are You A TV Snob?" July 17, 1953):
Maurice Evan's *Hamlet* got a 28.1, and *Billy Budd* an anemic 6.8 (Lucy
was in the seventies), but network executives felt a responsibility, in a
democratic society, to expose people to aspects of culture in which they
might well develop an interest. They were sugarcoating a vitamin, not
a pill, "and in time will remove the sugar." Through camera work, a
mood was easier to build on the set than on the theatrical stage. TV
promised a renaissance in quality drama.

Similarly, *TV Guide* championed the medium as a versatile aid to
classroom instruction. Because "You Are There" was so carefully re-
searched and documented (May 28, 1954), many teachers assigned it
as homework, confident that the show would not air "extremely soiled
linen" such as the Spanish-American War. To be sure, an occasional
error crept in—the knotted part of the noose appeared on the wrong
side of Nathan Hale—but what teacher was more accurate? *TV Guide*
took pains to refute the charge that TV kept youngsters from reading
or doing their homework. In Binghamton, New York, for example, kids
borrowed more books from the library in 1952 than in the previous
year. "Homework Can Be Fun If You Watch It on TV" (Sept. 28, 1957)
pointed to music class assignments that included "The Voice of Firestone" and Leonard Bernstein on "Omnibus," and it documented how
instruction in the sciences, social sciences, and literature benefited from
"Our Friend the Atom," "The UN in Action," "Money Talks," and
performances of Shakespeare. A year later *TV Guide* hammered away
at the medium's power as an educational tool by noting that Stendhal's
The Red and the Black disappeared from Manhattan bookstores when
New York University and WCBS offered a sixteen-week literature course
for a mere ninety dollars.

Not surprisingly, then, *TV Guide* heaped scorn on those "intellectual
typecrits . . . those who write for high-flown, low-circulation magazines"
and demean television's artistic and educational accomplishments ("As

We See It," Aug. 21, 1953). An egghead, it seemed, was a snobbish reactionary who refused to see the democratic possibilities associated with commercial television. In another instance it was noted that in *Harper's Magazine,* Bernard DeVoto, "like other stuffy critics," had demanded quality programs without commercial interruptions. "Even dreamy, ivory tower types should know," responded *TV Guide,* "that the man who pays the piper is entitled to call the tune" ("As We See It," July 24, 1953). And when Chaplain Louis King denounced TV as "a fever of the mind, tuberculosis of the heart and cancer of the soul," the magazine defended the medium (organ by organ) as a "mind-stimulating, heartwarming, soul-stirring gift" to millions, especially "shut-ins and the aged" ("As We See It," Sept. 4, 1953). Agreeing with intellectual critics did not come easy, no matter what they said. When "See It Now" went off the air, "that coterie of eggheads who do condescend to watch TV did an inordinate amount of crying in their beer," the reviewer reported (Mar. 7, 1959). "And rightly so," he noted with evident embarrassment, quick to defend the network by pointing out that "Small World" was at least as good.

At times "As We See It" dodged and dissembled as it defended television. To Carl Sandburg's assertion that more than half the commercials on TV were full of "inanity, asininity, silliness and cheap trickery," Panitt replied in an editorial that many were bad, "But more than half? We doubt it." The misleading commercials, the editor added in a search for the silver lining, actually "immunize our youngsters against blatant misleading advertising" (July 13, 1957). *TV Guide's* attitude toward intellectuals was quite complicated, as we shall see, but it was consistent in dismissing those who refused to acknowledge the medium's accomplishments or, at the very least, its potential.

Nor did *TV Guide* miss an opportunity to remind "critics who scoff" of television's public service achievements. On February 19, 1954, it indicated that an episode of "Racket Squad" on the illegal resale of used cars was being used as a training film by the Pennsylvania State Police. Three months later an editorial looked at the use of industrial TV on production lines, where it provided workers with eyes in places too dangerous for them to work. Cameras installed in the Houston city jail enhanced surveillance, while in the future they might enable housewives to watch their children asleep in the nursery. In July *TV Guide* revealed that after a tornado, television rescued viewers in the Midwest and New England by staying on through the night to handle Red Cross appeals, police bulletins, and transportation and housing announcements. In 1956 "As We See It" cited studies showing that mental patients who watched TV improved 16.2 percent over those who didn't and quoted a doctor who believed this economical treatment might well rank with tranquilizing drugs. As late as 1960 *TV Guide* was still full of the medical wonders of the medium, including an article about how television was about to gather cell-growth information in the war against cancer. Network television, *TV Guide* constantly concluded, provided more news and documentary analysis than was required of it, and the public service possibilities of the medium itself were just about infinite.

Highbrows were tempting (and toothless) targets for the self-proclaimed enlightened democrats of *TV Guide*. A more formidable foe of television was the motion picture industry, which quickly and accurately understood the threat posed by the small screen. Movie moguls responded to the upstart immediately offering 3-D, olfactory flicks, and stereophonic sound. They also tried to starve the new industry by refusing to sell films needed to fill out weekly programming. In spite of its enormous growth, the television industry and *TV Guide* at first adopted a defensive, at times conciliatory, strategy toward this rival.

"As We See It" recommended peaceful coexistence. Movie actors between films could keep busy and sharp making telefilms, which kept performers "close to the characterizations." But the editors cautioned Hollywood that it was "only a matter of time" before TV lured big stars (June 12, 1953). Already Lucille Ball was as popular as any movie matinee idol. This "just you wait" note became the *TV Guide* refrain as it became clear that the lion's roar covered a rapid retreat. Photographer Durward Greybill was not the only industry insider to intuit that within a couple of years TV would "out-dazzle theater." Strapped studios opened their warehouses, selling off more than bombs and B pictures. *TV Guide* smelled blood: television, "As We See It" boasted (Oct. 23, 1953), had forced Hollywood to shift from vehicles for big stars to better, blockbuster movies. Thanks to TV, consumers could look forward to quality pictures.

It was the film industry, of course, that sued for peace, far sooner than anyone, including *TV Guide,* expected. As early as July 17, 1953, "As We See It" noted a "sharp shift" in policy for MGM. Once "aloof" from TV, it now sought to capitalize on it. With the formation of Desilu Enterprises, the "often promised wedding" of TV and the movies was taking place in a form that would produce both feature films and TV shows.

Nor was *TV Guide* magnanimous in victory. On August 20, 1955, the magazine moaned: "TV gives, and the movie people take. And take. And take. It is time TV stopped playing patsy to the movies." At the end of 1957 "As We See It" commented on a new round of courtships—the acquisition of TV stations by the motion picture industry—that promised better telefilms. "Balderdash! Poppycock! Humbug!" the editors fumed. "Let the motion picture industry keep its cotton-pickin' entertainment philosophy off television programming." TV was not just "another way to exhibit movies," but a "unique medium of information and entertainment."

For nearly four decades now, *TV Guide* has been network television's biggest booster, showcasing upcoming specials, preaching the perils of pay TV, or refuting Newton Minnow's charge that the medium is a "vast wasteland." But neither Annenberg nor Panitt thought of himself as a mere booster; together they sought to make their magazine a conscience for the industry, an arbiter of taste, public morality, and, occasionally, private ethics. Only boosters, they believed, were qualified to be critics, for they would be caring, constructive, and balanced. These dual roles required *TV Guide* to walk a narrow path that sometimes doubled back upon itself or forked or emptied into a cul-de-sac. To be sure, Panitt was a cautious critic. When editors and writers pressed for permission to report on matters of substance, he sometimes asked them to wait until circulation hit three million, then four million. Nonetheless, especially in the fifties, *TV Guide* brought a missionary zeal to its carefully selected critique of the medium.

Types of shows that were cheaply reproduced or unimaginative or genres that hogged too much air time aroused the ire of *TV Guide*. In the days before heightened sensitivity to racism, *TV Guide* put its philosophy in the lexicon of Charlie Chan: "Big hit in television one season mean big trend next season. Also mean big pain in neck for viewer." Game shows were early targets, castigated for their callous treatment of contestants, especially of charity cases. On July 17, 1953, the magazine panned "On Your Account," a summer replacement show that forced unfortunate people "to pour out their family secrets." "Philanthropy is a good idea," the reviewer agreed, but not at the cost of a tasteless and maudlin invasion of privacy.

On the subject of the game show "Strike It Rich," "As We See It" (Feb. 26, 1954) indulged its instinct for righteous indignation. Viewers, it claimed, who are "unaware of the infinitesimal numbers of people picked from thousands who plead to get on the show; unaware of the many destitute people who spend their last pennies to get to New York in the faint hope of appearing on "Strike It Rich"; and unaware of the fact that the cases would receive better, more intelligent and more lasting assistance from unrecognized agencies, have been under the mistaken impression that "Strike It Rich" is a last resort for the poor." In the same issue *TV Guide* noted with satisfaction that the show had drawn fire from New York's welfare commissioner, Henry McCarthy. Perhaps soon the "public spectacle" of "Strike It Rich" would end.

Of course, *TV Guide* was not distressed with game shows primarily because of their impact on public policy. They were tacky, even grotesque, manipulations of the emotions of Americans—or simpleminded memory tests like "Concentration" (Nov. 11, 1958), "another childhood game transformed for television on NBC at a time when the medium is publicly crying its eyes out for inventiveness, imagination and originality." Perhaps some day soon the American housewife "would also be able to play Go Fish, Post Office and Spin the Bottle while watching TV." Game shows, according to Panitt, are a waste of precious TV time. "All they did was demonstrate vicarious greed. They pandered."

Daytime soaps were every bit as bad, at times evoking a more literary lambasting from *TV Guide*. In "Sobs and Suds" (June 5, 1953), the magazine mused, "maybe housewives haven't so much to do after all." The soaps kept women from the pots and pans but provided no Aristotelian emotional purge: "They have beginnings and middles. But they never end." "Search for Tomorrow" was typical. If the show represented the trials and tribulations of the normal American family, "then tomorrow had best be in the nature of an H-bomb and let's get it over with" (May 14, 1954). Five years later *TV Guide* reviewed the monotony of daytime TV in "The Torture Starts Early." Even at 3:30 p.m., wives remained glued to their seats while "the glucose continued to flow" with an unbalanced diet of giveaways, quizzes, and soaps (Apr. 25, 1959).

The popularity of these shows ("Strike It Rich," for example, appeared five mornings a week and once in the evenings) did not, in a sense, deter *TV Guide*'s crusaders for high quality. The imperatives of the market forced them to cover—and even showcase—series they had lambasted, as in the case of the much disliked but highly popular show "Peter Gunn." Thus *TV Guide*'s message was always mixed. But discerning readers could tell where the editors stood.

To be sure, the magazine was cautious with a popular genre like the western, which was the staple of the nighttime schedule. *TV Guide* waited to attack until 1958, well after many TV critics had already assailed the saturation of the screen with shotguns and saloons. Even then, *TV Guide* concentrated on the excesses of studio copycats: good westerns "are fine entertainment. The bad ones, awful. Worse, they are a real threat to creative drama on TV." In the course of recommending "Wanted—Dead Or Alive" (Nov. 15, 1958), the reviewer reminded readers, "TV Westerns seem to have reached the point where quiz shows were last year. There are so many that the newer one must have a gimmick." In

"Westerns Molded in a Cliché Factory" (July 26, 1958), *TV Guide* did mock the whole genre for its hackneyed plots and dialogue. About the only change has been to make Indians "so noble it's painful"; they now "blather banalities about 'Long Knife' being great white brother to Apache people. It's a revoltin' development."

To be constructive, however, *TV Guide* had to promote programs as well as point fingers. For many years the magazine needled the networks to provide better fare than fluff or reruns during the summer. As early as May 1953, *TV Guide* ran what would be an annual appeal that the summer be neither a hiatus nor a pale imitation of regular season shows, but a "tryout" for TV to "acquire stature as well as size, scope [and] more coverage." The next year, "As We See It" spiced its suggestion with a little sarcasm: "It's just that in our abysmal ignorance of the television business, in our obviously impractical idealism, we keep hoping against hope that you fellows may come up with something new this summer. Cheap, of course, but new." This was a battle that *TV Guide* lost, and by 1958 sober realism had begun seeping into its irony: "The dollar is mightier than the pen. . . . So there will be another summer of reruns and quizzes and giveaways. . . . Whether we like it or not, it makes economic sense" (June 21, 1958).

When something new did come along in the regular season, *TV Guide* tried to be ready with an endorsement. On August 30, 1958, the magazine found an antidote to the epidemic of westerns in the "new trend" of courtroom drama. "Realism is, of course, the keynote. The ordeal of a courtroom is at once more naturally dramatic than a western and more intimate than a soap opera. And it's particularly suited to television's special needs." Clearly, *TV Guide* was following the lead of the networks in trumpeting this "trend," but swinging the full weight of its increasing power behind shows like "Perry Mason" probably had some impact on their ratings. The September 6, 1958, issue contained a feature article on Raymond Burr and a review of "The Verdict Is Yours" that pronounced courtroom shows "exciting watching. The courtroom is an exciting place. It is also an intimate place [where] litigants and witnesses tend to reveal their strengths and weaknesses of character."

At times cautious in its criticism of television genres, *TV Guide* could be quite caustic in reviews of individual shows. As we shall see, the magazine could and often did hide behind the subjectivity, eccentricity, or even malevolence of its reviewers, insisting that they did not speak with *TV Guide*'s voice. Only rarely did "As We See It" blast a show or a performer as it did on June 25, 1954, in deploring Bob Hope's "vulgar," "crude" style of comedy: "Pawing, or being pawed by, beautiful women" might be appropriate for a show at an army base but not when women and children were in the audience. But reviewers were not at all reticent. On April 2, 1954, a short-lived show for youngsters called "Rocket Rangers" was dismissed as not "educational, informative or even entertaining. Unless violence per se is considered entertaining in these enlightened days of child guidance."

In the fifties, obviously with a go-ahead from Panitt, reviewers pulled no punches. The "Charlie Farrell Show" was summarily dismissed (Aug. 4, 1956): "Among other things, it suffers from lack of plot and motivation, bad writing, old jokes, over-acting and general ambiguity. Matter of fact, it's hopeless." And a western, of course, was in even greater jeopardy. "Broken Arrow" (Feb. 9, 1957) was no more than "a bunch of horsemen galloping off in one direction, then immediately galloping back in the other, continually firing rifles and side-arms. Sometimes they run in long enough to talk to each other: 'Look!' one of them is apt to say, 'On that ridge—it's Cochise.' " "Broken Arrow" "was a little too much for these old white eyes. It closed them completely." "The Investigator," to take one more example, was "an ill-conceived piece of mystery dramatics" that was "put on with the talent and enthusiasm of Miss Budgkins' summer drama school for girls. As an act of kindness in a world already too beset with troubles, names shall be omitted from this review." In this "artistic Neanderthal throwback" lines that "would barely pass a grade school composition test" seemed to be written illegibly on cue cards, an insurmountable problem for already inept actors (July 19, 1958).

As self-proclaimed constructive critics, the editors of *TV Guide* did not want to provide a platform for those who denigrated the value or potential of the medium itself. Merrill Panitt enjoyed exposing those who made television a scapegoat for the ills of American society. When dentists discovered "television malocclusion," an abnormal arrangement of teeth caused by cradling the jaw in one's hands as one watched the small screen, "As We See It" laughed derisively (June 5, 1953), as it did five years later when a dermatologist charged that adult westerns caused dandruff because nervous viewers scratched their heads. "Got a secret for you," the editor wrote: the dandruff shampoo company once sponsored a show placed opposite a popular western (Sept. 5, 1958).

TV Guide's reaction to those who simply denigrated or dismissed the medium was evident in the magazine's treatment of Red Smith. Already a well-respected sportswriter, Smith was hired to write a weekly column for *TV Guide*. Apparently no one knew that Smith believed that television had a pernicious impact on sports. Week after week he lashed out at the commercialization of sports, as aided, abetted, and accelerated by television, and cast doubts on whether the TV set provided a good view of athletic contests. Television, Smith argued, put neighborhood boxing clubs out of business, then forced the sport indoors, all because sponsors contribute "a bigger share of the swag than the customers do" (June 12, 1953). Because of TV's insatiable demand for matches, moreover, "any kid who shows a flash of promise is hustled up to the main event when he's scarcely more than an apprentice." Frequently, Smith added, the fighter's development is retarded or halted altogether, an ominous development for the sport (Aug. 7, 1953). Before long directors and cameramen, completely in charge of boxing, would orchestrate fights, forbidding first-round knockouts "lest commercials be crowded out" (July 24, 1953). Smith could not resist pointing out that it was "impossible to see a fight on television." The bodies of the fighters block the camera, which might in any event fail to show whether or not a blow landed. The viewer "is further confused by the commentator," who may be far off in the mezzanine but announces, nonetheless, that a boxer's eyes are glassy. "Turning off the sound helps," said Smith, who had an even better suggestion: "Be there" (June 26, 1953).

Baseball was equally vulnerable to the meddlesome medium. Commercial sponsors had seized the power to set the season's schedules, forcing more night games, for example, to accommodate brewers and cigarette manufacturers (July 17, 1953). On the field umpires preened in front of the "camera's all-seeing eye"; no longer content to call balls and strikes, they moved "in an aura of conscious grandeur" (Apr. 17, 1953). And baseball announcers, like those in boxing, were "absolute fakes," and brazen ones at that, who were even less inclined to tell the truth than radio play-by-play men, who could "tell" that a slider broke two inches outside because their operating philosophy was "what they can't see won't hurt." As always, Red Smith insisted that the camera, good as it was, could not see as well as the live observer in the grandstand (July 3, 1953).

By the end of 1953 Merrill Panitt printed articles that were, in effect, rebuttals to Red Smith's columns. On September 25, 1953, Gary Lebow, the vice president of the Sports Broadcasters Association, criticized Smith for "half-truths, distortion of fact and unbelievably irresponsible use of quotes" with reference to the broadcaster's ability to call balls and strikes. "Isn't it better," he asked, "to estimate a dance pattern from the back of a theater?" An unrepentant Smith fired back two weeks later: people are touchy when "called what they are"—that is, fakes. But other voices on sports increasingly appeared in *TV Guide*. Herman Hickman (Oct. 9, 1953) thought the living room chair the best place to "catch all the important action" in football, since the announcers left viewers uniquely well prepared to anticipate plays. Chris Schenkel, the Dumont Sports Commentator, taught viewers "How to Score a TV Fight" (Apr. 30, 1954): "Remember, it's a difference of opinion that makes matches[;] the opinion of an experienced TV viewer, while it does not determine the winner, can be as valid as the professional judge's." The more celebratory voices of Schenkel and Hickman were more compatible with the boosterism of *TV Guide* in the fifties than the sour voice of Red Smith. Eventually the Red (Smith) menace faded as the bland Melvin Durslag was installed as sports columnist. Although the magazine gave increasing latitude to big-name writers, throughout the fifties *TV Guide* never again offered a weekly column in entertainment, sports, or news and public affairs to a radical critic of the medium.

Most criticism of television originated outside of *TV Guide*. Some of it could not easily be ignored, especially by a magazine that aspired to be authoritative. Thus in the fifties *TV Guide* found itself embroiled in controversies over the social and political impact of television's violence and censorship. These weighty matters required a measured response, which the editors found in the concept of network self-regulation, an idea compatible with their staunch support of the free enterprise system, their boosterism, and their stance as conscience of the industry.

During the fifties public concern with juvenile delinquency prompted commissions and congressional committees to study the effect of TV violence on the behavior of American youth. For the most part, *TV Guide* denied that a correlation could be established, deriding those "who make a fetish of compiling statistics" on "how many shootings and head-crackings take place on the air in one week" (June 22, 1957). Gallup pollsters ("As We See It," Dec. 18, 1954) insisted on asking loaded questions such as, "Do you think any of the blame for teenage crime can be placed on the mystery and crime programs on TV and radio?" More important, the editors cited (July 17, 1953) studies by psychologists demonstrating that the children realized it was all play-acting. Benjamin Spock and Karl Menninger, for example, found that TV had no ill-effect on children. On the small screen "justice always triumphs, crime does not pay, and be sure to tell your mommy to buy crunchies." Violence on TV was "more of a bore than a danger," and youngsters were far more likely to respond to a real war scare than to a TV drama. And "sooner or later viewers will get tired of all the blood" (Nov. 15, 1958).

When viewers did not, *TV Guide* raised the specter of government regulation of network programming if the industry did not reverse "this disgusting trend." Pleading with parents to monitor their children's viewing habits, "As We See It" called on television to "clean its own house." The industry actually had a better record on this score than the movie or publishing industry, thanks to the code of good practice of the National Association of Radio and Television Broadcasters. More, of course, should be done, continued the essay: dramatic shows not intended for children should be so labeled by the networks. But voluntary compliance must be given a chance since state-run television was a remedy worse than the disease. *TV Guide* was not above using the impending intervention of Big Brother to prod the industry to action. Well into the sixties it kept up the pressure, reminding the networks of their responsibility to provide family entertainment. Network executives were "gold miners staking out claims on bonanzas," who would be well advised to protect their investments (e.g., Dec. 4, 1954; Jan. 29, 1955; June 22, 1957; Aug. 6, 1966; Dec. 7, 1968; Oct. 11, 1969).

Self-regulation frequently involved censorship, a topic covered extensively by *TV Guide* in the fifties. The magazine tended to believe that "he who censors least censors best" in a democratic society where viewers were the ultimate arbiters of substance and taste. Two months into its first issue, *TV Guide* blamed "creeping censorship" (an obvious reference to creeping socialism) for the death of topical humor and the spread of sappy sitcoms. About a year later an editorial (July 9, 1954) blasted the "unwritten but nonetheless binding rules" that half-hour drama shows must have happy endings. These taboos had not yet hurt TV, but "a steady diet of pap . . . may ultimately sicken viewers." Censorship was frequently held up for ridicule. In "To Kiss or Not To Kiss" (Aug. 21, 1954), the writer noted that even kisses between TV husbands and wives were "positively antiseptic" because network officials and sponsors feared to offend. The industry might save considerable confusion if an acceptable kiss were "limited to, say, one minute and 22 seconds." Even Woody Woodpecker had been chopped down to size by the censor, who had axed twenty-five sequences from fifty-two shorts because they depicted tipsy horses, tobacco-spitting grasshoppers, neurotic birds—and Negroes (Jan. 4, 1958).

Who was to blame? The culprits, according to *TV Guide,* were sponsors and organized pressure groups, the former timid, the latter tyrannical. Professional groups representing lawyers, teachers, bankers, and butchers protested real or fancied slights so vociferously that sponsors, already inclined to be cautious, bankrolled only the blandest fare. One could, perhaps, understand the hesitancy of Armstrong Cork Company to address the subject of racial integration, even if their explanation ("It can only inflame hatred in this country") seemed a bit bizarre. But when Helene Curtis cosmetics deleted a Zasu Pitts pledge that she "might burn off somebody's hair under a dryer but she'd never be a spy" because it might offend beauty parlor operators, *TV Guide* sensed that control of program content must be wrested from the sponsors (Apr. 20, 1957).

The solution rested, to some degree, with greater faith in the viewers, who were sophisticated enough to accept an occasional "damn" (or even the birth of an illegitimate child to deaf mute Julie Harris in "Johnny Belinda") and smart enough to turn off the set when they were offended. But *TV Guide*'s editors, it is important to note, were not libertarians. They accepted the necessity of some censorship for a home entertainment medium, as long as it was left in the hands of network officials. As we have seen, the magazine censored itself: Annenberg and Panitt believed in civility and decorum in a society that must be sanitized in order to be civilized. Difficult subjects should not be ignored, but harsh words and graphic pictures could not illuminate, let alone uplift. Implicit in *TV Guide*'s support for self-regulation was a view of taste, a way of thinking about culture, a paean to the golden mean, the moderation of the middlebrow. Television must not stray too far from the expectations of the "average viewer," nor subject viewers, even for the moment it took to change the channel, to the coarse, crude, or sexually explicit. Thus "As We See It" wondered whether Elvis Presley's "contortions" were appropriate for living rooms, then recalled the singer's popularity and concluded with evident relief that it was not the magazine's job to decide what to put on the air (July 7, 1956). As late as 1965 this sort of caution prevailed, as when, a staff writer told us, Walter Annenberg was shocked when he saw Billy Wilder's film *Kiss Me Stupid*. That waitresses in the film showed their navels, with jewels in them, was bad enough. But Annenberg thought unspeakably disgusting the scene where Kim Novak loses her jewel in a bathroom and crawls all around the toilet with Ray Walston trying to find it. Concerned that this smut be kept out of the living room, Annenberg suggested a *TV Guide* series on the need to exorcise these demons from the small screen. The three-part story, written by Leslie Raddatz, blasted Wilder as a "one-time gigolo" and a "sneering snob," whose films "verged on an, at best, unconventional and sometimes seamy borderline." (Raddatz was careful in *TV Guide* to refer to the infamous toilet as a "commode.") If Hollywood peddled this dirt to TV, Raddatz warned, Congress would not stand idly by while "Saturday Night at the Nudies" corrupted impressionable minds. A cartoon that accompanied the story made the point: "Boy, Dad! Carroll Baker has it all over Captain Kangaroo." The networks, Raddatz concluded, must keep trash off the air or lose their control over program content. It wasn't a very difficult choice (Apr. 10, 17, 24, 1965).

Throughout the fifties and well into the sixties, then, *TV Guide* called for close scrutiny by the networks. It was *TV Guide*, after all, that thought that a "You Are There" episode on the sinking of the Titanic would be "pointlessly sad" (May 28, 1954). In fact, the magazine had supported the shift from single to multiple sponsorship of a TV series because it meant that responsibility for scripts would pass to the networks. Between 1957 and 1960 *TV Guide* ran at least three feature articles on Stockton Helffrich, NBC's censor ("Just call me an umpire") in an obvious effort to show that network policy was sensible, restrained, and aware of modern mores: "We try to censor as little as possible." (Merrill Panitt now acknowledges, "He said it, but he didn't mean it.") If Rod Serling still complained that after the networks had finished with "Noon on Doomsday," his play about prejudice, "it said nothing and it dealt vaguely with nothing," (May 11, 1957), his was a lonely voice in *TV Guide*, refuted a few months later by Martin Manlius, producer of Playhouse 90, who didn't shy away from "illegitimacy, discrimination, or other touchy subjects" (Oct. 10, 1957). Self-regulation was so successful that "As We See It" discouraged the PTA from raising "a rumpus about programs that take you on a voyage of violence. . . . Heaven knows there are enough pressure groups telling television producers what not to put on the air" (June 20, 1959). In this cutthroat, competitive business, networks would be kept honest by their rivals—and by well-informed, selective viewers.

Behind the boosterism and the criticism of *TV Guide* was a democratic theory, a vision of powerful and discerning viewers practicing dialsmanship. Television was the quintessential democratic medium, which held an election every half hour of every day. The key to quality, the editors wrote over and over again, is in the possession of the viewers. The way to get better programs is to refrain from watching bad programs. *TV Guide* pronounced itself impatient with the argument that some shows were too good to be appreciated: "Who is to judge, if not the audience for whom the shows are designed?" (Jan. 25, 1958). In commercial television (the embodiment of laws of supply and demand) networks and sponsors had to bend to the will of the people, as expressed in the free marketplace.

TV Guide's editors, moreover, expressed confidence in the aesthetic judgment of viewers. It cited a study that loud and repetitive commercials alienate the public and do not help sales (Apr. 13, 1957), then expressed no concern about ads in which actors dressed as doctors peddled pills: "We've been exposed to so many men in white coats who contradict each other's recommendations, to so many sketches of the intestines, the bloodstream, the skeleton, the nasal tract . . . that we're all fairly immune—if not to ailments, then to the commercials" (July 7, 1958). Program choices also indicated good taste. "Everyone's a Long-hair," an article on opera announced: the loyal following of "The Voice of Firestone" "contradicts the theory that people who look at TV don't like music very much" (Dec. 8, 1956). The "respectable" rating of "Omnibus," which showcased *King Lear, Oklahoma,* and dramatizations of Steinbeck, Hemingway, and Thurber stories suggested that diversified cultural programming could be commercially successful (Dec. 18, 1953).

The people, however, could be manipulated, misled, and pandered to, and *TV Guide* was always careful not to appear to be leading its audience. Even its own review column made the editors queasy. To guarantee objectivity *TV Guide* reviews of New York shows came from Hollywood and vice versa. The reviewer had to see at least three episodes of a series before writing about it. No shows would be reviewed before the broadcast date because no one person was qualified to say what the audience would or would not like. At their best, reviews should tell readers what a series was about: although reviewers hired by *TV Guide* had good judgment and high batting averages, only viewers could make or break a show. Even so, "As We See It" once felt compelled, in the name of dialsmanship, to make fun of its own reviewer. When this critic "finally broke down and liked a show a few weeks ago," the essay confessed, "there was joy unbounded in the editorial offices. For a while we wondered whether the reviewers and the editors were looking at the same programs" (June 6, 8, 1957). More strategic than sincere, this column seems to us part of the magazine's desire to portray itself as authoritative but not authoritarian, a necessary information tool in the service of an empowered electorate.

Despite this rhetoric, however, *TV Guide*'s faith in viewers occasionally wavered in the fifties. Those noisy, obnoxious, hard-sell commercials worked, the editors noted, and advised irritated viewers not to bother to write with complaints: "If you were an advertiser you'd probably stick to the hard-sell too" (Aug. 8, 1959). Even more ominously, they acknowledged, most Americans shied away from news analysis, Shakespeare, and scientific subjects—"anything that smacks even a little bit of intellectualism." They "left deep-thinking to the deep thinker," who was then scorned "for being an egghead" (Feb. 15, 1958). The cancellation of "Matinee Theatre," "Seven Lively Arts," and "The Voice of Firestone" "will hardly disturb" the devotees of "Danny Thomas" and "Peter Gunn" (May 9, 1959). Once in a great while, *TV Guide* could be downright disdainful. The article "TV Viewers—Easy to Satisfy" (Oct.

23, 1954) claimed that television watchers will request anything when performers, no matter how facetiously, ask them to. Bob and Ray, for example, offered cracked phonograph records "dropped just a few inches off the delivery truck," invisible doughnuts ("all gone but the hole"), and chocolate Easter bunnies left near a radiator and now "moldable into any shape you want." The response was overwhelming, prompting Dave Garroway to offer a dead camera tube. Could such invincibly unsophisticated viewers be expected to turn on quality programs?

Even the collective character of viewers was occasionally called into question. "As We See It" (Oct. 19, 1957) thought the formula of westerns—hero wounds villain but brings him to justice—necessary because children needed standards in a modern world that provided them only intermittently. "If all our children could find a clear delineation between good and evil in the home life, it might not be necessary for TV western heroes to be quite so pat." Dialsmanship, then, might well usher in an aesthetic tyranny of a mediocre majority. *TV Guide* did not know what to do. On August 2, 1958, "As We See It" gave voice to its confusion: Ratings are "strictly a matter of what the majority wants—which doesn't necessarily make for the best in television; but at least it is democratic. Luckily we do have sponsors and networks that are not always interested in just the size of an audience." The editors took some solace in studies indicating a strong residue of good will toward sponsors of dramatic anthologies and documentaries. After all, ratings did not mention the intensity of viewer response to programs. When the Ford Motor Company traced the last fifty years of the American republic in song, dance, dramatic sketches, and film clips—without commercials—*TV Guide* predicted it would reap great rewards from an appreciative public. In the wake of the quiz show scandals of the late fifties, *TV Guide* demanded that networks take charge. Perhaps, just maybe, cultivating a smaller but loyal following constituted "smart business" for sponsors and good public relations for the networks, which were, in some sense, public utilities.

In the late fifties, then, *TV Guide* abounded in contradictions. Although it continued to advocate dialsmanship, it exhorted readers to watch quality programs and write to the networks about them; it lobbied to reserve Sunday afternoon for cultural and public affairs programming because in the evening the competition was too fierce; and it pleaded with the networks to educate and uplift, even if ratings suffered. Through it all, however, each *TV Guide* article had a confident, even assertive, tone, empowering viewers one week and acknowledging inexorable economic imperatives the next, each time blissfully unaware of what had been said before. By implication *TV Guide* seemed to say, with Walt Whitman: "Do I contradict myself? Very well then I contradict myself. I am large. I contain multitudes."

By 1960 *TV Guide* certainly contained multitudes of readers, if not yet advertisers. The magazine had not matched the phenomenal growth of the medium, but it had good reason to congratulate itself. A lofty, sympathetic guide to television and the TV industry, *TV Guide* thought itself "authentic and authoritative but . . . not autocratic or authoritarian." Readers praised the magazine for its balance, fairness, and impartiality, concluded the self-study (commissioned, presumably, to attract advertisers). "By and large it does not impose its 'tastes' in movies or TV shows on its readers; it tries to present them with 'facts' rather than with its own opinions." *TV Guide* viewers occupied a middle ground between highbrow and lowbrow, constant watchers and the somewhat disinterested. They were certainly not in the middle, however, "in using TV to best advantage—that is, as 'best' seems by their own standards. *TV Guide*'s *Selective Viewer Readers are the most determinedly rational consumers of TV in the Middlebrow world" (TV Guide: A Study in Depth).*

The terms *TV Guide* chose for itself—discreet, balanced, wholesome, calm—supported its carefully cultivated image of propriety, a magazine that helped viewers "attach more seriousness and weightiness to an area of behavior that might be easily viewed as frivolous and insignificant." This image was well suited to the complacent, conformist fifties, when walking the middle ground with the middle class was something of a national pastime, but it would be tested in the subjective and skeptical sixties, a decade of the New Journalism and the credibility gap, a decade in which *TV Guide* would continue its phenomenal growth even as it grew more uncertain about the taste, knowledge, and discernment of the masses.

2

The *Time* of Television: 1960–78

On September 29, 1962, *Business Week* noted that *TV Guide* had become the nation's largest-selling weekly, and "now, Madison Avenue [was] starting to like it almost as well as the viewing millions." The year 1961 marked a turning point, with a $6 million gain in advertising revenue, much of it from sources outside of the television industry. In 1962 *TV Guide* publisher James T. Quirk predicted a 10 percent gain for a total close to $20 million.

TV Guide had become a giant, impossible for the network giants to ignore. When Merrill Panitt visited Hollywood, he was treated like a king, wined and dined by Lucille Ball, Jack Webb, Jackie Cooper, and Sheldon Leonard and closeted with producers, studio executives, agents, and company presidents. One network executive told Panitt that a *TV Guide* "Close-Up," which showcased upcoming programs, was worth three rating points, a claim the editor appreciated despite doubts about its validity. In any event, *TV Guide,* once dependent on the good will of the industry, had come into its own.

As we have seen, from the outset Annenberg and Panitt tried to design a magazine that would do much more than supply program listings. They saw *TV Guide* as the chronicler of the greatest medium of the century, and occasionally, as its conscience. Above all, they did not want to publish a fan magazine. At its best, Panitt told his staff, *TV Guide* could show viewers that television was a business and remind the industry that the medium was an art form. At various times owner and editor told members of the staff that they aspired to be the industry's *Atlantic Monthly,* its *Life,* its *Harper's,* its *Time.*

They knew that *TV Guide* had not yet fully matured but were frustrated and angry when critics dismissed the magazine as supermarket schlock, or when, as staff writer Leslie Raddatz recalls, Terrence O'Flaherty of the *San Francisco Chronicle* called *TV Guide* "the big, fat queen of the fan magazines."

Determined to be taken seriously, Panitt and Annenberg began to change the content (without tampering with the form) of *TV Guide* in 1960, the year before advertising revenues began to climb. They focused first on profiles of television personalities. These popular pieces (according to Starch & Co., more readers read them than any other type of article) delivered what the cover photo promised—fresh insights into the stars of the small screen. Invaluable to a mass circulation magazine, the profile also made it vulnerable to critics who saw *TV Guide* as lightweight. In a respectable and respected publication, Annenberg and Panitt agreed, profiles must not gush or gossip; they must probe. In the dirty, sometimes sordid, reality beneath the glitzy surface of show business, ironically enough *TV Guide* found the material to polish its image as the objective, tough-minded authority on television and its celebrities.

If the *TV Guide* of the sixties did not deem all actors and actresses innately depraved, it did think that most of them were flawed. If performers were not neurotic, spoiled, or arrogant when they got to Hollywood, they quickly caught the virus. "In the halls of *TV Guide*," one staff writer recalled, "I always heard the word 'actors!' spat out venomously, contemptuously." In the early sixties, he believes, Merrill Panitt "hired people who shared his deepest feelings [and] heaped praise on writers who exposed celebs for what they really are." Although this account seems to us a bit conspiratorial, Panitt told us that while fan magazines lived on praise, *TV Guide* "looked for warts." "Most actors are difficult," Panitt believes. "Some of them are real bastards." In any event, the magazine did put on the gloves for celebrity combat at this time, no doubt confident that it could last in the ring against the network heavyweights.

Only rarely in the fifties had *TV Guide* turned tough in its profiles of the stars. A piece on November 21, 1959, innocently entitled "Betty Hutton Rules the Roost," proved to be a harbinger of things to come, as it carved up the popular actress with gusto. Noting that Hutton had gone through four producers, the article criticized a performer (especially a woman) who sought to control everything from writing to lighting. "To press her too hard on this point," according to *TV Guide*, "is to shorten the fuse on a critical mass of explosive Hutton atoms." The star's behavior probably had its origin in an unhappy childhood marred by her father's desertion and her mother's tough life as a "tack spitter" (auto upholsterer) in Detroit. To this gloomy portrait the article added evidence of Betty Hutton's insomnia, her regular visits to a physician and minister, and her third divorce.

In the early sixties Panitt hired writers who could produce probing, entertaining, informative, and accurate profiles while stripping away the mask donned by most performers. Equidistant from the fan magazine and the scandal sheet, yet with mass appeal, these profiles meshed with the mission of the magazine: to show the public the face behind the makeup and to illuminate the professional by understanding the person. Its writers should not wield a hatchet, but neither should they shrink from reaching for a scalpel. Sooner or later, Panitt lamented, writers were seduced by Hollywood and found it difficult to be objective about actors who had become their friends. A good writer "maintained cynicism and a sense of isolation." He found his ideal in a gifted freelancer by the name of Richard Boyd Gehman, whose frequent contributions helped change the direction of the magazine.

Dick Gehman was forty when he wrote his first piece for *TV Guide*. Born in Lancaster, Pennsylvania, he learned how to write as a copyboy and cub reporter for local newspapers and quickly turned to magazine writing and fiction. Over a short lifetime he would write over one thousand articles for popular magazines. When Panitt phoned, he had three novels to his name, books on Frank Sinatra and Eddie Condon, and the luster of having taught at New York University, Columbia University, Indiana University, Pennsylvania State University, and the Bread Loaf Writers Conference. *TV Guide* would not pay Gehman's standard fee, but it could offer him a huge audience and a way to enhance his already considerable stature as a commercial writer. The magazine, of course, got a byline it could be proud of—and a professional whose insight would not be arrested by surfaces, however shimmering.

Virtually every Gehman profile was grounded in popular psychology. Creative people, he apparently believed, were invariably insecure, neurotic, and unhappy. Emotional wounds could usually be traced to an unhappy childhood, which was also the source of a burning ambition to succeed. Sid Caesar's father, for example, "was a bitter, sarcastic man, made that way, perhaps, by his dominating wife." One day he reached into his pocket as if to give his son a quarter for the movies. "The delighted little Sid extended his hand, only to have Max Caesar give him a slap that bounced him off a wall. Such experiences—there were others—caused Caesar first to withdraw and then to attempt to find an outlet in performing." Psychoanalysis helped him to control himself "and even—a rather dubious reward—to talk on the telephone

without trembling." But Gehman's Caesar was a man given to self-
destructive excess, who drank to help "endure the captivity of his own
unarticulated problems," and who tormented his own writers: "Some
psychoanalysts claim that people unconsciously repeat the behavior patterns of their childhood, and it may be that he could function only if
all around him were arguing." Caesar's "Your Show of Shows" was
canceled, and a legendary figure of the medium was forced into exile
in 1958. As Gehman wrote, the comedian had begun his comeback on
Broadway in *Little Me* and on television in "As Caesar Sees It" and
longed to make himself "as comfortable and happy as I can." Success
and happiness were probably incompatible, Gehman wrote in an archetypal conclusion: "for if this comedian's strength comes from his
weakness . . . the ironic fact is that the unhappier he is, the happier he
makes the rest of us" (Feb. 16, 23, 1963).

In piece after piece Gehman stayed close to the couch. "That apparent ego" of Jerry Lewis, he intoned, "masked a frightened and insecure little boy . . . whose deepest motivation—he once said to me—is
fear" (Dec. 14, 1963). Even the apparently well-adjusted did not escape
psychological scrutiny. Arlene Francis (June 23, 30, 1962) was the per-
sonification of Rollo May's assertion that healthy people channel anxiety
into constructive work. In her husband, Martin Gabel, Francis had
found a father who was not at all condescending whom she could treat
"with a kind of flirting awe combined with a nicely fierce possessive-
ness."

The distinctiveness of Gehman's approach is evident in *TV Guide*'s
evolving coverage of Jackie Gleason. One of the top entertainers on
television, Gleason was a frequent focus of *TV Guide* in the 1950s. His
name popped up in articles about "Baggy Pants" comics (Feb. 26, 1955),
the plans of networks for mammoth TV cities in mid-Manhattan (Apr.
2, 1955), and the costs of shows (Aug. 20, 1955). When *TV Guide*
revealed that Gleason would sell cars for Buick, in an exposé of a feud
between NBC and an advertising agency, it left "The Great One" un-
scathed (Jan. 19, 1955). Articles on Gleason the showman were equally
unrevealing. In "It's All Done with Mirrors" (Jan. 29, 1955), the magazine explained the debt of the June Taylor dancers to Busby Berkeley.
When it concluded that Gleason had "gone overboard" in his use of
girls, especially the chorus line, *TV Guide* indulged in a fifties-style criticism: "It makes a great hit with the studio audience, but to the home
viewer with a small screen, its like sitting in the last row of the fifth
balcony, way off to the side" (Feb. 5, 1954).

Gehman was looking for the man, not the aura, in "Jackie Gleason"
(Oct. 13, 1962). The Gleason who was returning to television remained

creative, generous, and bombastic. In his "leafily prodigal behavior" and his insistence on imbibing in public, Gehman found evidence of "an immense craving for human companionship . . . rooted in a mulch of loneliness" that began in an impoverished youth. "Memories of old sadness" made Gleason aware of the essential tragedy of the human condition, a perception integral to the characters of "The Poor Soul," Reginald Van Gleason, and Ralph Cramden. As in the Sid Caesar profile, Gehman concluded that therapy's failure was comedy's gain.

If performers often made Richard Gehman sad, the arrogance of stars, many of them only marginally talented, made him angry. At the height of the popularity of "Ben Casey" (Sept. 22, 1962), Gehman operated on Vince Edwards. More "individualistic than talented," he asserted, "Edwards has been accused of being chronically late[,] of being possessed of an unmanageable temper[,] of coming in without having his lines firmly fixed in his mind." In a two-parter on method actor George Maharis of "Route 66" (Apr. 14, 21, 1962), Gehman blasted away at nonintellectual rebels who feel without trying to understand. Intensity was no substitute for craftsmanship or "the ability that comes as a result of care." In his haste to let his instinct govern, Maharis often became grotesque. With a dig at those ("future members of the Phoenix Junior League") who dug Maharis ("Our conformist mechanical society responds to the antisocial"), Gehman concluded his essay with a quotation that no doubt expressed his own views on the subject. George Maharis's love affair with himself, a photographer was certain, "will stand the test of time."

Gehman was only warming up. In "David Susskind Wants to Be Goliath" (Nov. 23, 1963) he declared war in his opening sentence: "Until recently David Susskind was the least controversial personality in the television industry. Nearly everyone hated his guts." In the rest of the profile he marshaled quotations to demonstrate that the producer was "still eminently hateful." As "immoderator" on "Open End," "which some call 'open mouth,' " Susskind postures as a self-appointed industry conscience; when someone says his passport exaggerates by setting his height at 5'9, "he gets almost apoplectic"; and he takes credit for other people's ideas ("creative kleptomania"). So great was his animus, that Gehman only lingered long enough on the psychic origins of his neuroses to insist that they must be there: "certain nameless and perhaps unidentifiable insecurities developed in childhood . . . churn on him continually." If Susskind stopped to find his self, to consider psychoanalysis, or even to think about how he gets things done, the producer's colleagues agreed, he might be far less productive. But Gehman gave himself the last word: "There seems to be no danger of that."

Few profiles were this acidic, but Gehman tried, in every piece, to puncture the pretensions of Hollywood personalities. Like most Americans, he loved Lucy, he explained to *TV Guide* readers, but she, too, bestowed "the Kissless Kiss," the quintessential narcissistic Hollywood greeting, which "consists of an actress pursing her lips as though to kiss someone, and extending her cheek for a kiss, and then forgetting to kiss as she looks around the room to make sure everyone has seen her arrival" (Sept. 5, 1964). To bolster his credibility, Gehman used a technique that became a hallmark of the New Journalism of Norman Mailer and Tom Wolfe. He placed himself near the center of each of his profiles: Lucy gave *him* the Kissless Kiss; "Literally *I* [Gehman] wept" as Sid Caesar recalled the trauma that was his childhood; although Susskind was said to have been born in Brookline, "to *me* he said it was Brooklyn." When readers sat in on the interviews, the interpretation was bound to appear authoritative.

Gehman's literate, even literary, style bolstered that authority. He was fully capable of alluding to Kafka, of depicting an unemployed Sid Caesar "stalking through the split level corridors of his own Elba," or of describing James Moser, the writer-producer of "Ben Casey," as "an angular Quixote" given to allegory. At first blush this parade of erudition seems out of place in a mass circulation magazine, but if anything, Merrill Panitt believes, it may have boosted sales. A magazine about a much-maligned medium, *TV Guide* needed some "snob appeal" to convince readers that it was worth their time. As we shall see, the new tone of *TV Guide* helped attract advertisers as well. In any event, Panitt insists that readers respected a magazine that didn't write down to them, even (or perhaps especially) when an occasional reference eluded them.

Merrill Panitt continued to call on Richard Gehman's free-lance services, but he moved to add writers of comparable quality to the permanent staff in New York and Hollywood. With Edith Efron, he hit the jackpot. Educated at Barnard and Columbia, Efron began her career in journalism at the end of World War II with the *New York Times* magazine section. From 1948 to 1954 she was the reporter on Central America for *Time* and *Life*. She then moved to *Look* for two years, serving as managing editor of special editorial departments, and then joined the public relations firm of Farley-Manning. In 1958 Efron became a staff writer on the "Mike Wallace Show." When the show was canceled, she answered a *TV Guide* ad in the *New York Times*. Interestingly, as she prepared for her interview by reading the magazine (for the first time, she told us), Richard Gehman's pieces jumped out at her, an observation she passed along to Merrill Panitt.

Like Gehman, Efron searched for and found a crisis of selfhood, a psychic void, as the defining essence of many actors. Lloyd Bridges, "a well-paid failure," did not pursue good parts because he lacked confidence in his ability. His role in "Sea Hunt," which brought him fame and fortune, "cannot be called acting at all," and his success was balanced by "a downward curve in terms of artistic seriousness" (Mar. 2, 1963). Barbra Streisand's success Efron attributed to "one traumatic fact: her ugliness." Wanting desperately to be pretty, Streisand pretended to like being homely and turned herself "defiantly into a grotesque." Even as a star she remained consumed with anxiety over her appearance; her manner "hedged around with her defense [was] almost stupendously non-charming," and her social behavior "mis-shapen." Streisand got little pleasure out of her fame because "in the last analysis" (but surely not *her* last analysis), she didn't like herself. "If Barbra Streisand's Nose Had Been a Half Inch Shorter" (July 22, 1967), Efron implied, she might well have been a happy, untalented homemaker.

At times an Efron profile seemed like a Gehman summer rerun. She, too, wrote about Arlene Francis, whose "bland, self-censored and syrupy chatter . . . slips millions into a gentle coma while giving them the illusion of hearing a meaningful exchange of ideas." She, too, looked beneath Francis's "gay insouciance," her life "dedicated to courting the favor of others," her insistence "to all and sundry that she is a remarkably happy woman"—and unearthed a soul-weary emotional distress, a regret that her desire for acceptance had prevented her from trying to be a serious actress (June 18, 1966).

Early on, however, Efron tired of profiles of actors "in chronic pursuit of what they variously term their 'egos,' 'identities,' or 'selves.' " Carol Burnett, she noticed, "confides the details of this quest to everyone who interviews her" (Feb. 23, 1963). Far more interested in ideas than ids anyway, she began to ask performers about their favorite books, the paintings they purchased, or their faith in God. Her profile of Jackie Gleason juxtaposed his public image as a "Rabelaisian caricature . . . a gross, bawdy Pagliacci" with his "unusually vivacious intelligence." Gleason faulted Plato for forgetting human desires in building his system. He wrestled with the moral tenets of Catholicism, with a faith that gives emotional certainty without proof and a science that supplies proof without certainty. "The strange truth," Efron reported, is that The Poor Soul and Crazy Guggenheim were satires on the Christian virtues, Gleason's versions of Dostoevski's *The Idiot*. As artist and thinker, then, Jackie Gleason was "a fascinatingly complex human being" (Feb. 6, 1965).

Most of the time Efron found the stars she explored vacant or gaseous. Barbra Streisand's cardinal sin was not her looks, nor even that she "name-drops bits and pieces of culture," but that she had neither the desire nor will to learn. Carol Burnett, pleasant and nonabrasive, had never been known to "converse in a sustained fashion on any subject which does not relate in some way to the entertainment world." Richard Chamberlain's "sole claim to fame is that he is famous." His career was "a duplicate of that of almost every other young actor," from the role of the Pied Piper in the third grade to work with a little theater group in Hollywood (Mar. 16, 1963). Efron went in with a chip on her shoulder, according to Merrill Panitt. She expected celebrities to prove themselves. When they didn't, "she killed them" in pieces clearly aimed at discerning, literate readers. Imagine the mismatch when Edith Efron met Troy Donahue and Connie Stevens, "the conventional stereotype of an ideal young couple—blonde, slender, vulnerable, infantile . . . adult children—lovely barbarians, 20th century style" (Sept. 1, 1962).

Efron did not enjoy shooting these fish in a barrel. A libertarian disciple of Ayn Rand, she relished combat with actors who mouthed the liberal platitudes of the sixties. Bud Collyer, "an inexorably humble man," Sunday school teacher, Boy Scout leader, and crusader against juvenile delinquency and racial intolerance, struck her as a man "who does not converse—he preaches." She added others' claims that Collyer was a phony, a boy scout, and a bluenose (May 26, 1962). Worse yet were the "up-to-the-minute politics" of Joanne Woodward, "as standardized for her circle as is rolling for the Holy Rollers." Borrowing Jack Newfield's phrase "the issue nymphomania of the white middle class," Efron rolled the credits of Woodward's causes: Adlai Stevenson, astrology, adopting a Chinese baby, Martin Luther King, yogurt, kibbutzim, guilt over having servants, wheat germ oil, and vegetarianism. Only "apparently" thoughtful, the "exhausting predictability and fashionable changeability" of her views "actually render her anonymity complete." In shucking her Southern identity for the "chic antiheroic world," Woodward had lost her way, the only hopeful sign her belated admission that she was not a serious thinker and was not qualified to take political positions (Nov. 27, 1971).

Even the saintly Captain Kangaroo, Bob Keeshan, was decanonized. Efron put his "sugar-coated vitamin pills" of religion and ethics under the microscope and found them not always "nonjudgmental." Some parents, she reported, objected to his deism; others disliked his endorsement of the United Nations. Behind the scenes, moreover, the "Social Institution with a Moustache" was a short-tempered tyrant, "a vest-pocket Messiah" (Mar. 19, 1966).

In a publication owned by Walter Annenberg, a staunch Republican and friend of Richard Nixon, a conservative political view was unlikely to hold back a talented writer. A year after her arrival at *TV Guide*, Efron had a preeminent position on the staff of the New York bureau, virtually an intellectual in residence, with wide latitude to choose her own stories. She was allowed an unprecedented eleven pages (profiles were rarely longer than four pages) to examine the legend of Loretta Young, "the fragile mystery star who is so solemnly at cross-purposes with contemporary fashion" and at the same time "the very embodiment of grass roots America." Young's commitment to American values might make her seem out of place "to a certain type of modern intellectual. But to the conservative, God-fearing, hard-working, hero-worshipping people who make up most of the American public, she is both intelligible and ideal" (Oct. 20, 1962).

In the middle and late sixties, as we shall see, Efron's interests took her beyond the profile. But as long as she was on the staff, she embodied the philosophy and tone Annenberg and Panitt wanted for their magazine. That she expressed views more vehemently and uncompromisingly than they was scarcely a problem. The magazine needed an enfant terrible. No writer, we believe, did more to shape *TV Guide*.

As *TV Guide* profiles changed, Merrill Panitt recognized that he had to beef up the Hollywood bureau. Dan Jenkins, the bureau chief, was too fond of show business personalities to write a Gehman-Efron piece. Jenkins "lived up to his reputation as being Mr. Nice Guy," remembers Martin Lewis, an aide to Walter Annenberg. "I don't recall he ever wrote a story about a television personality that wasn't complimentary." In the fifties Jenkins's leisurely style and familiarity with stars that dated from his days as TV columnist for *The Hollywood Reporter* seemed more than adequate. Early in the sixties he recognized that his days were numbered:

> I hesitate to use the term hatchet job, but that's where we were indeed heading. And I was simply incapable of writing such stuff. . . . When I got a memo which began, "Let's get Lucy," I fired back. Eventually Radnor fired back, with a letter which began, "I think it's time you started looking for another job." Another memo, in an effort to placate me . . . said, "The magazine changed direction and you didn't." I made one misguided effort to prove them wrong, turning out what might be called a minor sort of hatchet job on a young actress who certainly didn't warrant it. I later apologized to her publicist who, after a long pause, shook his head and said, "You're the first writer who ever said that to me." So I left.

To replace him, Panitt promoted Dwight Whitney, who had been a staff writer in Hollywood since 1958. Born in Hartford, Connecticut, Whitney was the son of a newspaperman turned public relations agent, and his mother was the dean of women at Beloit College. After graduation from Beloit, Whitney joined the staff of the *San Francisco Chronicle,* where he served for a time as drama editor. He then shifted to magazines, covering show business for *Time,* moving up to the post of assistant managing editor of *Fortnight,* and then going down with the ship as associate editor of *Collier's.* Whitney had excellent experience, he could write, and, most important, he knew which way the wind was blowing at *TV Guide.*

As he had for Richard Gehman, Vincent Edwards proved a convenient target. Whitney fired his first shot in "Anybody Know What Kind of Mood Vince-Baby Is in Today?" (Apr. 4, 1964): "Suddenly you get the picture of a very hungry man, hungry for acceptance, hungry for recognition, hungry for culture, hungry to find himself—and never quite knowing in which direction to look." Like Gehman, Whitney reviewed a troubled childhood in Brooklyn, where there was "no way to look down." Like Efron, he noticed the *Saturday Review* in one of Edwards's pockets and the *London Observer* in the other. And, in the spirit of the new *TV Guide,* he examined the actor ("*The New York Times* once said that 'Edwards has exhausted all conceivable methods for folding his arms to convey superiority, idealism and brutal loathing' "), the singer ("The record people, not to mention the critics, complained that he did not know how to sing"), the producer (he "has yet to produce anything except the good feeling of proprietorship"), and the man ("He once told [a friend]: 'When you let 'em wait, they appreciate you more' "). Either a masochist or a man without a memory, Edwards agreed to be interviewed again by Whitney less than three years later (Feb. 18, 1967). "Vince Baby Plays It Cool" was an instant replay, narrated by a man who had "known Vince a while longer than the press agent has." No longer Ben Casey, Edwards affected "a softer, less ferocious look" until, under Whitney's gaze, he became "his old fierce, scowling self," glaring as he admitted that "nobody has broken down any doors" to cast him.

Of course, Whitney did not always take target practice. In "The Seven Faces of Danny Kaye" (Jan. 9, 1965), he attempted a sympathetic analysis of a complex person. In an interview with Bob Hope (Sept. 16, 1965), he engaged in an Efron-like examination of the Catholicism of Delores Hope, the comedian's wife. And in a profile of Raymond Burr, he began with a recitation of philanthropy and public service that must have brought joy to a press agent's heart: "They include the direct support of 12 people, the indirect support of hundreds, including 13 foster children in five foreign countries. He is the director of the Freedom Foundation at Valley Forge, and he is actively involved in the Cerebral Palsy Association, the National Safety Council, the B'nai B'rith and the March of Dimes." The list continued for another two paragraphs (July 24, 1965). Whitney, moreover, was immensely proud of the fan letter he received from Red Skelton, with thanks for a graceful and gracious profile.

But it was the feistier profiles that won raves from Radnor. The only gift he ever received from Walter Annenberg, ĩ.ˮ ịtney told us, was a gold-plated straight razor, sent the week his profile of Jack Lord of "Hawaii Five-O" appeared (Sept. 4, 1971). Lord's compulsion to control everything, even time, was Whitney's theme. If he was born when his biography indicated, Whitney pointed out, then he was married at age 9. His image as a Renaissance man was simply self-promotion. This "Superstar," in sum, was a Lord with "a hundred transgressions."

Radnor's preoccupation with the darker side of Hollywood can be most conclusively demonstrated in the preparation of an article on the show business children of celebrities. On November 13, 1964, Whitney informed Panitt, with regrets, that the current crop was "relatively well-mannered." Marlo Thomas might be portrayed as a strong-willed woman, "the apple of her father's eye" in an industry "in which nepotism runs rampant," a female "whose lovers find her hard to manage as do her fellow actors, directors, producers, managers, and yes, photographers." Nancy Sinatra could be painted as "the Boots girl who took a page from her father's book." But "after that the pickings get slim."

> Dean's kids are fine. Ditto Jerry Lewis'. Ditto Bob Hope's. Ditto Lucy's. And that is not to say that they are angels or immune from the star syndrome. But monsters they are not. Liz Montgomery, headstrong though she may be, is a tough girl to put down, unless you're against touch football. . . . To find the real "ingrates" one has to go back to the Crosby boys (if, indeed, they are ingrates) and only one of them, Gary, is still in show business. Larry Hagman and James MacArthur? Highly doubtful as examples of filial disloyalty. My two brushes with the latter revealed only family fondness. And if Hagman is at odds with his mother, Mary Martin, we don't know about it.

To salvage weeks of research, Whitney proposed a story on the pressures brought to bear on the children of the stars, how they dealt with them ("sometimes badly," he reminded Panitt), and the role of nepotism in their professional and personal lives. Panitt was no longer interested and sent a four-word letter on November 9: "Forget 'The Young 'Uns.' "

When they appeared, of course, *TV Guide* profile pieces occasionally provoked angry protests from the stars who were stung by them. As

Hollywood bureau chief—and frequently as a writer—Whitney was required by Radnor to respond. Protected by an ever-increasing circulation and the support of Panitt and Annenberg, Whitney could be remarkably candid. In April 1974 Jean Stapleton complained about the "gossip, half-truths . . . innuendoes, [and] speculative opinions" in an article on "All in the Family." In his reply Whitney thanked the actress for her "eloquent" letter but stood his ground: "Alas, the 'truth' is a slippery commodity. Pinning it down is, as W. C. Fields once remarked, like trying to tie a hair ribbon on a lightning bolt. It grieves me that you, particularly, should feel the way you do. Maybe we should confine ourselves to seeing only the nice side of people, carefully camouflaging their darker side. But if we did we wouldn't be much of a magazine." Whitney went on to deny that there was anything speculative in his articles, but he had defined a key element of the *TV Guide* philosophy.

Over the years this philosophy was effectively communicated from Radnor to the staff writers. In weekly conferences the editors chose topics and made assignments. The writers were enjoined to interview their subjects at least three times, once without a press agent. In the profile itself, to establish the writer's authority and objectivity, the various venues of the interviews might be ostentatiously displayed, and the agent introduced, if only to demonstrate that his views had not been taken seriously. Articles were regularly returned to writers, with instructions to "dig some more." When Edith Efron interviewed Paul Burke of "Naked City" she found a "very open, very communicative, very emotional, expressive and intensely idealistic" man. When she handed in a "quite admiring" portrait, Efron "got a dry little note" from Radnor expressing doubt that Burke "could be quite that stupendous" and suggesting that she interview Burke's coworkers. She grumbled at the cynics who ran *TV Guide* but followed orders. When she talked with actors, producers, and directors on "Naked City" she "got the shock of [her] life," in the form of a consensus that Paul Burke was "closed, withdrawn, absolutely guarded, even taciturn." Evidently "the burst of intimate communication" Efron had gotten from Burke "was exclusively a result of the interaction of our two personalities." Efron revised her profile, which ultimately appeared with the title "Star with a Wall around Him."

Some staffers changed their stories even when they didn't change their minds. Assigned to cover a show in which Loretta Young played mother to a bunch of kids, Leslie Raddatz was "tremendously impressed . . . and made no bones about it" in the piece he turned in. It was promptly fired back to him with the comment that it was too adulatory.

Raddatz had said how bright the kids were. He added the phrase "maybe too bright," and that, he told us, made the difference.

With free-lance writers, the procedure was much the same. By the mid-sixties any careful reader of the magazine could see the direction in which it was headed. Thus young Carolyn See was a "cannon waiting to be pointed" when she got her first assignment, a profile of Walter Brennan, a reactionary even in the eyes of most conservatives. See discovered that she could produce a devastating piece simply by recording what Brennan said as the two looked at one another "across a forty-year generation gap and the whole muddy mainstream of American politics," he a subscriber to the *Liberty Lobby Newsletter,* she to the *New York Times Review of Books.* Brennan was nothing if not good copy, inveighing against a plot, "not just a plan but a plot," to take over the United States, an operation "run by the Communists, of course"; certain that "all this trouble with the Negroes is caused by just a few of them"; and proud that Mrs. Brennan had "almost single-handedly" closed down the educational FM station KPFK, a hotbed of dope addicts and beatniks. At the conclusion of the interview Brennan asked that something he had said be kept off the record: he wanted no one to know he had emphysema. Only too happy to comply, See wrote a penetrating profile that left Brennan, clinging to his beliefs in a trailer with a broken generator: "the system has got him again . . . and he's sitting in the cold half-dark" (Mar. 30, 1968). Carolyn See was *TV Guide*'s kind of writer.

In the ensuing years, See wrote profiles of the likes of James Garner and Diahann Carroll, pieces that, in retrospect, she considers unnecessarily harsh. Finally, in 1985 the inevitable happened: Carolyn found a subject in which she could see no evil. Everybody, including his ex-wife, liked Perry King, the star of "Riptide," who turned out to be, on close inspection, "incredibly handsome," a loving father and son, and a reflective and well-read man. See's story came back from Radnor with the suggestion that she had fallen for a "pretty moustache." Her ingenious re-write, "Six Reasons Why I Like Perry King More than Ever" (Jan. 26, 1985), was a revealing glimpse into the modus operandi of *TV Guide.* Casting her article as an open letter to the editors, See bristled at the assumption that she, "a reporter who honors truth," had been conned by a male starlet: "You wanted me to be 'more objective' the second time around, and here's the best I can do. . . . But the truth isn't always mean." And yet, as she listed King's virtues, See found a way to give Radnor what it wanted. Perry King, she noted, was too much the gentleman to take off his shirt in front of her, unlike Telly Savalas, who "during the course of a three-hour interview in a cramped motor home, tried on 27 silk shirts 18 inches away from my head. His chest was no picnic, I can tell you." Perry King was smart, unlike Don Galloway, who "could only tell me he was a pretty good poker player"; he had good manners, unlike Garner, who "pushed his index finger into my stomach as if to say that I needed to go on a diet"; and he was not narcissistic, unlike Audrey Landers, who "jerks her shoulders back to bring her breasts into prominence" when she speaks. These mean truths, of course, had more than a little to do with the decision to publish See's profile, although it came with an admonition that she not try this trick again.

Less combative writers pacified Panitt with a proper prologue. A well-adjusted or decent celebrity, they repeated almost ritualistically, was an exception that proved the rule of "galloping inflation—especially in the ego department" that came with fame (Apr. 6, 1968). When a star has a wholesome image, a profile of Mitzi Gaynor began, you can usually "lay odds that off camera she swears like a sailor and behaves like a shrew [and is] wholesome as a swamp. They'd kill you for a nickel, and if the right role were at stake, they'd kill you and forget the nickel. But not Mitzi" (Oct. 18, 1968). Digby Diehl made sure he registered his incredulity that beneath Karen Valentine's saccharine image lay a sweet farm girl who had never been propositioned by a producer and had fulfilled a dream of hers by singing "White Christmas" on a Bing Crosby special. "For an old cynic, Karen's uncompromising innocence was hard to grasp. . . . So what is an aging, jaded journalist to say? 'Golly' " (Mar. 15, 1975). TV actors lie when they praise the shows they're on, Burt Prelutsky insisted: "As a rule, dull and tasteless as they may be, they're aware of the fact that their show is a piece of cheese." But when Ralph Taeger, "a good simple American soul," lauds the late and unlamented "Hondo," "I'm afraid you'd better believe him" (Dec. 2, 1967). And in "The Greta Garbo of Dodge City" (Dec. 10, 1966), Robert DeRoos's preface threatened to overwhelm his profile. First, DeRoos wrote, TV actors "are nobody. Second, they get a series and become somebody. Third, they complain about their impossibly hard life. Fourth, they let it be known that television is a demeaning medium, that their series is beneath their talents and that they hear a higher call to play Hamlet. Once again, James Arness is not typical."

In essence, then, the *TV Guide* puff piece existed to undermine itself. As soon as readers learned, for example, how unusual Arness was, they discovered that Ed Ames had "reached new heights in the subtle art of the nagging complaint" when he declared the makeup woman's hands too cold (Apr. 6, 1968). By allowing praise in its profiles, moreover, *TV Guide* could eat its cake and have it too, as a balanced, objective magazine that was out to get no one, yet devoted to a single consistent theme: "stardom often results in the loss of all sense of life's values" (Feb. 12, 1966).

For two decades the *TV Guide* profile changed only in minor ways. In the mid-sixties writers turned on psychiatry as an affectation of the rich and famous, little more than celebrity conspicuous consumption. Gloria DeHaven spoke at an "almost non-stop analysis couch clip" of her fear of responsibility, the early divorce of her parents, and her marriage to John Payne at the age of nineteen (June 25, 1966). Pat Crowley told Robert DeRoos that she read *TV Guide*, "and all the people you talk about seem to be in analysis." Since she wasn't, what might she say (Jan. 29, 1966)? An insecure Red Buttons brought with him to the studio "headshrinker" Andrew Salter, "who writes books knocking Freudianism, while pitching 'conditioned reflex theory,' which viewed human frustration as Pavlov viewed canine salivation." Not surprisingly, Salter was no more effective as therapist than as self-appointed critic of the "plot nucleus of scripts" (May 28, 1966). That "Hollywood Dogs Go to a Psychologist" (Dec. 9, 1967) for treatment for "barrier frustration syndrome" and "allilo-mimetic behavior" did not surprise *TV Guide*.

The magazine's writers, like many readers, had come to believe that therapy might be useful as an analytical tool but that there was no substitute for willpower. Thus, a piece on John Davidson, son of a Baptist minister—which revealed that he had been taught to hide his feelings, was "running scared" that ambition might reveal him to be self-centered, and enjoyed clinging to pet monkeys because "they're totally dependent on me"—still had a place in *TV Guide*. But so did one on Kaye Ballard who "sobbed out her problems on a psychiatrist's couch" despite the fact, obvious to all but Kaye, that a "brassy ebullience . . . belies all those couches" (July 20, 1968). And happiest of all, a fitting end to the psychoanalytic sixties, was the tale of Florence Henderson, who went to a therapist thinking she was "supposed to" but was dismissed after four sessions (Feb. 7, 1970).

As celebrities made political pronouncements in the turbulent sixties and seventies, *TV Guide* profiles became outspoken in their criticism of current cant. Indeed, skepticism about psychology stemmed in part from its tendency to blur the lines of moral responsibility and erase the categories of good and evil. In a profile of Jonathan Harris of "Lost In Space," Dwight Whitney asked (a la Efron), "Where has all the Bad gone? Alas, in these psychologically oriented times, no one is really 'bad' anymore, merely 'victimized, the headshrinkers are fond of saying, by environment' " (June 18, 1966). An analysis of the modern western ("Frontier Freud") yearned for the days when the "villain did bad things because he was a Bad guy." Nowadays "the characters sit around and brood over each other's psychological navels" (Jan. 21, 1967).

If profile writers squirmed "under the nagging lash of the do-gooders" (May 9, 1970), they reserved a special contempt for radical chic. For many celebrities, they noted, it was a hypocritical pose. David Carradine, who lived in a decrepit shack with Barbara Hershey and his child, Free (born out of wedlock), drove a twenty-year-old car and was frequently stoned on marijuana. On the set of the films he made or owned, Bill Davidson noticed, he was alert, referring jokingly to directors seeing "his act." "An act?" Davidson queried. "Carradine said it. I didn't" (Jan. 26, 1974). More pathetic were the "up-to-the-minute" politics of Joanne Woodward and the insecurities of Will Hutchins of "Sugarfoot," who wanted to try LSD because it might improve his acting and who exercised diligently three times a week, in search of his "Vital Force." Like other silly celebrities, Hutchins's activities left him physically (and metaphorically) dizzy (Dec. 24, 1966).

To *TV Guide*, the cultural revolution began with impressionable boys and girls "reading and mulling the long, simplistic thoughts of youth" and ended in "hip and almost unintelligible" rhetoric, or worse, misguided, destructive social action (July 12, 1969). Michael Parks, "The Angriest Man on Two Wheels" (Dec. 13, 1969), was the magazine's archetypal radical: "If there weren't so many people vying for the honor, you might say [he] is his own worst enemy."

At this time, not surprisingly, *TV Guide* also found celebrity surrogates for its own political positions. At first Phyllis George (like *TV Guide*) did not discuss her politics. But in 1971 (Sept. 4), angry at people who criticize but present no plan for constructive change, she admitted she was a conservative, attacked campus riots, and lambasted "women's lib" for attempting to set standards for all women. Pat Boone also deserved praise for "Living the Good Life" (Apr. 1, 1978). A living contrast to Elvis, who died "bloated, drugged, alone," Boone resisted the temptations of women and liquor even when clean-cut crooners were out of favor with audiences. His wife, Shirley, helped draw him back to the church, and his career began to flourish again. The moral was clear: everyone wishes to send "audiences into paroxysms of ecstasy merely by walking on stage as Elvis did. But not playing by the rules sometimes leads to destruction of one kind or another. In this case, Boone seems to be saying, the good guy won."

Trips down psychiatric and political paths kept *TV Guide* profiles current and fresh without resorting to gossip. Readers, it seemed, had an insatiable desire to know everything stars thought and did. But the profiles never strayed far from their central aim—to depict the mean truths about the industry.

In the late sixties, when *TV Guide* profiles had established their combative, skeptical, debunking voice, Merrill Panitt decreed that no more than two of them appear per issue. He wanted the space to cover network news and its power to shape public opinion. Equally important, he thought, were articles analyzing industry-wide trends in entertainment, including network program planning, ratings, sponsors, and syndication. Above all, he repeated to his staff, readers of *TV Guide* must understand that television was a business as well as an art; all too often, in Neil Hickey's formulation, it was "a creature with two heads—the Muse and the Marketplace—each biting the other's neck" (May 7, 1966).

One way to address larger issues was to give Edith Efron more latitude. Throughout the sixties and early seventies, she was a one-woman libertarian lobby, lambasting the networks for undermining individual responsibility in the shows they broadcast—and those they didn't. It was probably inevitable that Efron would worry about censorship on television. In "Integrity and the TV Writer" (Apr. 21, 1962) she presided over a debate between Rod Serling ("The Twilight Zone") and Reginald Rose ("The Defenders") on the constraints imposed by network executives hesitant to broadcast controversial shows. Surprisingly, she seemed to agree that the medium provided considerable freedom, noting that Rose's "own career stands as a refutation of Rod's persistent charge." She even gave Rose the final, complacent word: 'I'm sure that a solid Rod Serling play illuminating a controversial issue would find its place in television.' [But he] is unable to keep a note of quiet condemnation from his voice, 'if you don't try, it's unfair to blame it on television.' " Serling, of course, had tried, and when Efron revisited the subject three years later, she had changed her mind and cited eight authorities who were not at all certain that television drama could survive the deadly viruses attacking it: in effect, the code of the National Association of Broadcasters, network censors, pressure groups, congressional committees, and the ratings had a numbing effect on television fare.

Even more disturbing was the impact these same forces—and a "floating political anxiety"—had on network coverage of news (a subject treated at length in chapter 4). Efron ticked off the taboos of "America's Timid Giant" (May 18, 1963): coverage of business and industry, strikes, and the stock market, and airtime for antiadministration sentiment. She dismissed official denials of self-censorship by pointing to "the artless admission that to break controversial stories requires 'courage,' 'brav-

ery,' 'guts,' and 'heroism.' " In light of its constitutionally guaranteed
freedom of speech, television was "that most anomalous of journalistic
entities: a censored medium without a censor." Efron did not have any
answers, but she demanded that the problem be publicly aired, once
and for all, and solved.

More consistent than the editorial position of *TV Guide,* Efron's opposition to censorship was rooted in her philosophy of individual responsibility. The First Amendment, she was fond of saying, "protects
the people whose opinions are not sanctified by the conventional wisdom, *above all.*" Even sex and violence, she believed, should not be
removed from television in the name of protecting the impressionable.
A survey of prime time, she wrote, should persuade even "angry, puritan
opinion leaders" that they retained "virtually uncontested control of
the airwaves." Indeed, the puritans were getting "precisely the TV 'sex'
they deserve." Thus the movement to censor sex would be a "pathetic
waste of time" even if it didn't increase the danger of government
regulation. In essence, Efron argued, all viewers must be their own
censor. No network edict establishing "a family hour" from 8 to 9 P.M.
could pen children in, unless "they're shackled to assorted table legs"
(Oct. 25, 1975).

Even more than sex, however, violence called forth contemporary
censors. Efron thought them more devious than rational, quick to rely
on spurious social science. She returned to the subject repeatedly, in
a multipart series in November 1972, April 1973, and June 1975, each
time dissecting reports on the impact of TV violence as "trash posing
as science." They hid behind vague terms like aggression and acknowledged that it was virtually impossible to isolate the effect of television
content—and then made a "tentative and limited" finding that TV violence and crime were connected, ignoring basic questions of cause
and effect. The studies, moreover, ignored evidence that the overwhelming majority of viewers identify with the heroes of television. To
say that the medium could turn normal people into predators was "plain
poppycock." If the cumulative "watching of evil is turning us all gradually into depraved beings, then the cumulative watching of good must
be turning us all gradually into saints! You cannot have one without the
other . . . unless you can demonstrate that evil is something like cho-
lesterol—something that slowly accumulates and clogs the system while
good is something like spinach, easily digested and quickly excreted."
To use scare tactics to censor, even in the name of ushering in a brave
new world without temptation or transgression, was as dangerous as it
was futile. Efron proposed to put the censors into the "archaic dustbin"

where they belonged, her task made easier, of course, by her demonstration that they were worrying about nonproblems.

Nonetheless, Efron did worry about the impact of television. In one of her occasional essays on the ideas and values embedded in series television, she took aim at depictions of the drug culture. TV softened or concealed moral horror by portraying users as "touchingly vulnerable characters," who should not be held responsible for their actions. "Neurotic," authoritarian parents who clung to the Protestant ethic, Horatio Alger, and the legal system pushed their innocent kids into antisocial behavior. No TV character, Efron acidly observed, tried to escape hypocritical *liberal* parents by turning to drugs. And no "squares" were ever excused from responsibility for their actions. Of course, Efron was not suggesting that such programs be censored, although she hoped to shame the networks into breaking the "anti-Establishment pro-drug-taker bias" that resulted from the left-liberal consensus among Hollywood writers. And once viewers were forewarned, they should be armed against an easy and ultimately destructive sympathy for lawbreakers (Mar. 13, 20, 1971).

Edith Efron did not always speak for *TV Guide*. Alongside her piece on the impact of television violence, for example, Panitt placed a "more moderate" essay by Neil Hickey, the bureau chief of the New York office. In fact, the two were paired so frequently that staff members dubbed them "righty and lefty." Nonetheless, Efron's analytical articles—on censorship, violence, and race (as we shall see in chapter 4—elevated the magazine's stature, in Panitt's view. That she lashed out at liberals was an added plus.

Edith Efron was not the only writer analyzing the industry for the magazine in the sixties and seventies. *TV Guide* demonstrated quite effectively over the years that television was a medium driven by money. As it did, however, the magazine found less and less room for the Muse, especially as the masses failed to practice "dialsmanship." As it increased analysis of the social and political implications of television and enhanced coverage of news and public affairs, *TV Guide* had less to say about the potential of network series. Merrill Panitt does not agree that *TV Guide* became "resigned" to the aesthetic potential of commercial television, preferring to say that it became "realistic," but in these years, it seems to us, the magazine was less and less the scrappy watchdog of the industry, demanding better programs and deploring the glut of trendy genres and the fatuousness of game shows or soaps. In the fifties *TV Guide* had brought to these causes a fervor born of the belief that the young medium could and would be better. But the magazine learned the lesson it was to teach its readers: network executives and sponsors, with both eyes fixed on the bottom line, were unlikely to rise far above the lowest common denominator.

Expressing dissatisfaction with television fare, it is important to note, had become a popular pastime by the 1960s. In 1961, after all, Newton Minow, Chairman of the Federal Communications Commission, asked viewers to turn on their sets for one full day: "I can assure you that you will observe a vast wasteland." This speech made Minow a darling of John F. Kennedy's New Frontier. He was invited on radio and television more than any member of the administration, except the president himself, and voted the top newsmaker in the field of entertainment in 1961 by the Associated Press Annual Poll of editors (previous winners included Marilyn Monroe, Grace Kelly, and Elvis Presley). As *TV Guide* became more critical of the medium, therefore, its editors could be fairly confident that they were not too far ahead of their readers.

As the sixties began, *TV Guide,* as we have seen, pinned its already halfhearted hopes on the networks. When a "Madison Avenue Meddler" controlled a show, invariably safe material was chosen to surround the advertising. Newspapers and magazines do not relinquish editorial control, "As We See It" (Oct. 28, 1961) pointed out; television could not be truly independent or creative until the networks restrained the sponsors. In the wake of the quiz show scandals of the late fifties, in fact, the networks did assume control. By airing longer, more expensive programs, moreover, they made it prohibitively expensive for an advertiser to sponsor a weekly program for an entire season. *TV Guide* applauded this development but added more than a few words of caution: No network, Panitt wrote, "will dictate too harshly to an advertiser who spends $15 million or $20 million a year" (Sept. 24, 1960). Panitt exhorted the networks to "lead as well as follow the viewers' taste," but he had trouble finding a stick to carry, as he spoke softly. "The moment they stop leading," he claimed, the government "commissars" and the amateurs ("pseudo-intellectuals who never watch it anyway") will take over (July 6, 1963).

Commercial television, with all its faults, was clearly preferable to state sponsorship. Government agencies like the Federal Communications Commission (FCC) could regulate "by lifted eyebrow" but should not "come roaring into the marketplace, disturbing all patterns of doing business," without a massive public mandate (Dec. 3, 1966). In Canada, *TV Guide* acknowledged, government subsidies produced more shows of high quality, but viewers stayed away "by the millions" from many of them. Such an approach was fundamentally undemocratic (Jan. 26, 1963). Equally dangerous was government control of program content. When the state steps in, "Taboos Take Over," *TV Guide* pointed out:

in Saudi Arabia, Lucy was banned because she was a domineering wife; in Cuba, Batista shot down "Gunsmoke" (Feb. 6, 1960). In the United States the "nannies" in Washington imposed the so-called "Fairness Doctrine," which effectively curtailed discussion of politically controversial issues, and they also dictated the doctrine of prime-time access, which prompted local stations to dust off antique game shows. They proposed to usurp child-rearing responsibilities, too, by advocating a ban on commercials for highly sugared food on shows directed at children under twelve. Who knew how far they would go if given half a chance? Government, moreover, was usually inefficient. Now that the Swedish government pays for medical bills, "As We See It" pointed out, the wait is up to two years, and the Swedes "are no doubt asking 'Why doesn't the government do something?' " (July 5, 1975). So it was with television, where free enterprise was the best guarantor of freedom and where network entrepreneurs were compelled to respond to the will of the people. Commercial television wasn't very good, but *TV Guide* never wavered in its belief that, like democracy, it was better than any alternative.

For a time *TV Guide* tried to declare victory for network television by seeing evidence of "adolescence if not maturity." But the evidence was meager indeed. As courtroom dramas and medical melodramas replaced westerns, violence and bloodshed subsided. Scripts in general "sound better even if they have little of significance to say." Network and sponsor interference was declining: Bob Newhart made fun of the PTA and supermarkets; "Route 66" brushed aside sponsor objections and produced an episode on the radical right; criminals were not always caught; and divorce and abortion became television topics. Censorship remained a problem, with sponsors turning down 10 percent of all script synopses on "Alcoa Presents" and with "Manhunt" straining to depict no smoker or automobile unfavorably. If *TV Guide* acknowledged that writers still avoided controversial subjects and if it admitted that affiliates still censored, it sought solace in a "New Trend: Adult TV." Still, it was difficult to rejoice in a conclusion that pronounced the medium a "swampland," not a wasteland, because it had promising growth (Mar. 3, 1962).

The dreariness of season after season made this argument difficult to sustain, and *TV Guide* tried another, albeit contradictory, approach. As advertisers discovered they must reach specific audiences to sell specific products, they might abandon ratings, which reveal the size of an audience but not its purchasing power. Hallmark paid twice as much for the "Hall of Fame" as other sponsors did for "Wagon Train" and the show had half the audience. Nonetheless, "As We See It" gleefully noted, Hallmark's revenues had increased 100 percent a year since 1951, the debut of "Hall of Fame" (Feb. 20, 1960). Sponsors, especially those with "considered purchases" (refrigerators, autos, etc.), were finding that support of ballet and classical music might lead them to the "right" viewers: "It's a pleasant prospect" ("As We See It," May 26, 1962).

But it didn't work, as "The Story behind Armstrong Circle Theater's Sudden Demise" (June 1, 1963) demonstrated. The sponsor was satisfied with the show and its selective audiences. The network was not, however, because it charged advertisers based on cost per thousand viewers. So Armstrong made way for Danny Kaye. The incident left little doubt "that the networks are the most powerful single voice in television" and, even more ominous, made "one wonder whether [they] are really interested in 'serious drama.' " *TV Guide* had come full circle but remained lost. The best it could do was hope: "Somebody's going to figure out how to give this medium more satisfying content" (July 24, 1971).

In the bottom-line culture of network television, moreover, neither producers, performers, directors, or writers were likely to agitate to raise aesthetic stands. *TV Guide* articles relentlessly revealed the subordination of artistic considerations to economic ones. "Hugh O'Brien: Actor and Businessman" recognized that he was a marketable product, "a tube of toothpaste." The industry sold him to the public as Wyatt Earp, "and they can easily build someone else." Using the earning power of his name was, therefore, O'Brien's principal aim (Feb. 9, 1957). Even when actors came to Hollywood to make their mark as serious artists, the results were frustration and cynicism: "It's happened too many times to count," and it happened to Paul Michael Glaser of "Starsky and Hutch" (June 3, 1978). Secretly, Glaser, like countless actors who preceded him to Hollywood, "craves the big money, and the big audiences and the attendant fame—a bigger than life kind of life." Glaser discovered television and complained all the way to the bank. Because actors were hired guns, they were perennially uptight, so anxious about making it that they made a pathetic sight at parties as they worked a room making contacts ("The Grim Business of Having Fun," Dec. 26, 1970). More often than not, their interest in their art was a pose. When Robert Horton of "Wagon Train" complained that he was not taxed as an actor, Dwight Whitney sneered, "As if he was somehow expecting" he would be (Mar. 5, 1966). Glaser, too, "naturally pooh-poohs" fame and "talks loftily of artistic commitment." Most revealing of all was "The Starlet" (Apr. 15, 1967), which condemned the typical TV actress for trotting out the "kit shtick" at some point in her career—adding to plastic mi-

plastic microskirt, sunglasses, and boyfriend, the "protestations of high seriousness and the aspiring to thespic art." The article noted that its subject, Karen Jensen, with back turned to the false and phony, goes "to the sea in slacks for introspection." Sometimes a failed romance causes it, "nothing really ghastly, mind you, but something sad enough to pluck the heartstrings." When Karen emerges, she yearns to "give people lives they have never seen or become."

TV writers, although their desire for creative expression was greater, were no less prisoners of the system. When Neil Hickey journeyed to Yale University to observe a class in writing for television, he found "something bizarre, antique and valiant about a handful of young men—protected and sequestered in the placental warmth of a university atmosphere—learning how to be the world's best crossbow archers in an age of overkill." A student play about sin and authority, Hickey observed, "conflicts with everything Desilu, Four Star and Universal are looking for" (May 7, 1966). The professionals agreed. Edith Efron presided over a blistering attack on TV fare by four dramatists. "You will be punished for writing well," they agreed, because programming "doesn't even aspire to the trash art of movies." Once a year, one writer, who admitted that he had become a hack, sat down to write something just for himself. "And it goes nowhere."

American viewers seemed to want what they were getting. In the sixties and seventies *TV Guide* abandoned its faith in an enlightened public transforming the medium. At first the magazine used surrogates for its strongest criticism. In "You, the Public Are to Blame" (Nov. 26, 1960), network executive Hubbell Robinson held one hundred million passive Americans accountable for "the belt-line assemblages of repetitive inanity." Writer-producer Robert Arthur gave the public "Creative Rating—Zero!" (June 17, 1961): "As long as 50 to 60 million red-eyed lumps sit or lie, uncomplaining and unselective, they will only get more of the same dreadful pap." Newton Minow, chairman of the FCC, believed that the "best leadership cannot take people where they do not want to go" (May 13, 1961).

By 1965 (Oct. 23), "As We See It" joined the chorus, asking viewers to tell the truth and admit they enjoyed series television. Three years later staff writer Dick Hobson explained that "Television's Brain Drain" originated in the "dictatorship of the proletariat," the insatiable appetite of "addicts of mediocrity." Most viewers, writers insisted, didn't know what they wanted and settled for what they were shown. That the masses remained unsatisfied, their yearning to enrich their lives unfulfilled, was not much consolation (June 15, 1968). In the same issue, in fact, staff writer Richard Doan was even more gloomy. Commercial TV, network executives now admitted, was "no place for minority tastes, and nobody's making any more bones about it anymore." In fact, *TV Guide* reported, most viewers watched the "least objectionable program" and exhibited little desire for cultural or educational enrichment. When all three networks ran public affairs programs, then and only then did sizable numbers of people watch them. Complaints about TV fare abounded, but when two networks aired a documentary, vast numbers switched to entertainment (July 24, 1971). *TV Guide* had met the enemy—and it was us.

At one time *TV Guide* had appealed to the people to keep good shows on by practicing dialsmanship and writing to networks and sponsors. It had sought to empower the people and had run afoul of the tyranny of the majority. Now it believed anyone who expected much from series television "disingenuous or naive" ("As We See It," Oct. 28, 1967). Attempts to beat the numbers game were futile. "He and She" was canceled, despite the largest number of letters CBS had ever gotten, Doan reported, because the ratings were too low. Scheduled opposite "Laverne and Shirley," "The Paper Chase" didn't have a prayer because it was axiomatic that a show with "intellectual characteristics" had as much chance against a hot sitcom as did "Anita Bryant proselytizing in a gay bar." "As We See It" wished "The Paper Chase" well but feared "it is about to be tripped up by an axiom" (Oct. 14, 1978). "The Law and Mr. Jones" was rescued, but the idea that the affair was "strictly grass roots" was a "pleasant conceit" conceived by producer Sy Gomberg and actor James Whitmore (May 5, 1962). Viewers didn't understand that by the time word got out that a show was canceled, the decision was irreversible. Letter writers seemed uninformed and even pathetic, "the mail girls agreed," when they complained that their program was the most popular on the air. Grateful for the form letter response, some sent back a Christmas card (Sept. 21, 1974).

A mass circulation medium itself, *TV Guide* was reluctant to denigrate the taste of the masses. And yet they found ways to do just that, often, as we have seen, by using surrogates, and sometimes through humor. "View from a Saucer" (Apr. 22, 1967) provided an alien's view of the United States, based on the depiction of reality on television. There's life on earth, he reported, "but I wouldn't exactly call it intelligent." Cartoons often carried the same theme. In one "TV Jibe" (Mar. 16, 1968) a producer says to his associate: "I think the pilot script is vacuous, inane and insulting to any viewer's intelligence. Now let's hope the sponsor likes it too." In another cartoon (Aug. 31, 1968), a youngster asks his father: "But how will I know what wheat is unless I look at the chaff?"

Since few readers identified themselves as part of the mediocre masses, these jibes may have been less risky than one might expect. *TV Guide,* moreover, surrounded its sarcasm with assurances that it actually looked down on those who looked down on television addicts. Highbrow hypocrites, it seemed, watched TV too. In one "TV Jibe," an intellectual, eyes glued to the "Flintstones," says: "TV? Bah! The only things worth watching are the news and Leonard Bernstein" (Sept. 1, 1962). One "TV Snob" insisted that he owned only one set: "Of course there's an idiot box in the children's room and a boob tube in the kitchen" (May 9, 1970).

Even more important, as *TV Guide* accepted network program content as a given, unlikely to change, it became avuncular in its criticism, though occasionally it was wry and wistful. "As We See It," for example, suggested giving the American people "a much-needed vacation during which they would [be] free to . . . enjoy TV without having to worry about what a big problem it is" (Jan. 18, 1972). Once a crusader against reruns, Merrill Panitt now objected to an FCC inquiry on the subject: "if reruns really bother viewers, let the entrepreneur use them at his own risk" (Jan. 26, 1974).

And the magazine developed a technique, not dissimilar from the one Carolyn See would use in the eighties, of undercutting its own tough talk. In a clever article on "Hee Haw," which, according to critics, brought new meaning to the term lowest common denominator, Neil Hickey managed to address discerning readers, adopt an air of resignation, and find something to praise in the program (Mar. 7, 1970). "Hee Haw" had replaced the Smothers Brothers, a politically conscious satirical hour, Hickey sighed, but there was "no point at all in my sitting here being patronizing about 'Hee Haw,' nor in your feeling superior to it. It's bigger than both of us, so we might as well knock off the effete snobbery and accept 'Hee Haw' as a fact of life, like Brussels sprouts or the measles. Oh sure. You and I have refined tastes and we spend a lot of time reading Yeats and listening to Mozart, but how about the less fortunate. . . . Well, a hell of a lot of them watch 'Hee Haw.' " Hickey, however, made a detour en route to his inevitable destination. He had a "nagging suspicion" that Shakespeare, "that most shameless purveyor of bad gags would have loved it. Now don't that sop your gravy."

The master at using the mean truth only to undercut it with a puff was Cleveland Amory, a *TV Guide* reviewer from 1963 to 1974. Amory was fully capable of a moral indignation reminiscent of the reviews of the fifties. The "Jerry Lewis Show," he wrote, ran "two mortal hours," making the comedian's five-year contract "an appalling thought." Lewis's "screeches, his tongue waggings, his eye-crossings" might, perhaps, appeal to people over 95 or "for generations yet, and for quite a while yet, unborn" (Nov. 9, 1963). "The Tonight Show" had "become the know-nothing party of this century. . . . Nowhere, repeat nowhere, do you have even a chance of learning anything [because] the immutable law of 'The Tonight Show' is that the emcees must know nothing."

Amory's most critical reviews appeared in the early sixties. After that he tended to blast only game shows and soaps, perennial *TV Guide* targets. People who like "The Newlywed Game" evidently existed, he wrote. "These are not necessarily people beyond help. They are just beyond outside help. It is quite possible they can help each other" (Mar. 2, 1968). Of the alleged "reality" of soap operas, Amory asked why, then, they never die "no matter how sick they are." He concluded the column with a parting shot: "Finally, a word about the writing. The word is 'no' " (Apr. 25, 1970).

Most of the time, Amory found something positive to say in reviews where puns began to crowd out analysis. As he mellowed, however, he found ways to give the impression that he hadn't gone soft. He found the game show "To Tell The Truth" agreeable, then, noting that it appeared on daytime and prime-time TV, cautioned viewers who wanted to avoid it to "shut your eyes, keep moving and don't talk to strangers." For good measure, Amory added a gratuitous shot at a show he wasn't reviewing, "What's My Line," which "along with smog, exhaust and general noxiousness [is] one of the leading causes of air pollution" (May 28, 1966).

This Janus-faced approach became a trademark of Amory's reviewing. He began with tough talk about a tired genre, then found something valuable in the specific show. TV didn't need another adventure-filled, action-packed series "involving undercover work in a 'fun war,' " but "Jericho" was the best of its kind (Oct. 22, 1966). Despite a "second-hand idea," "third degree violence," and "ludicrous one-sidedness," "Garrison's Gorillas" was (completing the numerical imagery) a "first-rate show" (Jan. 20, 1968). "Lancer," at first glance, was a ready-mix recipe western: "To your proposed batter of Bonanza add a cupful of the High Chaparral, beat vigorously with The Big Valley, and then season carefully." The result you might get, "if you're lucky . . . will be Sonsmoke, or Half Son Will Travel." Yet "Lancer" turned out to be "the most satisfying" western of the season (Oct. 26, 1968). Similarly, "Lost in Space" seemed no exception to the endless number of shows written for children, "but also apparently—so it seems!—by them." Actually, Amory loved the show (Feb. 5, 1966). And finally (though this list could be easily expanded), in the early seventies virtually any lawyer or detective show made a hit, it seemed to Amory. If "The New Perry Mason Show" was new, "we're Baby Snooks," but the program was "interesting, well developed" (Sept. 29, 1973).

Amory found a way to say something nice about "Captain Nice," a show he pronounced bereft of a sustaining idea. "We warned you about spoofs of spoofs," he began. "This time we're not going to warn you— we forbid you to watch it." And yet the reviewer raved about the "fine, fun and genuinely satiric" characters and the scripts, which he thought "more than nice—they're terrific" (Feb. 4, 1967). If readers reached for a reason to watch, they could usually find one in an Amory review.

In his rhetorical bag of tricks, Amory found other costumes of the curmudgeon. "The Jonathan Winters Show," he groused, just might be too great. Then, of course, "by Amory's law, it will go off the air" (Feb. 17, 1968). In his annual "Mailbox" column he printed letters from readers who took violent exception to his reviews. In 1967 (May 27), for example, the first seven were quite critical. "What is a Cleveland Amory?" one reader complained. "He never has anything good to say to anyone, at any time." To the last correspondent, who called him "the greatest," Amory responded: "Thank you, Karen, keep that letter coming." A year later the "Mailbox" was much the same, with the only positive letter acknowledging "how many letters you get from people saying how rotten your reviews are. But I would like to tell you that no matter what anyone says about you, I think you're boss and so do the boys of our class 5A-1" (May 4, 1968).

Nasty letters increased the credibility of a reviewer, Panitt agreed, and "As We See It" went out of its way to distance itself from Amory, as it had with the reviewers of the fifties. In a column on *RT*, the Soviet Union's *TV Guide*, Panitt derided charges that the Voice of America broadcast "falsehoods." Nonetheless, he quipped, *TV Guide* would be willing to exchange critics. "How'd you like Cleveland Amory for a few weeks, Voitekhov?" (May 21, 1966). The editors frequently disagreed with Amory "violently," another editorial claimed. "But he is our critic and we respect him and we print what he writes. This does not mean we endorse what he writes. Not by a long shot. And never by a longer shot than this week," when impenitent Amory had picked "He and She" as television's worst comedy (Apr. 27, 1968).

Actually, Panitt and Amory were aligned in their attitudes toward the medium, if not always in their evaluation of specific shows. As *TV Guide*'s faith in networks and viewers faded, Panitt used the magazine to plug those high-quality programs that were aired, tacitly abandoning its much-trumpeted neutrality. "We told people what to watch," the editor acknowledged with a chuckle, "but we did it in a pleading way, so you couldn't call us authoritarian." Tentatively and apologetically, "As We See It" announced in 1962 (Sept. 22) that programs of "unusual interest" would have a double check mark next to them in the listings. Panitt denied that *TV Guide* was predicting whether they "will be good or bad, whether you will like [them] or not. We have never prejudged programs—nor do we intend to start now."

This was not a very artful dodge, and the double checks soon disappeared, but the editorial staff of the magazine continued to recommend programs directly through "As We See It" and indirectly (though consciously) through their choice of feature articles. From its inception, for example, *TV Guide* showcased PBS programs in far greater numbers than their ratings merited. Its very support of public broadcasting, an exception to its otherwise blanket opposition to government interference in television, marked a recognition that the networks would not risk ratings to elevate taste. Panitt feared that PBS would further release networks from a sense of responsibility but thought that having a public station was the only way to increase the number of good programs. "With certain exceptions," commercial TV must be bland in order to reach huge audiences." As long as PBS was independent of government, it deserved a place on the airwaves (June 19, 1971). Television was what it was, the magazine seemed to say; the best service *TV Guide* could perform was to locate the small but solid core of quality programs so that no person who was inclined to watch would miss them. Each year the magazine named the honor roll—in 1974, for example, "Jane Pittman," "The Execution of Private Slovik," "The Glass Menagerie," and "The Merchant of Venice." Evidently TV was too much a business to consistently be an art form, but enough could be as good as a feast for the selective viewer.

In the sixties and seventies, then, *TV Guide* had two different but complementary tones. Its profiles were sharp, sassy, and skeptical, up-to-date and increasingly appropriate in a journalistic climate of credibility gaps, where personal peccadilloes were fair game. Ironically, the meanest truths were comparatively risk-free for the magazine, for in show business, it seemed, there was no such thing as bad publicity. In the rest of its coverage of the industry, the magazine was resigned and realistic about the aesthetic promise of dialsmanship and the artistic potential of network television. In 1977 (Feb. 19, 26, Mar. 5), Panitt examined "Television Today: The State of the Art." The once-crusading voice was now cautious and chastened. A seller's market, TV cashed in at the rate of $100,000 a minute. Thus, not surprisingly, the creative people deferred to the marketers in setting the network's schedule. Television news was "directed to the mass audience, programmed to provide maximum income, with minimum thought given to improving either the cultural level of the audience or the stature of the medium." As a whole, TV, once considered a guest in the nation's living rooms, had become "to some eyes, at least—pushy and ill-mannered, almost contemptuous of its host." If tens of millions of Americans turned off their sets, the networks might be forced to change "the inordinate amount of mediocre entertainment" they served up. But, Panitt ruefully concluded, "we will continue to watch the medium that informs and entertains us just about as well as we deserve." *TV Guide* had lost its missionary zeal, but it was, more than ever, Merrill Panitt believes, an authoritative but not authoritarian organ of the industry, even if it was largely impotent.

"Television puts the viewer down," Merrill Panitt told us, "but we tried not to." In fact, throughout the sixties and the seventies *TV Guide* tried to implement for itself the advice it gave to the networks—to help create a demand for a high-quality product by occasionally making read-ers reach. In the profiles, as we have seen, *TV Guide* raised the literary level. In 1960 Panitt began to offer space in the magazine to a veritable "Who's Who" in American letters and politics. Attracted by the prospect of preaching to huge audiences, many accepted, including Isaac Asimov, Henry Steele Commager, Betty Friedan, J. Edgar Hoover, Robert Hutchins, Jacob Javits, Max Lerner, Margaret Mead, Malcolm Mug-geridge, Louis Nizer, Chaim Potok, Ronald Reagan, Nelson Rockefeller, Leo Rosten, Arthur Schlesinger, Jr., Eric Sevareid, Benjamin Spock, Arnold J. Toynbee, John Updike, Gore Vidal.

According to Panitt, what he and Annenberg "wanted to do for aesthetic reasons also turned out to be good business." In the fifties *TV Guide* had a relatively difficult time attracting advertising outside of the television industry; indeed, most of the magazine's ad revenue came from promotions of upcoming shows. Advertising, Panitt believes, is sold less on circulation or even demographics than it is on emotion and psychological climate. At first, advertisers thought the medium frivolous and suspected that *TV Guide,* a fan magazine, was read in the dark while the set was on: "That's what killed us." In desperation, Panitt "caved in" in the fifties, allowing a regular food column in the magazine in an effort to attract advertisers with the promise of color displays of their product. In 1960, however, he was confident enough to stress the "in-tellectual quality" of *TV Guide.* Big-name writers lent stature to the magazine, and surveys showed that their articles were "read almost as much as our popular profiles." To make sure that Madison Avenue appreciated the aesthetic appeal of *TV Guide,* Radnor distributed, through its own sales force, glossy booklets with excerpts of interesting articles. Invariably intellectuals were ostentatiously—and disproportion-ately—represented in these brochures. *Nine in Feb.* (1967), for example, gave top billing to Malcolm Muggeridge, included two pieces on Viet-nam, and a piece on Africa by a *Newsweek* correspondent. It worked: advertising revenue shot up, eventually propelling *TV Guide* to the top, and, most pleasing of all, circulation continued to skyrocket. Economic success bred editorial freedom, of course, and Panitt never had to look back.

At first Panitt asked these distinguished writers to assess the me-dium—and must have swallowed hard before publishing the essays they submitted. Leo Rosten's rosy view that television was beginning to rec-ognize the importance of the kind of people who watched and didn't watch and his opinion that in the long run education outweighed es-capism were not shared by most of his colleagues (Oct. 6, 1962). TV had the capacity to keep people well informed and perhaps even "change the dimensions of human participation," according to Mar-garet Mead. But the networks were timid, "accustoming people to dreary half-attention" (Mar. 10, 1962). Malcolm Muggeridge also bowed to TV's potential, but surveyed the cultural wasteland of TV's actual offerings "with distaste bordering on horror." Although the most pop-ular shows were "in terms of fatuity . . . a lower level of entertainment than any hitherto publicly provided," the standard continued to decline visibly from year to year. With characteristic perversity, Muggeridge found solace in a world-weary view that it all made little difference anyway. It "is not saying much," he sighed, but the proportion of worth-while offerings on TV was at least as high as in other mass media, which might well be "intrinsically inimical" to art, literature, and thought. "We do not expect tabloid magazines to serialize Kierkegaard. . . . As well complain about Coney Island's lack of rural amenities." Fortu-nately, Muggeridge impishly concluded, television's impact was small: even those who watched it compulsively were influenced superficially (July 23, 1966).

Muggeridge was an optimist compared to Arnold Toynbee and Louis Kronenberger. In "The Lion that Squeaked" (Dec. 4, 1965), Toynbee depicted TV as a pseudo-alternative for working people upon whom industrialization had placed the curse of boredom. Of interest to those bereft of a loftier vision, television would inevitably sink lower if ad-vertisers had their way. In "Uncivilized and Uncivilizing" (Feb. 26, 1966), Professor Kronenberger agreed with a vengeance. With the ex-ception of the educational stations, he thought television squandered our "supreme cultural opportunity" by catering to "mediocre tastes and mass reactions," pandering to venality, commodifying knowledge, and glorifying violence. Televised versions of *Othello* and Beethoven's *Eroica*, much praised by "As We See It," Kronenberger dismissed as "esthetic distortions," culture with a stopwatch that was punctuated by "grotesque and vulgar intrusions and interpolations—the commercials." His conclusion was unrelenting: "There has been nothing too elegant for it to coarsen, too artistic for it to vulgarize, too sacred for it to profane."

We can imagine Merrill Panitt's ambivalence as he read these words. In his darkest moments, as we have seen, he shared these sentiments. Yet a sweeping, unqualified indictment, reminiscent of the Red Smith philippics of the fifties, was disquieting. Arthur Schlesinger, Jr., to cite another example, took on dialsmanship in the pages of *TV Guide*. "Repelled" when democratic principles were trotted out as cover for a medium that was degenerating into "electronic vaudeville," Schlesinger insisted that cultural democracy begged the "question of how public wants come into being" and ignored the fact that in television, supply creates demand. Disturbed by the fatalism of industry spokesmen, he reminded readers that "artistic excellence is not . . . determined by majority vote" (Dec. 12, 1959). Evidently Panitt felt compelled to respond, although in his editorial in the same issue he addressed only Schlesinger's call for the FCC to raise standards through the granting and renewal of stations' licenses. *TV Guide* believed that program control should be freed from the constraints of antitrust laws; if networks could cooperate, excellent programs might be introduced.

In the sixties, however, the present and future of television was not a matter for debate. The topic was played out. As Henry Steele Commager put it: "Most Americans regard criticism of television like criticism of the weather. It cannot be other than it is" (June 25, 1966). Not coincidentally, we suspect, articles by distinguished Americans in 1967 carried an editor's note: writers had been asked to confine themselves to the "positive aspects" of the medium.

Fortunately, *TV Guide* had other uses for famous writers and experts in psychology, law, and public affairs. To provide authoritative coverage of an issue like TV violence, Panitt solicited contributions by people with a wide range of views. Benjamin Spock worried that violence brutalized children or raised their threshold of tolerance, perhaps even paving the way for the bombing in Vietnam, where women and children, "however unintentionally," were burned along with enemy soldiers (May 28, 1966). Dr. Paul Witty, however, found that TV violence, though it might be a problem in irresponsible families, did not harm children (Feb. 13, 1960).

Obviously these articles blunted the editorial thrust of *TV Guide*, a result acceptable to Panitt, who was not sanguine about "As We See It" 's influence anyway. "We believe," he announced, "a publication should not only take a stand on an issue, but should inform its readers as to the arguments on the other side" (June 17, 1961). In the kaleidoscopic sixties and seventies, in fact, *TV Guide* had difficulty finding its own side on the perennial issues of violence and censorship. To crusade against the former, of course, was to incline toward the latter, a fact that rendered editorials confused and self-contradictory. Thus Panitt commended Mexico for banning thirty-seven violent shows, though he could not "endorse any government action that smacks of censorship" (Nov. 2, 1978). "Violence on Japanese TV" attributed low crime rates in Japan to tight family bonds and heightened civic responsibility. The conclusion, however, was a nonsequitur: "perhaps no amount of TV violence can ever hurt a good kid—whether he's Japanese or American" (Jan. 28, 1978). But *TV Guide* was not ready to take an unambiguously strong stand against censorship, though on occasion it seemed to. Thus "As We See It" pointed out that the TV Code, about "as restrictive as Kate Smith's old girdle on Twiggy" and enforced "with all the rigid discipline of a doting grandmother," was about to be loosened still further to allow ads for "intimate products" (July 27, 1968). Ever-mindful that his readers included churchgoers in Iowa, Panitt was not pleased. Unlike newspapers, he wrote, "it's impossible not to see and hear "television commercials, possibly during dinner." On another occasion the editor remembered that "a panel of thought monarchs" was un-American, finding it disturbing that 60 percent of Americans surveyed supported a review board to keep shows of questionable taste off the air. "Face it," he chided, "a review board is only a euphemism for censorship." By turning the dial—presumably even during dinner— "every man can be his own censor" (Nov. 17, 1973).

With such thorny problems, it is not surprising that *TV Guide* found safe haven behind famous and authoritative signatures. Readers could find in the magazine positions to agree or disagree with on issues that appeared intractable. "As We See It," by the 1970s, was losing its reason for being.

In 1972 Panitt found a way to use name writers without embroiling them—or *TV Guide*—in controversy or recrimination. For upcoming cultural, historical, and public affairs programs, most of them on PBS, *TV Guide* commissioned background articles by "authorities" in appropriate fields. These pieces became a regular feature in the magazine, much to the delight of staff members, who enjoyed tracking down eminent professors or favorite novelists and persuading them to contribute articles to *TV Guide.* Backgrounders such as one by J. Edgar Hoover on the FBI and another by Senator S. I. Hayakawa on the internment of Japanese during World War II added luster to *TV Guide,* but the emphasis was as much on expertise as name recognition. John Garraty, Irving Howe, and Chaim Potok were not well known in most *TV Guide* households, but they were well qualified to set the context for programs on World War I, *The Red Badge of Courage,* and *David.* The editors, of course, informed readers about the credentials of their authorities; most of all, they were delighted that they could publicize good shows, educate readers, and enhance the prestige of their magazine.

Merrill Panitt is justifiably proud that *TV Guide,* far more than TV, provided balanced offerings in a mass medium, including educational and even esoteric fare. That achievement, we must add, was accompanied by outbursts of anti-intellectualism that seemed calculated to provide a balance of their own. While giving space to artists and academics, *TV Guide* simultaneously reinforced popular stereotypes of them. In a spoof on PBS cultural series, for example, host Sir Arbiter Soup, replete with pipe and sherry-filled decanter, introduces "The Saga of Culture": "Some posit that the climb out of the primordial soup began in Olduvai Gorge, some say Jersey City. . . . Perhaps together we can stumble upon some answers, or at least pick up a couple of bimbos." The piece concluded with a word from Joe Garagiola: next week Anthony Hopkins will interview Alistair Cooke about "why there's always an Oriental rug backdrop for BBC interviews. In the meantime, this is pledge week" (July 26, 1975). When writers regarded by the public as intellectuals poked fun at intellectuals, *TV Guide* had an added bonus. Gilbert Seldes, director of the Annenberg School of Communications at the University of Pennsylvania—and *TV Guide*'s reviewer—merely mocked "The Petulant Highbrow and TV" (Jan. 2, 1960), but Eric Sevareid really blasted "professional intellectuals" as hypocrites, "telling each other what they like and dislike" and only "pretend[ing] that their concern is with the great mass of people. With longshoreman-philosopher Eric Hoffer, Sevareid prayed that intellectuals never be given power "because they want people to get down on their knees and love what they really hate" (Dec. 30, 1967). And John Leonard celebrated his retirement as a television critic as an end to "remedial seriousness." Only reviewers or accident victims with multiple compound fractures that prevented them from changing channels were obliged to watch "documentaries on killer bees and Nepalese mating rites." Nor would he any longer be required to attend seminars on the future of TV, Leonard gratuitously added, with "a sociologist whose graduate students compile violence profiles, a psychologist who adumbrates sex roles, a Marxist who babbles on about how the class relations of a culture help determine its deepest communal fantasies, an educator who deplores." "What a relief it is," Leonard gushed, "not to think about what I'm watching when I watch" (Dec. 23, 1978). Intellectuals were welcome in *TV Guide,* then, but the magazine worked hard to put them in their place. They were silly savants—pompous, prescient, and powerless in a democratic society—who merited a hearing but not necessarily a following. In any event, they disagreed about absolutely everything. They were in *TV Guide* but not of it, for *TV Guide* remained the magazine of the people.

In 1978 *TV Guide* was twenty-five years old: it had much to celebrate. According to *Publishers Information Bureau,* the magazine had surpassed all its competitors as a money-maker since 1975, when it earned well over $127 million (*Time* earned $117.3 million; *Newsweek* $88.2; *Sports Illustrated* $67.2; *Reader's Digest* $64.7). And *TV Guide* was still growing: in the first seven months of 1976 it was $14.3 million ahead of its earnings for the same period in the previous year.

In the 69 million television homes in the country, *Business Week* reported (Sept. 20, 1976), approximately 24 million women and 20 million men chose the shows they watched with the aid of *TV Guide*'s Fall Preview Issue. For this single issue, which broke all circulation records by selling more than 20 million copies, the advertising revenue was $5.3 million. In a quarter of a century, *TV Guide* had achieved remarkable penetration into the daily life of Americans, especially those clustered in the largest urban TV markets: it entered 37 percent of the homes in New York City and over 38 percent in Los Angeles. Only in Chicago, where the *Tribune* ran a supplement called *TV Week,* and ironically in its hometown, Philadelphia, was its reach relatively small, at 17.5 percent and 13.8 percent.

Asked by *Business Week* to explain the magazine's phenomenal success, Merrill Panitt modestly pointed out that *TV Guide*'s program listings provided a basic service, available at 300,000 checkout counters, newsstands, and other outlets. But, he continued, every newspaper in the country now provided program information. "There must be something more. Let's face it, you can't sell a billion copies a year unless there's a need for it." Asked to speculate further as to what that "something" might be, Panitt gave a "measure of credit to the magazine's editorial changes over the last decade, when it began to run fewer 'fan' pieces about TV performers in favor of serious articles on such topics as TV violence, the Federal Communication Commission's role in broadcasting, biased news coverage, and educational television." A brilliant editorial balancing act, Panitt did not say, made *TV Guide* an acquired taste and a habit for millions across the economic, educational, and occupational spectrum—and for Madison Avenue as well.

These were the best of times for *TV Guide* and for television. By 1977, 97 percent of all American households had a set; 43 percent had two or more. And Americans were watching those sets over six hours a day. Tiny, dark clouds were appearing on the horizon, in the form of competition by the mighty Time, Inc., and the threat posed by cable TV. But no one noticed. Network television and *TV Guide* were the heavyweight champions of the world, unbeaten, untied, and as yet, unchallenged.

3

"It Was Never the New York Times Review of Books": TV Guide, 1978–91

In 1976 with *TV Guide* riding high, publishing over a million more copies each week than *Reader's Digest,* Merrill Panitt hired David Sendler to replace the ailing Alex Joseph as managing editor. The first outsider to land a top position in Radnor in a quarter of a century, Sendler brought not only a B.A. degree from Dartmouth College and an M.A. from the Columbia University School of Journalism, but also editorial experience with mass circulation magazines including *Sport Magazine, Pageant, Today's Health, Parade,* and *Ladies Home Journal.* Although quiet at first, Sendler impressed Panitt as an imaginative editor; before the decade ended he was executive editor, responsible for the articles in the national edition, with Merrill Panitt close at hand as editorial director. For a dozen years David Sendler wielded great power over the articles in *TV Guide.*

The new editor saw no reason to make radical changes in a stunningly successful magazine, but he sensed that *TV Guide* was a bit stodgy for the seventies. Sendler sought to make the magazine at the same time more substantive and more fun. Faced with competition from Time, Inc.'s highly touted *TV Cable Week* and other program guides for the small screen, Sendler found himself scrambling to retain readers while preserving the delicate balance between serious journalism and the *People Magazine* style readers seemed to prefer. Under his direction, we believe, *TV Guide* simultaneously grew harder and softer. And ironically, in the end, some of Sendler's innovations paved the way for *TV Guide*'s return to the fan magazine style that followed with Rupert Murdoch's acquisition of the magazine in 1988.

Like Merrill Panitt, Sendler relished pieces that "mined better minds" about television in the United States. Along with Managing Editor R. C. Smith, who had taught English at Northwestern and Texas A&M universities, Sendler increased the frequency of "Background" articles, recruiting the likes of John Updike and Alfred Kazin to write them. When Elie Wiesel balked at preparing an article, Sendler and Smith coaxed him into sitting for an interview. The editor even introduced "TV Bookshelf" in 1980, a regular column with reviews of books on the television industry.

As it had in the sixties and seventies, *TV Guide* continued to dig for the hard truth beneath the glamorous façade of Hollywood—debunking dominated. A profile of Carroll O'Connor claimed he was a journeyman actor and playwright before he hit pay dirt as Archie Bunker but "now seems to think himself a consummate actor who *created* the part, who can write better than the writers, direct better than the directors" (Jan. 6, 1979). O'Connor was emblematic of "The Three Stages of Hollywood Stardom": at first friendly and even grateful, rising stars begin to demand special treatment and then artistic control. At the third stage, when nothing seems right, "Exit star, enter lawyer." As one agent put it: "Once I get them where they want to be, where the air is rarified, they become deified. That's when I get nullified" (Oct. 9, 1982). Susan Littwin concluded a positive profile of Cathy Podewell of "Dallas" by insisting that she had not been fooled: "I know that as soon as I'm gone, she will snarl at the propman for giving her the wrong napkins. . . . Soon she will demand that her salary be tripled and that a limo drive her to work. The tabloids will show her tossing a drink at someone. I mean, she's an actress, isn't she?" (Oct. 7, 1989).

When actors weren't arrogant, *TV Guide* reported, they could be downright pathetic. Against the "myth" that stars enjoyed a carefree existence, *TV Guide* depicted drinking, drugs, and divorce as the prices they paid for their success (July 18, 1987). Fantasy helped cancel out the life of soap opera actress Brenda Benet, Mary Murphy informed readers. In the real world, her first husband, Paul Peterson, testified, Benet would have been in a mental hospital, but in Hollywood she was a star. When Benet's son died in a medical mishap, she turned to unorthodox religion and then to alcohol. Nothing helped: even playing a villain did not, this time, allow her to escape the traumas of her life— and she committed suicide. "With the homage it pays illusion," Hollywood, Murphy concluded, was a contributing cause (Mar. 12, 1983).

Even television's top performers remained insecure in Hollywood, fretting about keeping a job, gaining weight, paying taxes, growing old, and even bad lighting. Ironically, stardom often fed neuroses by reminding actors how far they had come and how much they had to lose (Jan. 16, 1982). The writer of "Congratulations, You're a Star—Let the Suffering Begin" asserted that very few successful performers landed on their feet. The hazards of fame moved Barry Manilow to don a moustache in an often futile quest for anonymity; more ominous, it kept Jonathan Winters and Robert Blake "going around the bend and coming back," and it destroyed Freddie Prinze and John Belushi (July 16, 1988).

In Hollywood, contract-breaking, theft of ideas, and embezzlement were everyday occurrences, and the word was spelled ETHIC$. As Fred Allen said, all the morals in town could be "rolled up and fit in a gnat's navel and still have enough room for an agent's heart." It was no place for the squeamish and naive (Jan. 16, 1982). Yet they came by the truckload, approaching "auditions with the faith of a soldier charging a hill, certain that it is *he* who is special and blessed and that it is the man running next to him who will be shot down. The conviction has the substance of a cloud but it is peculiarly sustaining." Some of these neophytes ended on the casting couch; others toiled on till talent commanded attention, refusing to believe that capriciousness and favoritism often governed the industry. After four auditions with "Buck Rogers in the 25th Century," Eddie Benton kept asking himself what they wanted. What they wanted was a brunette. And "another hundred people just got off the train" (Nov. 3, 1979).

These articles were familiar fare to the *TV Guide* faithful. Sendler decided to revise the recipe. To show readers that television was a business, Sendler pushed staff writers into the offices of the network executives responsible for the fall lineup. *TV Guide* revealed how series had become more powerful than stars. When "Charlie's Angels" survived the departure of Farrah Fawcett, for example, the magazine reported that the networks began to play hardball with pouting prima donnas, preparing in each series an elimination episode to let stars know they were eminently expendable (June 30, 1979).

With "NBC Confidential: Inside TV's Power Decisions," *TV Guide's* readers accompanied Brandon Tartikoff as he chose the programs the network would put on the air. They learned from a master in a *TV Guide* exclusive how important a lead-in was to a new show, how prestige programs were scheduled opposite blockbusters on another network, and why advertisers looked beyond the ratings numbers to "demographics." In writer Richard Turner's hands, *TV Guide* gave specificity to its assertion that Hollywood honored only the bottom line: for program executives like Tartikoff, "special scorn seems reserved for shows with high pretensions but not enough 'larger than life' characters or situations, not enough 'promotability'—buzzwords for traditional commercial appeal." Readers watched as Tartikoff turned thumbs down on pilots "The Big Five" and "The Shooter," shuffled "Family Ties" to Sunday, and paid homage to producer Aaron Spelling, then denied his show "Nightingales" a spot in the fall (Oct. 8, 15, 1988). Few executives were as courageous or crazy as Tartikoff, so these scoops were rare. However, in other articles *TV Guide* took a hard look at casting decisions, the sale of "The Cosby Show" for syndication, and the negotiations between the networks and the NCAA over college football.

As *TV Guide* pushed into the boardrooms, it also lingered more often backstage. Neither Sendler nor Panitt had any desire to turn the magazine into a scandal sheet, but he was more willing to publish stories about sex and drugs in Hollywood, and even to name names, especially when connections could be made to what appeared on the small screen. This kind of exposé journalism, according to Sendler, was not at all incompatible with the middle-class respectability to which *TV Guide* aspired, not at a time when Americans palpitated over the peccadilloes of John F. Kennedy and Gary Hart.

In a cover story on "Hollywood's Cocaine Connection," Frank Swertlow called drug use in the television community an "epidemic." He described young performers, rich and famous, bored and immature, attracted to a subculture that had become "a status thing" in Hollywood. Often barely able to function when the cameras began to roll, these performers, insiders feared, might well "destroy the TV industry" (Feb. 28, Mar. 7, 1981). The other scourge of the eighties, of course, was AIDS. In a fascinating story, Mary Murphy demonstrated that gay actors were having difficulty finding work in television because their straight colleagues were petrified of exposure to the virus. Every embrace, every on-screen kiss had become an occasion for negotiation. One executive told Murphy, "The one thing we need is to make a safe place in this world for people who have AIDS, and it's not safe for people to have AIDS in Hollywood" (Oct. 22, 1988).

Articles on drugs and AIDS made Sendler's *TV Guide* more topical and trendy while reinforcing the theme that television was a business, grim as well as glamorous. Staff writers, however, could not often attach names to quotations because performers feared retribution, and the magazine's forays into investigative journalism often seemed shallow. The sources for "TV's Daring Stunts: Are the Thrills Worth Dying For?," who charged the industry with recklessness and a failure to report accidents, remained anonymous (Mar. 13, 1982) as had those who talked with Swertlow and Murphy. More often than not, *TV Guide* placed the "mean truth" in a morality play straight out of the fifties, discussing drugs, for example, in profiles of performers who claimed to have kicked the habit. Johnny Depp of "21 Jump Street" had gotten into trouble for breaking and entering, used drugs, lost his virginity at the age of thirteen, and dropped out of high school during a misspent youth in Florida. But the "Bad Boy" had become a "Role Model," proud that his show taught kids about drugs and safe sex (Jan. 23, 1988). A similar message headed another article: "Ray Sharkey Would Die before Using Drugs Again." Although producer Stephen Cannell insisted that the former heroin addict who had often overdosed be tested regularly while on the set of "Wise Guys," Elaine Warren reported that Sharkey was back in control, helping others as part of his own therapy (Aug. 6, 1988). *TV Guide* was not breaking stories, but it was keeping up with the news while preaching safe sermons to a church of the already converted.

As it took readers behind the scenes, with mixed success, Sendler's *TV Guide* also tried to make them more conscious of the values embedded in prime-time television. Articles demonstrated how television changed with the times. CBS had resisted a black costar on "Mannix," Mary Murphy maintained, but reversed itself the day after Martin Luther King was assassinated (Aug. 13, 1983). For years, Dan Wakefield reported, the words "condom" and "birth control" could not be mentioned on the air, but in the age of AIDS the networks had loosened up, arguing that sex education was a public service as well as an aesthetic and artistic right (Nov. 7, 1987).

Still, the networks reacted cautiously to cultural trends, *TV Guide* pointed out. Television in the eighties depicted neither sex nor nudity, Stephen Birmingham pointed out, and subjects like adultery were treated with old-fashioned morality even on prime-time soaps. In his view, organizations like Donald Wildmon's Coalition for Better Television (a fundamentalist lobby prepared to boycott companies that sponsored objectionable programs), had identified the wrong target (May 22, 1982).

For the most part, *TV Guide* confined itself to a description of cultural trends in television. Doug Hill charted the change among network censors from a doctrinaire to a situational approach to sex. Hill implied that with audience expectations liberalized by movies and cable, they had little choice, although AIDS may have sent the pendulum in the other direction. Officer Cagney, Hill observed, was no longer sleeping around (Aug. 8, 1987). Howard Polskin agreed that television was getting sexier, pointing to the bondage scene in the made-for-prime-time movie "Favorite Son." Although he acknowledged that this was a disturbing thought to some, Polskin concluded that as long as audiences tuned in, even at "moderate levels, it may be anything goes for a long time" (Jan. 7, 1989). Mary Murphy revealed that "Hollywood's Forbidden Subjects" included romance between old people, astrology, and lying among military service members. Taboos are necessary, she editorialized ("TV cannot provide a forum for hatemongers"), and, for the most part, television was responsive and responsible (Aug. 13, 1983).

In a sense, of course, articles on these subjects, especially with titles like "Prime Time Sex: Hotter or Cooler?" (May 22, 1982), contributed to the sensationalism and decadence that some deplored. Nonetheless, *TV Guide* occasionally made its cultural sympathies clear to regular readers of the magazine. In calling for television without restraint, Ron Powers stood virtually alone. "Take away violence, take away sex, and you have taken away the two main motivating impulses of the long history of human drama" (Aug. 5, 1978). More representative was "Family Viewing: Proceed at Your Own Risk," which lamented television's treatment of premarital sex as an ordinary, everyday affair. In "Eight Is Enough," for example, one character discovered that "everyone in her school was on the pill." The article concluded that television should not return to "Ozzie and Harriet" but that children should remain children a bit longer (Aug. 11, 1979). Eight years later the world of the Nelsons seemed even more attractive to David Handler. Ozzie and Harriet's town was "safe, clean, prosperous and fair. No one died of cancer. No one *died*. There was no poverty or racial injustice or divorce or rape or suicide. . . . Those were the days of blessed ignorance [and] lately I've been feeling strong pangs of nostalgia for the '50s" (Nov. 14, 1987).

In the early eighties, *TV Guide* provided a column to psychologists Dorothy and Jerome Singer, who advised parents on how best to use television for their family. In their counsel of moderation and restraint, the Singers seemed to reflect the views of the men in Radnor. By watching shows like "Little House on the Prairie" and "Happy Days" with their children, the Singers suggested, parents could find examples of friends exhibiting genuine concern for each other. Conversely, the Singers looked askance at small children who watched horror movies: "Although your daughter does not show signs of being afraid now, research indicates that sometimes frightening images can remain to haunt a child as she gets older. We suggest you steer her in the direction of more appropriate programs." The Singers worried that children might learn from television that sex was more closely related to "violence and vulgarity than love and intimacy." Thus they praised the episode on sex education on "Archie Bunker's Place" and fretted about a "CHIPS" show about a male stripper ("make certain such video incidents never go without comment"). For young children, parents should preselect suitable programs, they advised. "With older children you may have to play a more active part" (July 11, 1981; Aug. 7, 1982).

Of course the Singers were concerned about programs for children. It seems clear to us, however, that *TV Guide* deemed wholesome programming sufficient and salutary for all ages. The magazine had long since withdrawn any overt sympathy for the censor, but, like David Handler, it preferred (but did not demand) less complicated, less explicit, less relativistic culture than the one that was slipping, albeit slowly, onto the small screen.

The most discerning cultural analysis in *TV Guide,* not surprisingly, was the least didactic. A four-part series, "How TV Helps Shape Our Values," by Joanmarie Kalter and Susan Littwin, provided a particularly perceptive look at prime time. In family shows, Kalter argued, kids were self-styled and independent, invariably more sensible than their parents. The programs of the eighties reveled in individuality but concluded on a note of community that might not ring true to audiences (July 23, 1988). Littwin agreed that television created a world of unbridled individualism where the uncertainty of relationships, even within families, was accepted. Even being a couple seemed unnatural. Each week Sam and Diane ("Cheers") and David and Maddie ("Moonlighting") affirmed that individual freedom must not be sacrificed to a relationship. In the subtext of the small screen, moreover, good and evil, love, and principles seemed melodramatic, while personal gain seemed the only plausible motive for action. The visual message was that style really counted, as exemplified by the wardrobe of Sonny Crockett ("Miami Vice"). "For without social support, ethics become vague and ideals evaporate into cynicism and irony" (July 30, 1988).

Littwin also chronicled the disappearance of the hero on prime time. Television not only had fired the western marshal but had also abandoned stories of ordinary people who made courageous choices in realistic settings. Well-intentioned characters in the eighties tended to be flawed, weak, and ineffectual. Programs seemed too bathed in irony to take heroism seriously. Thus when Joe Gardner of "A Year in the Life" saved the attorney general of the state, he was made to gather his family around the TV set to watch the evening news and look foolish when the story failed to appear on the air. Modern-day protagonists, Littwin observed, viewed the members of the establishment as an enemy as formidable as the criminals they battled. "The Equalizer," for example, was part entrepreneur, part vigilante; on "Hill Street Blues," Steven Bochko's cops compromised and clawed in the urban jungle (Aug. 6, 1988).

This series of fine essays, despite its title, did not demonstrate that television was a value *setter,* but it made viewers more aware that popular programs, however entertaining, also contained a view of the world. Cultural analysis had appeared in *TV Guide* before, often written by Edith Efron, but during Sendler's tenure such articles surfaced more frequently and evidenced greater sophistication. No one could be sure how readers reacted to these more cerebral essays, but as long as circulation remained high and Walter Annenberg and Merrill Panitt encouraged him, Sendler indulged his instincts as a journalist. "We did things that weren't always commercial," R. C. Smith acknowledged, but "we thought readers should have more substance." *TV Guide* would never be mistaken for *The New York Review of Books,* but at its best, it provided an informative, insightful assessment of television.

By the time David Sendler came to *TV Guide,* dialsmanship had been relegated to a ritual affirmation in "As We See It." As already noted, Panitt had come to accept television as it was by the 1960s, but in editorials throughout the seventies and eighties he continued to exhort his readers to raise their standards—and to hope. The editor blasted game show producer Bob Stewart for flashing answers to contestants on the assumption that audiences with "diminished IQs" wanted to be entertained rather than tested. Stewart had "his facts backward. The audience hasn't changed. What has diminished is the quality of the game show product: sleazy, exploitative programs put together by producers who hold their customers in contempt" (Nov. 4, 1978). As he had done countless times before, Panitt praised PBS for doing Shakespeare, and he lobbied for high ratings (Feb. 10, 1979); he attacked as naive the assumption that advertisers would support programs if, despite meager audiences, they attracted critical acclaim (Nov. 18, 1978); and he insisted that since people with a college education on average watched television two hours and thirty-one minutes per day, the medium "must be doing something right" (May 5, 1979).

But by the late seventies "As We See It" was running on empty. Panitt tried to salvage dialsmanship by adopting the definition of excellence advanced by Fred Pierce, the president of ABC. "Quality is not in the form but in the execution," Pierce insisted. "It is not necessarily in the intellectual level of the message but in its effectiveness. Does the show do what it's supposed to do. . . . As viewers, we need to quit feeling guilty about how someone else thinks we should spend our leisure time." By this standard Pierce—and Panitt—judged "60 Minutes," "Laverne and Shirley," and "Little House on the Prairie" excellent shows (Dec. 16, 1978). In essence, "As We See It" was equating quality with popularity, but Panitt sounded more resigned than convinced.

By the eighties, "As We See It" had become an occasional, rather than a weekly, column. Months might go by without an editorial in *TV Guide*. When Panitt picked up his pen, he assessed the medium and the masses in the same schizophrenic way. In 1986 he observed that the ratings of nighttime soaps were down, while the "bastions of the literate" ("Moonlighting," "The Golden Girls," and "Murder She Wrote") were up. Maybe, "just maybe," he mused, "underestimation doesn't carry the profit margin it used to." Optimism, however, did not last through the end of the editorial. "No one ever went broke underestimating the intelligence of the American public," he sighed, and agreed that the adage was not yet "ready for the ashcan" (Feb. 16, 1986).

Two years later the same sentiments surfaced, in a slightly different order. The cancellation of shows with sensitive writing and plots and characterizations that broke new ground ("Cagney and Lacey," "St. Elsewhere," and "A Year in the Life") prompted Panitt to make a "wildly unscientific and highly subjective survey" that revealed that some viewers "rather bitterly contemplate" abandoning network TV altogether. Evidently, however, Merrill Panitt was not one of them. Other good shows remained on the schedule, he pointed out, and the world had not ended when "Lou Grant" and "The Mary Tyler Moore Show" went off the air several years earlier. But the editor was as uncomfortable with complacency as he was with threats. If a new crop of promising programs did not spring up, he predicted, "brokenhearted fans won't weep for long. They'll simply dry their tears and turn to cable and local channels, where their favorites are being rerun" (June 18, 1988).

David Sendler did not believe he could use *TV Guide* to change programming practices or viewing habits. To be sure, he hyped PBS programs with "Background" articles as Panitt had, and no doubt he endorsed Neil Hickey's spirited defense of public television against a Reaganite challenge. Half of PBS's viewers, Hickey reported (Dec. 11, 1982), came from households that earned less than $20,000 a year, and the federal government spent less in support of the network than the Pentagon did on 103 military bands. Sendler believed that viewers did not—and would not—control television programming, but neither did he think that the quality would improve if they did. Because television is a business, *TV Guide* repeated, "given a choice between a splendid humanistic drama and a piece of total trash, worthless and degrading," network executives choose the one that promises higher ratings (Nov. 18, 1978), and viewers select from the options they are given. During Sendler's tenure the magazine was less likely to balance its assessment of the mediocrity of the medium by trying to flatter or empower or implore readers/viewers. In a skeptical, adversarial, sometimes cynical age, *TV Guide* may actually have reached out to readers by showing them that no matter how much television insulted their intelligence, many of them came back for more.

In his typically acerbic style, staff writer Laurence Eisenberg summarized the contempt television producers had for their audience. When they turned best-sellers into TV movies, producers assumed that the average viewer was "too simple-minded to sit still for dramatic development or complex dialogue." Early on, "without taxing the intellect of a hamster," they set the theme, flashing pertinent plot information "like Trivial Pursuit answers" (Apr. 26, 1986). The image of the "boob tube" was so pervasive in American culture in the eighties that sarcasm was meant to amuse, not enrage, readers, or to get them to demand better programs. For a quick laugh, a "TV Jibe" aimed at the vacuous video was frequently inserted into *TV Guide*: "Due to the Idiotic Subject Matter of the Following Program Viewing Discretion Is Advised" (Jan. 6, 1979); "Because of the puerile nature of the following show, viewer discretion is advised" (Nov. 24, 1979); [two kids chatting] "Sometimes I wish I had a shorter attention span so I wouldn't have to watch so much of this stuff" (July 3, 1982).

Occasionally a guest columnist like critic John Leonard did plead for a little more meaning in prime time. "Three's Company" did not turn teeth green, he admitted, but neither was it a good way "for millions of English-speaking peoples to punch a hole in their Tuesday nights, when they could be out at a drive-in watching *Porky's IV* or being stomped on at a Clash concert." When real emotions and problems disappeared from the screen, Americans were anesthetized into accepting that nothing happens and never will in the "Romper Room" in their home "where the prats fall like apples of unknowing" (Sept. 24, 1983). If Leonard's elitism did not reveal him as a card-carrying intellectual, his prose did. He, too, was in the magazine to arouse readers, we suspect, because he took it all so seriously. "Better Think Twice before Asking Academics to Explain TV," Merrill Panitt warned (Nov. 5, 1988). Did he mean to include John Leonard?

TV Guide's tough talk about TV, then, came with a recognition that even ardent watchers agreed that the medium was mediocre; a sweeping indictment offended few. While reviewer Robert MacKenzie felt free to be critical of the quality of network programs, as Leonard had, he

'Because of the puerile nature of the following show, viewer discretion is advised.'

did so as a populist, making common cause with the reader/viewer and asking, as *TV Guide* used to, for something better. TV doesn't often move us or illuminate life, he wrote, because we don't want it to, "and maybe that's wise of us, day to day. But sometimes, after a day of walking around pretending that nothing scares us and that life is a joke, we come home with a need to hear something true about human existence, even if it costs us an emotional investment" (Apr. 23, 1983). MacKenzie devoted whole columns to this subject. "Why Don't We Talk about Television?" he asked, answering that it had become a self-contained medium, with love-boats, supertrains, and fantasy islands, "a pleasant

place to pass some time, but one that hasn't much to do with our lives."
Television achieves its aim, pleasant pacification, with consummate skill,
but MacKenzie continued to hope that viewers were "ready for a shot
of adrenalin." The best assurance he could give was that television could
be worse, but he insisted there was a better way. "Switch off the schlock
and read a book or paper the bathroom. Better yet find a program that
charges your mental batteries instead of draining them" (Apr. 28, 1979).

The last missionary in *TV Guide,* MacKenzie presented himself as a
tough critic. And, as Cleveland Amory had, he luxuriated in angry reactions to his reviews: "Most of my mail has to be handled with tweezers,
since it blisters the skin on contact . . . people whose favorite series I
have panned have an understandable urge to dip me in hot fat" (June
11, 1983). But in fact, in his reviews MacKenzie tried to identify the
qualities in shows that made them popular, and as he moved from the
generic to the specific, he softened, generating increasing sympathy for
the status quo. He often could not bring himself to pan even the programs he didn't like.

MacKenzie's reviews worked on two levels. To discriminating viewers
they seemed to say, "This popular show is pretty bad, but let's agree,
it's bigger than both of us." But they also reassured fans that what they
liked was likable. Although the plots of "Father Murphy" were "pat
and predictable and schmaltzy," MacKenzie found them satisfying because "corn is another word for sentiments we all respond to" (Jan. 2,
1982). Despite the fact that "We Got It Made" was a "bit of fluff" in
the distinguished tradition of "airhead comedies" derided from coast
to coast, MacKenzie decided to like the show. "It features the cutest
blonde in television, and who needs a better reason than that?" (Nov.
12, 1983). Even the atrocious "A-Team" escaped MacKenzie's frying
pan. The show's glorification of destruction seemed obsessive, but he
acknowledged that "tired guys who have spent the day drilling teeth or
putting fenders on Fords may find an hour of uncomplicated diversion
here" (Mar. 26, 1983). When Robert MacKenzie claimed that viewers
need not fear "cerebral cramps" if they returned from a hard day at
the office and watched "BJ & the Bear," he was describing, not decrying,
the show (Sept. 29, 1979). In reviews of specific programs, it turned
out, MacKenzie was not much of a missionary at all.

In 1985 MacKenzie gave way to Merrill Panitt, who used the pseu-
donym Don Merrill to prevent anyone from assuming that reviews had
the editorial imprimatur of the magazine. Panitt occasionally advised
readers to watch programs that were good for them. Anyone who missed
"The Story of English" forfeited forever the privilege of deriding television "as a boob tube filled with nothing but bubble gum for the

mind" (Oct. 4, 1986). And once in a great while Panitt could be roused to righteous wrath reminiscent of the reviewers of the fifties. About 'Divorce Court,' he inveighed: "Is this entertainment in America today? Is this how we get our jollies in a civilized country? Divorce Court, exploiting as it does the distress of failed marriages, is revolting, it's trash and it belongs in a garbage can, not in our homes" (June 14, 1986).

"Divorce Court" was not a prime-time show, and Panitt more typically wrote his reviews with one eye on the Nielsen ratings. Even more than Robert MacKenzie, he confirmed and legitimized viewer's choices, putting into practice the Fred Pierce principles he had once endorsed in an editorial. "So what if it isn't Shakespeare?," Panitt wrote of "A Different World." The sitcom provided "light entertainment for people who have nothing better to watch or do. . . . As such, it's doing its job" (Jan. 16, 1988). He liked "Matlock," despite the courtroom drama's "derivativeness and thin stories, because there's such a pleasant feeling about it. . . . Nothing to tax the viewer's legal knowledge" (Dec. 20, 1986). And the once arch-foe of game shows now said of "The $100,000 Pyramid," "There are times for all of us when mental stimulation is the last thing we want [and this is] a pleasant enough way to spend a half hour" (May 30, 1987). As for "Wheel of Fortune," "despite incessant product plugs, studied enthusiasm and blatant materialism [it] turns out to be fun for the viewer" (Oct. 5, 1985).

Don Merrill came very close to saying that some programs must be good because they were popular. He was tempted to suggest more substantial plots and better production values for "My Two Dads." "We're tempted—but the obvious answer is: 'Don't carp. The show's successful' " (Jan. 2, 1988). With the fabled "Dallas," Panitt marveled at how the professionals responsible for the show kept it "fascinating to its audience. Its viewers *care* about what happens . . . enough to keep it among the top 10 shows on television and that, after all, is the accolade that counts" (Feb. 15, 1986). Don Merrill might just as well have revealed his identity; he was saying precious little to offend.

As television condescended to viewers, *TV Guide* prided itself on the respect it retained for its readers. That the magazine no longer crusaded for better programs was a sign of realistic, objective journalism. Among his significant accomplishments, David Sendler listed the sophisticated and graceful prose he and the professorial R. C. Smith brought to *TV Guide*, not only from famous guest columnists, but from staff writers and free-lancers.

As long as circulation increased, no one at Radnor worried about the anomaly of articles on J. S. Bach in a magazine for the masses. But sales of *TV Guide* peaked at about eighteen million per week in the late seventies. When the mighty Time, Inc., announced the birth of *TV Cable Week*, Walter Annenberg opened his wallet and approved Sendler's request to add eight pages to the national edition. *TV Cable Week* died in 1983, six months into its infancy, but the "Insider" section added to *TV Guide* in the eighties remained and, we believe, started it on a long journey back, in content and style, to the fan magazine. *TV Guide* was not immune to the trend in mass media that substituted the snippet for the essay and made *People Magazine* and *USA Today* enormously successful.

The "Insider" appeared on colored paper that was filled with photographs. The section allowed *TV Guide* to provide weekly coverage of soap operas, sports, and home video releases. The "Insider," according to Sendler, was the "playground" of the magazine, providing "quick little nuggets, juicy little things that were happening around town." He thought it gave *TV Guide* a new look and feel; in conjunction with the longer, more thoughtful articles, "Insider" made for a more balanced national edition. An immediate hit with readers, it became the "most read" section in *TV Guide*. "If you want to call it soft," Sendler told us, "that wasn't the intention."

Merrill Panitt did acknowledge that the "little gossipy items" in the "Insider" constituted "fan magazine stuff." And indeed it was just that, often in the form of squibs reminiscent of *People Magazine* and *USA Today*. "Insider," for example, breathlessly reviewed the results of a poll on whether Ann Romano of "One Day at a Time" should get married; some thought she should live together with her partner out of wedlock— "naughty, naughty" (July 2, 1983). Two weeks later, "Grapevine" revealed that after working together on "Male Model," Jon-Erik Hexum and Joan Collins "were seen together looking very chummy at two recent Hollywood dinners." For just-pubescent fans, "Grapevine" giggled that Scott Baio and Heather Locklear, who met on "The Battle of the Network Stars," had become "Jocks in Love" (July 16, 1983).

On the last page of the "Insider," the section "Cheers 'n Jeers" in effect replaced "As We See It" with four or five editorials of 100 to 150 words each. The column clung to familiar and inoffensive themes. With a mangling of tenses, it predicted that the clustering of commercials "may increase network revenues, but if it results in a turned-off, tuned-out audience, maybe the strategy is back-firing" (Oct. 8, 1988). It jeered steamy promos during the family hour (8 to 9 P.M.) for soap operas because children might watch them: "Little pitchers have big eyes, as well as big ears" (Nov. 5, 1988). To sophisticated readers, "Cheers 'n Jeers" brought new meaning to the word insipid. The editors praised Wilma Flintstone as a role model because she resisted Stoney, "A Marijuana-Smoking Neanderthal." The message of the cartoon was important, *TV Guide* cheered: "Just say yabba dabba don't!" (Sept. 17, 1988). But the prize for vacuity was won hands-down for the jeer to the "Santa-bashing" of "Probe," which had shown Parker Stevenson announcing: "the hard evidence says the guy's bogus." *TV Guide* brought down its editorial wrath on such muckraking during the family hour: "If you want to puncture childish fantasies, do it later in the evening" (May 28, 1988).

For decades, Merrill Panitt and David Sendler agreed, *TV Guide* was not interested in the diets or sex lives of the stars. The magazine worked hard to gain the respect of readers, advertisers, and industry insiders. In the eighties, they glimpsed into the future, and it worked.

In August 1988 Rupert Murdoch, the titan of tabloids, purchased *TV Guide, Seventeen,* and the *Daily Racing Form* for $3 billion, by far the biggest deal in the history of publishing. Born in 1931 in Australia, Murdoch had inherited the *Adelaide News* when he was twenty-one years old. Within a few years he had amassed vast holdings in news corporations and publishing companies. Then, in the United States, he acquired, among many other holdings, the *Chicago Sun-Times,* the *New York Post,* the *Boston Herald,* and the Fox Broadcasting System.

In almost every venture Murdoch was accused of promoting sensationalism in order to attract readers and viewers. In *TV Guide,* the jewel in Annenberg's crown, Murdoch acquired a magazine that was still widely read in the United States (approximately 17.2 million readers per week in 1987), with huge annual advertising revenues ($331.2 million). Murdoch announced to the press that he would not tinker with *TV Guide,* nor would he use the magazine to promote the Fox Broadcasting Company, which he also owned: "I'm not that silly. I paid a lot of money for that property. I'm not about to destroy its credibility. I plan no changes at all there."

Nonetheless, signs began to appear that *TV Guide* was slipping. In the first half of 1988 circulation fell to 16.3 million (attributable, perhaps, to an increase in the cover price from 60 to 75 cents) while advertising revenue leveled off. Joseph Cece, newly installed as president of *TV Guide,* rushed to rectify the illusion that it "is broke and needs to be fixed," but the Murdochians were scrambling toward what *Time* magazine was to call "The Tarting Up of *TV Guide*" (May 29, 1989).

Murdoch's people stressed circulation rather than advertising. In a meeting with the editors soon after he took over, Murdoch labeled the magazine "too cerebral." Cece and Roger Wood, the Murdoch lieutenant who revamped the *Chicago Sun-Times* and the *New York Post,* assured Smith and Sendler that they, too, thought "middle-class respectability" essential to *TV Guide*'s success. But actions spoke louder than words. Wood grumbled that articles on news and public affairs were too long or too boring. Sendler read the handwriting on the wall and discontinued the "Background" feature. Within a year, the new management had doubled the number of personality profiles, added more photos, inserted a soap opera summary, and even offered a horoscope (where readers followed Uranus, the planet that rules television). *TV Guide* had not run one-page profiles for decades; R. C. Smith thought them "unbelievably sappy." In the new *TV Guide,* brevity became the soul of wit—and wisdom.

Of all the sections in the national edition, the "Insider" was least in need of alteration, given the emphasis on fun. If anything, its tidbits grew more childish. For example, on September 2, 1989, it revealed that Vanna White considered her greatest beauty flaw to be her ugly toes and that Robin Leach stole soap from hotels. And nastiness now accompanied the childishness more frequently. Consider the following examples of how gratuitous *TV Guide*'s insults became: "Overheard in New York's Maurice Restaurant: 'Every time Tom Brokaw hits an L he sounds as though he's gargling' " (Jan. 7, 1989); "What's Arrogant But Pretending Not to Be? Bryant Humble" (Feb. 4, 1989); Robin Leach would not have to take sleeping pills on airplanes if they would show a Robert Urich movie (Dec. 3, 1988). On David Cassidy, spotted in a Baltimore parking lot entertaining at the wedding of a couple who had won a local radio contest: "We'd say he has his work cut out for him [but] hey, if Donnie Osmond can make a comeback, anyone can" (Aug. 11, 1990).

Even "Cheers 'n Jeers" descended further into triviality. In an editorial that seemed to confuse fiction and fact, *TV Guide* jeered CBS's "Guiding Light" for bringing back to the soap the wife beater, kidnapper, and rapist Roger Thorpe. "A swell villain, sure, but to see him charming much of the cast . . . makes us sick. Alexandra marries the guy without questioning his reprehensible behavior toward his ex-wife, Holly, then appoints Thorpe president of her company. We smell trouble with a capital T" (May 5, 1990). Was this a cheer, a jeer—or simply hype for a returning baddie? It was certainly light years from "As We See It."

In essence, the tabloid-thinking Murdochians expanded the "Insider" to the rest of the magazine. They reduced the time from layout to the newsstand to twelve days so that articles could be fresh. Whole issues, with cover stories like "Knockout Nov." and "What a Week," alerted readers to upcoming specials. In 1990 even though the fall preview was spread over four issues, profiles dominated. With astonishing speed, wrote Tom Shales of the *Washington Post,* the "magazine went from a certain seriousness to an undiluted frivolousness. The whole thing is kind of swamped in star gush. . . . It's beyond lightweight." To make *TV Guide* a livelier product, articles examined the best and worst Oscar parties, Geraldo Rivera's "Compromising Tattoo," horoscopes of the hottest TV stars, and "Designing Women's Guide to Prime-time Men." A cover story told readers Dixie Carter would speak out on "TV's nastiest on-set feud" in "Designing Women" (December 15, 1990). Borrowing directly from *People Magazine, TV Guide* put the faces of the sixteen top television personalities of the eighties on the cover and ran stories on the top twenty shows of the decade, as well as the "twenty moments that shaped and shook" it (Dec. 9, 1989).

The Murdoch team thus created entertainment news as much as they covered it. For several weeks the editors asked readers to vote in the TV Beauty Poll. On August 25, 1990, they put Jaclyn Smith, Dana Delany, and Nicolette Sheridan on the cover. "Is one of these women the most beautiful on TV?" they teased. Only in the article did *TV Guide* reveal the surprising result: "And the winner is . . . Kathie Lee Gifford. Perhaps there's been some mistake." Something less than a Greek goddess, Gifford was never photographed from the rear, *TV Guide* ungraciously observed, adding that Victoria Principal had once told an audience "just where the hostess needed work." Gifford, however, had campaigned for the *TV Guide* title, using her own show to solicit votes. In condemning her, the magazine struck a solemn pose: "*TV Guide* set no rules that prohibited campaigning. We assumed good taste and self-respect would preclude such unsportsmanlike behavior." Of course, Gifford's gimmick was a godsend to *TV Guide,* enabling the editors to put a bevy of beauties on the cover and a plot twist on the inside, with a soupcon of cattiness thrown in for good measure.

As the Gifford piece suggests, gush in the eighties and nineties, when there was no such thing as bad publicity, did not mean praise but attention. Fan magazines these days luxuriate in the torrid and the lurid, and *TV Guide* has been no exception. A January 14, 1989, cover showed Cybill Shepherd and Bruce Willis considerably less than fully clothed. Merrill Panitt's command "Airbrush nipples" no longer applied. Three articles in the October 14, 1989, issue showed the dark side of Hollywood, Murdoch-style. "Mama Was a Rebel . . . Papa Was an Addict," introduced readers to Chynna Phillips with some old news about her parents. "I've Been Through . . . Several Layers of Hell" was a savage swipe at demanding, petulant Faye Dunaway. And "Why a Comedian? Louie Anderson Recalls His Tormented Life with Father," included Louie's memory of hiding under the table when he was five years old while dad, an alcoholic, was beating mom.

Speed was now so essential that more and more material was placed in the program section of the magazine, where copy could be inserted at the last minute, rather than in the national edition. In "TV Guide Plus," for example, readers could learn about which series were canceled or what executive had been cashiered, or they could accompany staff writer Mary Murphy, who was "Desperately Seeking Roseanne: Media Barred from Her Wedding." Reporters fanned out across the city, Murphy reported, "including the drug-and-alcohol rehabilitation center where [Tom] Arnold had just checked out—just in case he and Barr decided to tie the knot where he'd detoxed" (Feb. 3, 1990).

On May 23, 1989, Managing Editor Dick Friedman implied that investigative reporting was no longer valued in a memo to the bureau chiefs in New York, Hollywood, and Washington: "We feel that the overwhelming majority of our pieces require no more than two weeks to write and report." The memo had a chilling effect on the holdovers from the Panitt-Sendler regime, when even a simple profile often involved two dozen interviews and several weeks of digging.

R. C. Smith ran up against the new system when he tried to edit a story on the on-again, off-again relationship between Don Johnson and (the then pregnant) Melanie Griffith. The piece submitted was deemed unsatisfactory by Murdoch's people, who called in Phil Bunton of the *Star.* According to Smith, Bunton "wheeled into action," called for the *TV Guide* clips from the archives, and whipped out a story "full of overripe clichés." Smith tried to edit out some of the "heavy breathing," but he knew he could not last much longer at *TV Guide.*

The race to get the stars while they were hot made Murdoch editors less sensitive to the "fact-checking" of the magazine's research department. According to free-lance writer Richard Slattery, this department for decades had been "thorough to the point of nuttiness." On one occasion Slattery had joked that an actor spoke like Charlie Chan. The *TV Guide* research staff insisted that they listen to a tape before allowing the story to run. After much consultation the department approved the reference, although no one ever told Slattery if the actor sounded like Warner Oland or Sidney Toler. Under Murdoch, however, the Research Department was consulted less and less. Haste may also have contributed to a much-publicized gaffe in 1989: the cover issue of *TV Guide*'s August 26 issue showed Oprah Winfrey in a revealing, glittery gown, but the cover artist, Chris Notarile, had used a publicity photograph of Ann-Margret as the basis of his illustration. Hired at the last minute, Notarile claimed that he did not have sufficient time to get a recent picture of Oprah. "Diet or no diet," the *New York Times* reported (Aug. 30, 1989), "Oprah Winfrey's head does not belong on Ann-Margret's body." Media critics had a field day, speculating that the real Oprah wasn't sexy enough for *TV Guide*, while an embarrassed David Sendler promised that there would be no return of the body snatcher.

This incident, however, did not slow the momentum for change. Within a year, Katharine Seelye of *Columbia Journalism Review* reported (Nov./Dec. 1989) that most of the staff from the Annenberg era was gone: three of five writers in the New York bureau had left, and three of six in the Hollywood office had departed. John Weisman, the Washington bureau chief, quit in July. "They used to say, 'Go get 'em John Boy,' " he remembered, but in a magazine where news and public affairs barely mattered, "They don't say that now." R. C. Smith also gave notice that he was leaving but was cashiered after his contribution to *Time* magazine's "The Tarting Up of *TV Guide*" became public. David Sendler hung on, defending the Murdochians: "The philosophy is that we're in the business to sell magazines, and the philosophy is that shorter stories and more personalities will help us sell more magazines and make us livelier." But Sendler, too, was on the way out. At odds with Wood and Cece since the takeover, he resigned in September 1989 but remained on the Murdoch payroll as a consulting editor. Seelye suggested that Merrill Panitt was probably delighted he had reached retirement age. Valerie Salembier, publisher of *TV Guide* for five months before she left to become president of the *New York Post*, explained personnel changes that also included a thirty-person reduction in the sales staff and the departure of fifty people in the advertising promotion and research department when they refused to move from Radnor to New York: "I found a sleepy corporate culture there [in Radnor], and it needed to be energized." And, of course, Murdochianized.

It is not clear that the Murdoch approach is working. In 1990 circulation dipped below sixteen million per issue. In the first quarter of the year advertising pages dropped 10.1 percent from the same period in 1989. To make matters worse, *TV Times*, a weekly television listings magazine, appeared in February 1990. Its publisher, TVSM, planned to invade other markets around the country and reach a circulation of two million. For about three dollars per month *TV Times* offered subscribers current listings for all channels on a cable system—and only that system. By sharing profits with cable system operators and simplifying listings, TVSM executives thought they could mount a credible challenge to *TV Guide.*

Rumors circulated that *TV Guide* was up for sale, but Murdoch vehemently denied that the magazine was on the block, offering to pay *Ad Age* publisher Crain Communications one million dollars if it could verify the story or identify anyone with whom he had held discussions. But *TV Guide* was in trouble even though, as Joseph Cece pointed out, it remained the most profitable magazine in the industry. He admitted that nothing was now held sacred and even entertained the possibility of replacing its pint-sized pages with a 7-by-10-inch version. Indeed, in 1991 he announced that a larger edition would be test-marketed, while acknowledging that it would result in a price increase that might depress circulation still further.

The only certainty was that *TV Guide* would remain a fan magazine, offering little to readers interested in news and public affairs, public television programming, or decision making behind the screen. "Every bone in their body," said R. C. Smith of the Murdoch staff, tells them to "downscale" the magazine. Although Cece feels the magazine's trade ads have been designed to change the image of the *TV Guide* reader from "a couch potato who lives in a trailer park" to an upscale consumer of video cameras, the look and content of *TV Guide* seems to confirm Smith's judgment. On June 17, 1989, the magazine cover beckoned readers with a coupon-clipping offer: "Save $$ 16 Pages of Shopping Coupons Inside." Two years later it announced: "Win $1 million! Look inside and play Quest for the Best!" Meanwhile, the articles have grown shorter and shorter, and less and less substantial.

Yet, significantly, even R. C. Smith, who thought the mental worldview behind the new *TV Guide* "childish," believes that "readers probably love them." Perhaps (as Smith thinks) Roger Wood and Joseph Cece have given up on the national edition, concentrating their energies and resources on improving the program listings, increasing previews of upcoming shows, and supplying, in "TV Guide Plus," news of who is hot and who is not in Hollywood. But *TV Guide* probably needs articles on entertainment wrapped around the program listings. And the Murdoch philosophy is that of the tabloid thinkers, who are not likely to make readers stretch by venturing beyond the visual equivalent of the "sound bite." So in the nineties, *TV Guide* will gossip and gush and taunt and titillate, as it reaches for the stars and a lower common denominator.

Walter Annenberg, founder of *TV Guide* and owner until he sold the magazine in 1988. (Courtesy of the Annenberg School of Communication, University of Pennsylvania)

Merrill Panitt served, in essence, as editorial director of *TV Guide* for more than thirty-five years. (Courtesy of Merrill Panitt)

The *TV Guide* Publicity Office worked hard to get celebrities to pose with the magazine. Here Noel Neill and George Reeves spend a break from filming "Superman" with the magazine. (Courtesy of Martin Lewis)

The fall preview issue was *TV Guide*'s best seller. Here Jack Webb of "Dragnet" reminds readers that the magazine was read by the stars. (Courtesy of Martin Lewis)

Ayn Randian conservative Edith Efron was the most influential writer on *TV Guide*'s staff in the 1960s and early 1970s. (Courtesy of Edith Efron, taken by William Kahn for *TV Guide*)

Neil Hickey was "lefty" to Efron's "righty" in the eyes of *TV Guide* staffers. Hickey is chief of the magazine's New York bureau. (Pach Bros. photograph, courtesy of *TV Guide*)

David Sendler edited the national edition in the late 1970s and 1980s. (Bachrach photograph, courtesy of David Sendler)

Rupert Murdoch acquired *TV Guide* in 1988 as part of the largest transaction in the history of publication—$3 billion. (Courtesy of News America Publications)

Part 2

America in *TV Guide*

4

"Afraid of the Dark": Race in *TV Guide*

In the fifties, when *TV Guide* was born, an increasingly vocal civil rights movement began to force the United States to confront what Gunnar Myrdal called an "American Dilemma." World War II, a struggle against the racism of the Nazis fought by segregated armed forces, made many whites aware of the anomaly of political disfranchisement, job discrimination, and social oppression in a democracy committed to equal justice for all. Blacks returned from combat and became more insistent that the federal government guarantee integration and equal rights. In 1948 the armed forces abolished segregation. In 1957 Congress passed the first civil rights bill in almost a century. Equally important, the attitudes of whites began to change. In 1942, 40 percent of the white population deemed blacks as intelligent as whites; by 1956, 80 percent held this view.

Nonetheless, the pace of reform was very slow in the fifties, and blacks took to the courts, the streets, and the lunch counters in quest of their rights. The Supreme Court in *Brown vs. Board of Education* (1954) concluded unanimously that in the public schools the doctrine of separate but equal had no place. Separate educational facilities were inherently unequal because they produced a feeling of inferiority in black children. Although the Court did not demand immediate compliance, waiting a year before ordering the desegregation of schools "with all deliberate speed," the decision energized blacks throughout the South. In 1955 Rosa Parks, a seamstress in Montgomery, Alabama, refused to follow the Jim Crow practice and surrender her seat on a bus to a white. When Mrs. Parks was arrested, local black leaders decided to boycott the public transportation system. They persuaded Martin Luther King, a twenty-six-year-old Baptist minister, to direct what was to be a year-long struggle in the glare of national publicity. The successful Montgomery strike was followed in 1957 by federal intervention to protect black students at Little Rock Central High School in Arkansas. The same year, in the Civil Rights Act, Congress created the United States Commission on Civil Rights.

Many whites, including President Eisenhower, did not welcome a vigorous civil rights movement. Although personally opposed to segregation, the president opposed government coercion to achieve equal rights for blacks. He said he understood southern anxiety about seeing that "sweet little girls are not required to sit in school alongside some big overgrown Negroes." Reluctant to intervene in Little Rock, Eisenhower federalized the Arkansas National Guard only when violence seemed imminent. He did not protest when Little Rock officials closed the public high schools in 1958 and 1959 rather than bow to a court order to desegregate them. Not surprisingly, in 1963 only 9.2 percent of black children in the South attended integrated schools.

As southerners defied and resisted implementing desegregation decrees, many white Americans from all sections of the country followed President Eisenhower's lead and downplayed or ignored "the Negro Problem." In the fifties to dissent was to be un-American; only troublemakers, unwitting dupes of the communists (or worse) played on racial oppression. In the land of the free, many Americans convinced themselves, segregation and discrimination were the heavy baggage of the past, about to fall of their own weight. To ignore racial problems was to resolve them, some rationalized, while others no doubt dismissed distant issues of little interest and of no benefit to them.

On television, more than anywhere else in the fifties, blacks were invisible. Held hostage by their local stations in the South, the networks dared not risk integrated casts or programs with racial themes. Viewers might glimpse a black singer or dancer on "The Ed Sullivan Show" or a black cook or chauffeur in an old movie, but with one notable exception—"Amos 'n Andy—the color line was not broken in situation comedies or series dramas. "Amos 'n Andy" was a storehouse of stereotypes, with the scheming George C. Stevens, the screeching Sapphire, the lazy lunkhead Andy Brown, and the Step 'n Fetchit look-alike "Lightnin'," which made it offensive to advocates of civil rights. Racial insensitivity appeared in the most unlikely places on the small screen. One day in 1960, as a novelty, Art Linkletter assembled a panel of black children for the "Kids Say the Darndest Things" segment of his popular afternoon show "House Party." Instead of the usual parting gifts (a doll, a wagon, or a game), Linkletter gave each little boy a regulation outdoor shoeshine kit and told them all, "Go out and earn some money." In commercials, moreover, the collars—and everyone inside them—remained whiter than white. With network news limited to fifteen minutes of talking heads, viewers could look forward to a white middle-class world on the small screen in both entertainment and public affairs. One way to eliminate racial strife was to wish blacks out of existence.

Like other mass circulation magazines mindful of their southern market, *TV Guide* also avoided racial issues. Early in his career Merrill Panitt wrote an editorial for the *Philadelphia Inquirer* praising football as a force for integration. A supporter of civil rights, he attributed *TV Guide*'s inattention to blacks to television's timidity in giving them airtime. The "magazine covered what was out there," Panitt insists, but he did not explain the failure to write about "Amos 'n Andy," its detractors, or any of the black entertainers who appeared on variety shows. In the early fifties, of course, *TV Guide* was not alone in avoiding race, but in our judgment it was slower than other organs of popular culture in covering black performers or civil rights in the industry.

No "Close Up" appeared, for example, on the "mammy" character of Beulah the maid or of Willie Best of "My Little Margie" and "The Stu Erwin Show" or of the sharp-tongued Rochester of "The Jack Benny Program." *TV Guide* did not examine the appearance on TV of Farina, Stymie, and Buckwheat in reruns of the "Our Gang" comedies of the twenties and thirties; nor did it refer to the thirteen-week run on ABC in the fall of 1952 of "The Billy Daniels Show," the first sponsored network musical show hosted by a black. It did not cover the five days of hearings of the House Committee on Education and Labor in the autumn of 1962 on discrimination in media employment practices, where Sidney Poitier and Ossie Davis testified about the barriers black performers faced and Dick Gregory quipped, "The only television show that hires Negroes regularly is Saturday Night Boxing." Twice during the decade the magazine denounced discrimination: "Fearless Ed Sullivan," a profile noted, deserved praise for presenting ballet and opera stars, taking a gamble on politically controversial performers (who had refused to cooperate with the House Un-American Activities Committee), and showcasing black performers. Sullivan, the profiler wrote, was at first swamped with letters of protest but then received an avalanche of apologies (June 19, 1953). Doing the right thing, according to *TV Guide*, wasn't really risky. A review of "The Ann Sothern Show" six years later (Mar. 14, 1959) commended the program for departing from the stilted situation comedy format by taking a stand, singling out an episode in which a bigot learned that American Indians had been "maligned in history."

Throughout the fifties, however, "As We See It" remained silent on the issue of blacks on television. And between 1953 and 1963, when other popular magazines were beginning to cover civil rights, *TV Guide* published but one feature article on a black performer. "Nat King Cole: An Important Role on Television" was unambiguously integrationist, as the subtitle, "A Step in the Right Direction," made clear. The first black after Daniels to star in his own regular network show, Cole reassured *TV Guide* readers that he was not a crusader. The article's author, inclined to sympathize with those who urged caution in combating prejudice, understood the "passive prejudice" of networks and sponsors, which both feared adverse reactions in the South to blacks on TV and implicitly endorsed Cole's decision to appear before segregated audiences (Sept. 7, 1957). This single benign attempt to address race stands alone, not to be repeated until a preview of "An Evening with Harry Belafonte," when the magazine invited readers to tune in to a portrait of black life ("Negro," as it was then termed) in America, told in song "with a great deal of sub-meaning" (Dec. 5, 1959).

In 1960, the year students sat in at lunch counters in Greensboro, North Carolina, until they were served, *TV Guide* took a strong stand against segregation—in South Africa. "As We See It" protested apartheid and attacked the government in Johannesburg for interdicting American television, which was beginning to show an occasional black face (July 30, 1960). From the first, *TV Guide* was color-blind and objected to those who weren't: the magazine's stand was liberal when it was whites who refused to be color-blind, conservative when it was blacks. No editorial addressed the efforts of the Congress of Racial Equality in 1961 to test segregation by sending "freedom riders" throughout the South or the violent reception they met or the preparations for the massive March on Washington in the summer of 1963, even though the march was televised.

Apparently the second feature article on a black performer in *TV Guide* came as a surprise to the editors in Radnor. According to staff writer Leslie Raddatz, the men in the Hollywood Bureau, noting that the "pretty girl pages" in the magazine were lily-white, "decided to try to slip a black girl" past their superiors. They had decided to feature her "on the basis of her resume and did not realize she was black until they saw her picture." The magazine editor, Alex Joseph, was "furious," not because he was bigoted, Raddatz believes, but "because we had put one over on him." Significantly, Panitt agreed to run the piece, in part to test the reaction in the South. "Actress Kim Hamilton" appeared on September 7, 1963, the month after Martin Luther King, urged on by

Mahalia Jackson, told the marchers on Washington of his dream that blacks would be "free at last, free at last."

Even more than Nat King Cole, Kim Hamilton was a gradualist on civil rights. She played Andy's girl friend in "Amos 'n Andy" and defended the show, which was under assault by the NAACP at the time. The characters on "Amos 'n Andy" were not stereotypes, she insisted, but men and women with "real wisdom." At a time when jobs were in short supply, moreover, the show "gave a lot of negroes work." In the sixties, Hamilton asserted, the television industry was providing equal opportunity for blacks. Her part in "Ben Casey" had not been written for a black, and she had been hired after competing with white and black actresses, one example of a "growing trend in casting negroes as people, not just negroes."

Hamilton's confidence came at a time of broad public support for federal guarantees for civil and political rights for blacks, generated by the peaceful and moving March on Washington and by the passive resistance to the attack dogs and water cannon of "Bull" Connor, the sheriff of Birmingham, Alabama, who could have come straight out of central casting. Media coverage of determined and dignified blacks built momentum for the sweeping Civil Rights Act of 1964, which outlawed discrimination in public accommodations and in hiring, firing, and promotions. A year later the Voting Rights Act made actions by individuals or governments to disfranchise black voters a federal offense.

In this climate *TV Guide* commissioned its first serious analysis of blacks in television, a two-parter by free-lance writer Richard Gehman (June 20, 27, 1964). Gehman used what was to become a trademark *TV Guide* approach: he pilloried prejudice but placed it mainly in the past, pointed to progress, and located solutions to the problem in the sum total of individual acts of discipline and responsibility.

Network officials, not surprisingly, told Gehman of their sincere efforts to tear down the color wall, although, somewhat paradoxically, they insisted that "none exists." Blacks, of course, were less sanguine, pointing to tokenism and endorsing Nat King Cole's characterization of advertising agency men as "afraid of the dark." Not a single black entertainer, even of the stature of Sammy Davis, Jr., Gehman reported, had "not felt the sting of sponsor discrimination."

Although opportunities had been limited, progress had clearly been made, a point Gehman hammered home. "Negroes admit that television long has been receptive to their talent." They "concede" that in 1964 producers had made an honest effort "to expose Negroes in dramatic shows as human beings." In fact, Sidney Poitier predicted that 1964 would be "the year of the Negro." Slow advances had even been made in commercials with the commitment of eleven agencies to use blacks. All "but the most hostile or worst-wounded," Gehman concluded, "admit it's getting better," although he was careful to exclude the technical trade unions, where blacks constituted half of one percent of the members, from his optimistic forecast. Even the best-educated, most well-adjusted, successful Negro had good reason to be bitter, Gehman acknowledged. But the temptation must be resisted for the good of race relations in America. Gehman marveled at the "eternal resilience" of Negroes, epitomized by Sammy Davis, who didn't have a network series despite his enormous talent and versatility, yet didn't get sore about it. Negroes must be patient; the promised land was in sight.

Discrimination persisted in the United States, Gehman acknowledged, because the roots of fear and hostility in the prejudiced ran "very, very deep." But he did not belabor bigotry, perhaps because he (and his readers) took its existence for granted. Instead he focused on the responsibility of the victims for their plight: "Some Negroes, because of hostility, fear, carelessness or ignorance, must assume some of the blame for the slowness of . . . integration." Gehman could understand the unprintable comments of some of the performers he interviewed, but he was clearly outraged by the refusal of some to speak with a white man. More important, Gehman agreed with a producer who charged that the behavior of some Negroes "draws out latent prejudice" and insisted that he would employ more Negroes "if they would show up on time." Four directors, Gehman told readers, made the same point. Another asserted that Negro actors didn't "do their homework" and relied too much on blind intuition; another informant thought Negroes overly sensitive to criticism. Gehman quoted comedian Godfrey Cambridge's quip that Negroes were late because they couldn't get cabs in order to read into the record a director's humorless retort that he would take a subway or a bus to be on time even if he had to sit in the back. The message was clear: if blacks wanted the same rights and responsibilities as other American citizens, they must do more to earn them. Unconsciously or not, Gehman's articles appealed to the passive prejudice of readers and protected the southern flank of *TV Guide*.

The honeymoon for the civil rights movement in the United States was remarkably short-lived. By the mid-sixties, the spotlight had shifted to the North, where economic and social inequality, as well as de facto segregation, were not easily addressed through legislation. Remedies like "affirmative action" in employment, with its goals, timetable, and quotas, and court-ordered busing to achieve racial balance in schools, convinced many Americans that blacks were moving too far, too fast.

Black leaders, moreover, appeared increasingly militant, even revolutionary. While Martin Luther King aroused the ire of Lyndon Johnson by denouncing the Vietnam War and focusing on economic exploitation with a poor people's campaign, Stokely Carmichael demanded black power, insisting that integration was irrelevant, and nonviolence futile and foolish. Huey Newton and Bobby Seale went one step further: their Marxist Black Panther Party, founded in 1966, armed and trained members to defend themselves. And finally, scores of American cities erupted in racial violence—Watts in 1965, then Detroit and Newark—in a seemingly endless series of long, hot summers.

Amid black anger and white backlash, both extensively covered on each evening's network news, a great number of *TV Guide* articles on black performers and race relations were published. Relatively silent during the first phase of the civil rights movement, the magazine became politicized by the upheavals of the sixties. As television employed more blacks, *TV Guide* wrote about them, often in ways that staked out a clear, consistent position on the best way to achieve racial equality in the United States.

As on so many other issues, Edith Efron acted as the quintessential *TV Guide* voice on race relations between 1966 and 1973. She was assigned many profiles of black performers, as well as several articles analyzing the progress of blacks in television. On this issue, Efron had, in her own words, a "profound, *personal* stake." Married in 1947 to a Haitian businessman, she gave birth to a son a year later. In the mid-fifties she brought her mixed-race youngster to the United States. All the positions she took on race in her articles, Efron told us, "were determined by what I thought would be good for a young, vulnerable black child." Disturbed by the changing strategies toward achieving racial equality in the sixties, Efron remained the same on her position: "*Always*, I was in favor of equality of opportunity *and* meritocracy. Meaning, among other things, that I was as critical of crap from blacks as I was from whites, and *used the same standards to judge both*. That is definitional of *not* being a racist. One judges individuals, not their color!!!" Thus, Efron was as passionate about black power as she was about theories positing the genetic inferiority of blacks because each accepted the group instead of the individual as the appropriate unit of analysis and action: "Essentially I was always protecting my child from two kinds of racism: the *bestial* kind common in the South and the *inverted* kind characteristic of the North. Both contempt for all blacks *and* glamorization of all blacks are detestable, and *both* damage blacks."

The key to equality of opportunity in a meritocracy, according to Efron, is universal, high-quality education. Without it, legal guarantees of equal treatment are "an empty shell." Poorly educated blacks "could not profit by the newly opened doors" because they could not compete successfully. Efron found assertions that blacks should not be subject to "white" standards specious. And lowering standards in education and employment was anathema: in affirmative action, she saw the condescension of white liberals and the cynicism of black radicals, who in the long run were guaranteeing "helplessness and failure." At bottom, the achievement of equality for blacks was very difficult but not terribly complicated: once government purged discriminatory laws and provided good schools, blacks must work harder and longer. "There is no other solution."

Efron's point of view came through clearly in her *TV Guide* essays. In "Negroes in the Broadcasting Industry," she argued that "finding Negroes for the jobs" was the principal problem facing television executives. The networks had been "affirmatively aggressive," seeking to increase the pool of qualified blacks by establishing the Broadcast Skills Bank in conjunction with the Urban League. Ironically, while black leaders denounced the broadcasting industry as discriminatory, jobs and training slots "have gone begging from coast to coast." Unlike Gehman, Edith Efron did not blame the victims for their low representation in broadcasting, but she did suggest that a psychological block, traceable to a time when blacks were not welcome in television, made blacks reluctant to apply for positions. Because blacks were not adequately educated in sufficient numbers, Efron concluded that it would take a long time for them to achieve "mass employment" in broadcasting (July 30, 1966).

In a three-part series six years later, Efron revisited "Blacks in Broadcasting," this time to assess the charge of the Congressional Black Caucus that promotion, hiring, and firing on television news programs was racist. Discrimination, she insisted in a direct challenge to advocates of affirmative action, cannot be determined by numbers alone. Efron investigated two stories of firings of blacks and reported that in both cases the action was justified. Three realities, she concluded, governed black employment: "black unpreparedness due to historical racism," "contemporary network efforts to improve the black position,"and "contemporary racism." Yet while documenting the first two, she had, by omission, to some degree slighted the third. Without being given evidence of discrimination, readers were free to conclude that it no longer hindered blacks.

At the same time Efron blasted attempts by black activists to get quotas in hiring and proportional representation in total programming by challenging the licenses of recalcitrant television stations. This ap-

proach "is dangerous. . . . it is quite simply an extortionist trend." Efron
applauded a Washington, D.C., Court of Appeals decision that instances
of discrimination and a conscious policy of exclusion, not simply numbers of blacks employed, must be proven if the courts were to intercede;
no law, the Court added, required a station to devote 20 percent of its
broadcast time to address the needs expressed by 20 percent of its
viewing public (Aug. 19, 26; Sept. 2, 1972). When the Supreme Court
expressed a different view of affirmative action, Efron remained adamant: black equality had to be achieved from the bottom up, through
education, one determined individual at a time, rather than by government fiat.

In 1973, furious that leaders of minority groups were "fiercely indignant as ever" in their complaints about TV stereotypes, Efron was
almost ready to declare victory. The louder the voices of extremists, it
is worth noting, the more militant Efron became in defending the good
intentions of the television establishment. The industry, she wrote, was
"probably the most concentratedly integrated area in the United States
of America." On the small screen, moreover, virtually no blacks were
portrayed as inferior. Even "a cursory view" of programming, Efron
concluded, showed substantial improvement; "many of the hysterical
charges . . . are lacking in factual foundation, in balance, and in recognition of what has been accomplished" (Oct. 27, 1973).

In profiles of black performers Efron also treated racial problems as
the struggle of individuals to overcome adversity, a struggle that could
be successful but that, in essential ways, had to be fought alone. The
life of Diahann Carroll, for instance, was the "classic Horatio Alger
success story" of the daughter of a New York subway conductor who
became a star. Nonetheless, Efron felt compelled to add: "The truth is
that there are thousands of white celebrities who have struggled far
harder and waited far longer." The real struggle for Carroll was a race
consciousness that threatened her individuality: sadly, she was a Negro
first, Diahann Carroll second. In feeling "the pull of the protective
security of the ghetto and the thrilling challenge outside its walls,"
Carroll married a white man, then divorced him; joined the Student
Non-Violent Coordinating Committee (SNCC); resisted jazz because it
was racial. Only in her work, when she placed herself before her race,
did she find "inner satisfaction" (May 27, 1967). Carroll's desire to turn
herself into what she was, in Efron's existential world, was the most
interesting and important struggle in everyone's life, and all the more
difficult when blacks trapped themselves in a collective identity.

Unlike Carroll, Robert Hooks of "N.Y.P.D." had apparently achieved
inner peace along with success. The actor, therefore, wasn't "snapping

his fingers in quite the same angry way. He's GOT IT." In the hands
of another writer, Hooks might appear arrogant and materialistic; to
Efron he was a triumphant and heroic capitalist. Brought up in a Washington, D.C., slum where he was bitten by rats, Hooks now lived in a
chic Manhattan tower with a doorman in uniform who bowed defer-
entially when the actor arrived home from work. To his credit, Hooks
had reached out to help other black actors by founding a free dramatic
workshop and producing plays written by blacks. At ease with himself,
he could shrug off those who now attacked him for being "insufficiently
angry with the white world" as easily as he did those who thought him
too angry. In Hooks's entrepreneurial energy, Edith Efron saw an important element in the solution of racial inequality: the country "needs
a good many more 'businesslike browns' " who invest their energies in
their "talent, not [their] anger" (Feb. 10, 1968).

With very few exceptions, staff and free-lance writers in *TV Guide*
viewed race relations as Efron did. Indeed, the subject was treated with
a solemnity not extended, for example, to the women's rights movement,
which was often the butt of jokes in the magazine. Only Cleveland
Amory squirmed at the excessive seriousness of civil rights activists.
Noting that the words of "Kentucky Baby" had been changed, Amory
lamented that "we can't be pro civil rights and still be allowed a few
old songs" (Sept. 4, 1965). Even the hiring of blacks, a sacred subject
for *TV Guide,* was fair game for Amory. In a swipe at TV tokenism the
reviewer cracked: If "you're inclined to think that Ironside's 'legs,' his
aide-de-camp, Negro Mark Sanger, is in the show merely for the sake
of being—well, in it—you are going to find his performance is both
different and convincing" (Nov. 18, 1967). And when the western series
"The Outcasts" featured a black, Amory announced: "Nowadays we
may not always have equal stardom under law, but here we sure have
it with outlaws" (Nov. 30, 1968). "Julia" deserved congratulations for
breaking the color barrier, but the racial self-consciousness of the show
gave Amory such a "fast pain" that he quoted the sarcastic line uttered
by Lloyd Nolan on one episode: "Have you always been a Negro—or
are you just trying to be fashionable?" (Oct. 12, 1968). Often at odds
(for other reasons) with Merrill Panitt, Cleveland Amory was all alone
among *TV Guide* writers in treating minority rights with a jocular tone,
although it is significant that the pokes he took were usually aimed at
affirmative action.

Articles on race relations stuck to several closely related themes during the sixties and early seventies. They urged the industry to employ
more blacks, not only as performers but as technicians, writers, and
managers. Blacks were rarely cast as executives or professionals, Art

Peters reported in "What the Negro Wants from TV" (Jan. 20, 1968). The number of black reporters and editors, Neil Hickey revealed, remained pitifully low (June 8, 1968). In testimony to the United States Senate, summarized for *TV Guide* by Richard K. Doan, former CBS executive Mike Dann, "a man who should know," asserted that television had little to be proud of in its treatment of minorities (Aug. 8, 1970). On the small screen, moreover, news programs paid little attention to racial issues other than riots, arson, and looting. In bringing to the attention of *TV Guide*'s readers the controversial findings of the Kerner Commission on Civil Disorders, appointed by President Johnson after the urban disturbances of the mid-sixties, Neil Hickey agreed that television's depiction of blacks was "shoddy, shallow, [and] misinformed" (June 1, 8, 1968).

Around these charges, however, *TV Guide* established a reassuring context. Television was putting its own house in order. Paradoxically, Art Peters wrote, "the sound and the fury" over black employment was coming at a time when the networks were redoubling their efforts. Neil Hickey agreed, a bit more grudgingly, that 1968 might well be the year white Americans "began to comprehend in significant numbers what's needed to defuse the ticking time bomb of racial disharmony." "Knowledgeable" Detroiters told Hickey that news coverage was gradually, "perhaps too gradually," getting better.

Part of *TV Guide*'s optimism was due to the tautological situation of the magazine. Its attention to the black stars it interviewed was proof that they had *already* achieved professional recognition, and for these privileged few, a personal sense of injustice could be felt only in retrospect since they had already overcome its effects. *TV Guide* was therefore likely to be more optimistic than the prevailing situation of blacks warranted.

In 1968 Doan reported that the Negro had become "something of a status symbol in TV. The show without one isn't with it. . . . By fall it will be a rare evening program that doesn't have a Negro in a role intended to make everybody feel good except the adamant bigot" (May 18, 1968). Indeed, in that year at least one black regular character was featured in twenty-one of the fifty-six network dramatic series. Three years later Doan crowed that "Newscasting No Longer Is a White Man's Club." Although integration was "late in coming and sometimes painful," station managers were now eager to hire blacks. Some executives told Doan that the situation had improved so dramatically—and, they thought, permanently—that the training program established by Columbia University with funding from the networks did not need to be continued for a fifth year (Dec. 4, 1971).

Although few *TV Guide* writers joined Doan in declaring victory, many thought it not far off. Black athletes, according to "As We See It," were slowly "but inevitably . . . changing bias into acceptance. . . . On the playing fields, all men stand equal. Those with superior ability stand out" (Nov. 14, 1970). Although television took twenty-two years to recognize blacks, "surely the slowest double take in history," Martin Maloney wrote, bigots "don't seem to have as much clout as they once did." Maloney remained concerned that blacks continued to be cast in "essentially white roles and white stories," but his caution paled before the title of his article, "Black Is the Color of Our New TV" (Nov. 16, 1968). And expanding opportunity was clearly the theme of "An Open Door for Minority Writers," the story of a program that proved that "you *can* get through doors once thought to be shut." The article ended with the acceptance of Blanche Franklin's script for the situation comedy "Julia": "And skin color had nothing to do with it, either" (Apr. 24, 1971).

Nothing angered *TV Guide* more than European television journalists who seemed bent on distorting race relations in the United States. Imperfections should never be hidden, but credit should be given not only for sincere efforts, but for accomplishments. The British, however, persisted in covering urban riots, but "not the temporizing fact that more Negroes get higher education in America than Whites in England" (May 27, 1967). In failing to provide a context for British viewers, newscasters left the impression that "blacks are toting bales of cotton up Broadway or clashing with the police." Many blacks in America made lots of money, a fact never mentioned by "loquacious American liberals" or "opportunistic radicals" intent on crying woe about their country or besmirching it by "anchoring the color problem . . . in an apartheid" framework. The America haters had credibility only because they monopolized the airwaves in England and much of the Continent; their half-truths were in fact lies (Oct. 2, 1971).

Good intentions and impressive results, according to *TV Guide*, definitively answered the complaints of black radicals and their white allies. Nonetheless, black power got under the skin of the magazine. Vocal extremists like Stokely Carmichael and H. Rap Brown, far more than the "less theatrical but saner voices of moderation," Neil Hickey observed, knew how to manipulate the television cameras to gain attention for their demands. TV had certainly "fanned the embers" that set Harlem, Bedford Stuyvesant, and Los Angeles on fire (Sept. 16, 1967). Extremists fed on publicity—indeed they could not survive without it— yet *TV Guide*, like television, could not ignore a story with such dramatic voltage. Throughout the sixties and seventies the magazine tried to deflate and diminish black power radicals without paying too much attention to them.

Other than pointing to progress, *TV Guide* constantly equated black power with extremism, comparing the view of "responsible" black leaders with the demagoguery of "self-styled" leaders. Another approach was to enlist a prominent black American to endorse working within the system. In a preview of the 1968 Olympics, for example, Jesse Owens acknowledged the severity of racial problems in the United States but then pointed to "the many things both blacks and whites have done to alleviate these conditions." Sports, in particular, had been good to blacks, giving them the resources to help themselves and others. Owen appealed to black athletes not to express their discontent at the Olympics (by raising their fists in a black-power salute while the national anthem was played): "I'm not in favor of cutting off the one area of understanding we have. Negroes have a right to be proud of the disproportionate percentage of black athletes representing the U.S." To embarrass one's country "in so conspicuous a world arena," Owens implied, was to shed doubt not only on one's patriotism but on one's sense of decency and fair play. After all, no one had more right to show his anger than a black Olympic runner in Hitler's Germany in 1936. Dignified restraint, however, had captured the world's imagination as no aggressive or defiant act could have (Oct. 12, 1968).

In profiles of black stars, *TV Guide* tried to demonstrate that black power was unnecessary as well as dangerous. In overcoming discrimination, virtually every article implied, these men and women provided irrefutable evidence that it could be done. The blacks singled out by the magazine as role models were talented, hard-working, and patient; the message appeared to be that the meek, not the militant, would inherit the earth.

Everywhere it looked, *TV Guide* found a black Horatio Alger. By disposing of the bad times in a few breezy sentences, profile writers made it look easy, even when they emphasized that it wasn't. Sammy Davis, Jr., sneered at as a "dirty nigger" while serving in the army, showed the way as a black who persevered in benighted times and then took up the fight "to win over every bigot in the world. For every nine he wins over, it's the one who got away that bugs him" (July 16, 1966). Davis's batting average, however, seemed impressive indeed. Comedian Godfrey Cambridge followed much the same path, making a "giant step from ghetto life," where his dad dug up streets for Con Edison. The only black at Hofstra, Cambridge joked his way uptown, but he, too, vowed not to forget less fortunate people, "and I'm not just talking about Negroes" (May 11, 1968). In a profile of Don Mitchell of "Ironside," Leslie Raddatz found a vignette that epitomized the *TV Guide* paean to individual effort. When Mitchell complained to his grandmother about the struggles of an actor, she replied, "You asked for it . . . now do it." And, Raddatz raved, "Don did it" (Nov. 30, 1968).

The parents of many black performers, according to *TV Guide,* taught self-reliance by word and deed. Hari Rhodes's father was a laborer; his mother, a domestic, scrubbed white people's floors. A stint in the Marines helped give Rhodes the discipline he needed to fight his way to stardom on "Daktari" (Apr. 20, 1968). Similarly, Godfrey Cambridge's mother pushed him to be "somebody." Gail Fisher's mother, widowed in 1937, raised five children and ran a catering business in New Jersey. Not surprisingly, neither "competition nor handicaps seems to have impeded" any of the Fishers, who prospered in their chosen fields. Before her big break in "Mannix," Fisher worked without complaint as a domestic, manicurist, and secretary (Oct. 19, 1968). Occasionally parents forced themselves to bestow an even tougher brand of love. As Lloyd Haynes grew up in South Bend, Indiana, working in his family's struggling undertaking business, he received little attention from his mom and dad, whose apparent insensitivity was designed to help him survive. Haynes, like Hari Rhodes, joined the Marines, who then financed his education at San Jose State. With his leading role in "Room 222," Haynes finally felt "like I escaped, definitely, no question about it. I escaped from South Bend." But, like so many black stars, he did not forget the ghetto, participating in Seven Steps, a foundation dedicated to rehabilitating former convicts (Nov. 1, 1969).

The more stoic the black stars were in the face of adversity, the more *TV Guide* admired them. Ellen Holly had good reason to be "appalled and inflamed by a grim personal vision of waste, suffering and racism." With her mixed African, French, English, and Shinnecock ancestry, she observed that her paleness excited a "morbid fascination" in these days of "zany inversions of blacker-than-thou racial one-upmanship." To some whites, however, she was black enough to be thrown out of a diner and told to eat in the back with the pigs. "Surprisingly," Ross Drake noted, "it didn't harden her" (Mar. 18, 1972). Men and women who shuffled, tap-danced, rolled their eyes, or mangled the language in the forties and fifties were often derided in the sixties as Uncle Toms who sustained stereotypes; *TV Guide,* however, praised them as pioneers. In a profile of the Harlem Globetrotters, Melvin Durslag gave player and executive Inman Jackson the last word: "We started out going up the fire escapes of hotels and wound up going in the front door. . . . We integrated seating, even in the South. . . . We have played for countless

Negro charities, helping crippled children, the ill and the aged. What have our critics done except talk?" (Jan. 24, 1968).

In Flip Wilson, *TV Guide* found an impeccable role model, who had to fight off charges that he was insufficiently militant. In three profiles (Jan. 17, 1970, Jan. 23, 1971, Jan. 8, 1972), the magazine summarized a gruesome childhood in Jersey City with an alcoholic father, a wayward mother, and seventeen siblings. Assigned to a "spirit-killing succession of foster homes," Wilson ran away from home thirteen times, did a stint in reform school, and joined the Air Force at sixteen. It took him a long time to make it, but he was used to hardship. Amazingly, at a time "when many blacks speak bitterly of yesterday and today, and tomorrow with skepticism," Flip, whose life gave him "plenty to grouse about," retained no rancor, resolutely snubbing "the bitter, placard-carrying comedy" of a Dick Gregory in favor of a "gentle spoof of race relations" made "without puncturing anyone's skin." Writer Bill Davidson watched with admiration as Wilson wrote down a line for his act—"The Negro didn't give the blues to America; America gave the blues to Negroes"—only to scratch it out: "too bitter." The comedic truths he used, Robert Higgins predicted, "will prove more decisive in reversing racial attitudes than all the sermonizing and demonstrating put together."

Repeatedly *TV Guide* emphasized that blacks and whites working together, within the system, could make dramatic progress just by saying "no" to racism and "yes" to color-blind employment. Like most of those who befriended Flip Wilson, Monte Kay, his agent, was white. In agreement with this client that "funny knows no color," Kay "wangled his boy" into performing on "The Tonight Show." Bill Cosby's white angel was Robert Culp, described as teaching him how to act on "I Spy" (Oct. 23, 1965).

The system showed how responsive it could be with the creation of "Julia." Producer Hal Kantor traced the origin of the show to a speech by Roy Wilkins, executive director of the NAACP: "Wilkins spoke calmly, yet firmly, about solutions to the crisis in the cities, in contrast to the demagoguery of his more militant contemporaries. His simple eloquence, reflecting optimism rather than despair, visibly moved many of those present." Kantor cast Diahann Carroll as a single parent, working as a nurse, and promised a character with love interests and realistic emotions. Predictably, "Julia" was criticized for failing to focus on black American problems while reinforcing "the castration theme" in its depiction of a fatherless black family. Kantor responded by acknowledging that he had not produced a civil rights show; nor was he convinced that a "stupid bumbling father" was better than no father at all. More im-

112 America in *TV Guide*

portant, "Julia" boasted three black writers and, in addition, at the insistence of Diahann Carroll (an SNCC contributor) "racial aspects are on the upswing." In the past, writer Richard Warren Lewis concluded, bones were thrown at black actors. Now meat was on the bones, though Carroll was not ready to call it sirloin (Dec. 14, 1968). Black and white together might well overcome someday—soon.

Against this backdrop of progress, *TV Guide* portrayed black militants as agitators without an agenda. The magazine did not define extremism, though clearly it had in mind criticism of the capacity or desire of those who controlled the major institutions of the United States to treat blacks equally. Unlike black stars, extremists wallowed, unproductively, in resentment and anger. *TV Guide,* and most of its subjects, had little patience for the "big talk" of militants. Only a fool, Hari Rhodes exclaimed, fights a system too big for him to handle; bitterness is a "consuming, cancerous quality." Gail Fisher lamented that the Stokely Carmichaels and Rap Browns got publicity instead of positive, productive people like her mother. Even Harry Belafonte, "one of the most active—and oftentimes impatiently abrasive—leaders in the civil rights movement," according to Robert Higgins, pointed to the substantial achievements of the sixties. "Better than most," Belafonte knew that injustice still existed, but even in the wake of the assassination of Martin Luther King and the accession of Richard Nixon to the presidency, he was optimistic and cautioned against precipitous action (Mar. 21, 1970).

The rare expressions of sympathy for black militancy were invariably undercut by *TV Guide* writers. Otis Young of "The Outcasts" refused to allow his character to say "Ain't nothin' like darkies for prayin'," insisting that if he did, "the next thing they'd have up there is Step 'n Fetchit." Blacks who "are praying instead of doing" were damned fools, according to Young, who added his dissatisfaction with "I Spy" and "Julia": "Negroes should have pride in their own negritude." Dick Hobson liberally quoted Young but added that the actor was a quiet moderate when he was hired, bursting forth as a fiery militant only in the twelfth episode (Mar. 1, 1969). To this image of Otis come lately—and fashionably—*TV Guide* added an article a few months later that refuted the assertion that Young was a militant at all. On the day of the interview, costar Don Murray insisted, Young had just had a bad day: "You know he's more optimistic about a lot of the American scene than I am." Young should realize, writer Carolyn See implied, how far blacks had come in the United States. After all, on contemporary television "to be the white man on a black and white show is to be in second place" (Aug. 9, 1969).

Less indirect was the discrediting of Chelsea Brown, supporter of the Peace and Freedom Party in the national election of 1968. Brown owned up, not only to her own use of racial epithets as a youngster (Asians were "Buddha faces"), but also to allowing her emotions to govern her politics. Moreover, how seriously could readers take the political pronouncements of a woman who was sorry Senator Edward Kennedy got caught at Chappaquiddick (Nov. 21, 1970)?

As they derided militants, *TV Guide* writers also gave the back of their hand to blacks who seemed aggressive or arrogant. With the exception of Edith Efron, the Ayn Randian individualist, writers preferred humility over hubris, especially for blacks. Cassius Clay and Bill Cosby, for example, aroused an animus that was, at least in its allusions, race conscious. Armed with "modest skills" and "childlike" doggerel, Clay ascended the ranks in boxing, "like a gasbag," according to Melvin Durslag. Although Clay had "fastidiously avoided dangerous opponents," he was about to meet his match in burly, surly Sonny Liston, the heavyweight champion. With no pretense to neutrality, Durslag dispatched Clay with a poem of his own: "Cassius may be tricky / And rapid with a pun / But we dread to see the Nielsen / Of a man who goes in one" (Feb. 15, 1964). Cassius Clay did not endear himself to Durslag when he became heavyweight champion, nor when he became Muhammad Ali. The sports writer revisited Ali in 1975, when he was making stupendous sums "fighting mediocrities like Chuck Wepner, the Bayonne Bleeder," and lecturing on college campuses as "the voice of reason" opposing the Vietnam War, "which he sidestepped adroitly, saying such conflicts ran contrary to his religious beliefs." What Ali actually said, Durslag could not keep himself from telling readers, was "I got nothin' against them Viet Congs" (May 10, 1975).

Ridiculed in *TV Guide,* Muhammad Ali could not quite match the sustained hostility received by Bill Cosby. First the magazine bristled at his materialism. When Cosby confessed that "money is of the utmost importance to me," Robert DeRoos found a theme for "Bill Cosby, the Spy Who Came in for the Gold" (Oct. 23, 1965). Four years later Richard Warren Lewis was repelled by a superstar ostentatiously enjoying his success. Without using the phrase, Lewis described the lifestyle of an "uppity black." The piece opened with a reference to Cosby's $500,000 house and his "fleet of seven cars," including three Mercedes and a futuristic 400-horsepower Ford. "While a white-jacketed butler answered the ornately carved front door, another servant could be heard vacuuming the $12,000 antique rug that carpeted the cavernous room." When Cosby emerged to meet Lewis, he was a character right out of "Amos 'n Andy," wearing "only blue pajama bottoms and a yellow terry cloth robe. One hand held a fat Havana cigar. The other grasped a telephone receiver." Although Cosby had hired eleven black stagehands, grips, and cameramen for his show, Lewis stressed his recent conversion to the struggle for black equality: "Millions of dollars later, contemptuous observers say, Cosby has finally revealed his social conscience." Better belated than never, perhaps, but Lewis relentlessly pursued his quarry, lest anyone think that Cosby might also have become a nice man, revealing that he had jettisoned his manager when he reached the top and abruptly resigned from the Campbell Silver Cosby Corporation amid rumors that large sums of cash had disappeared or had been misused (Oct. 4, 1969).

Not surprisingly, Cosby's interest in black power became an occasion for *TV Guide* to find a misanthrope behind the professed egalitarian. In 1973 Cate Ryan observed that Cosby liked to wear a black liberation flag in his suit lapel. The wardrobe man had trouble placing the flag where Cosby wanted it, and the star, instead of taking matters into his own hands, took it out on the hapless employee: "Five times he got it wrong. And Cosby counted" (Feb. 3, 1973). Everyone at *TV Guide* with whom we spoke insists that the treatment of Cosby, Ali, and every other performer was color-blind. The magazine, after all, told the "mean truth" about whites as well. Nonetheless, conscious or not, the writers of articles about them played to a pervasive fear and anger that blacks had become too demanding and too likely to lord it over whites whenever they had the chance. In the pages of *TV Guide*, if not in American society, no black was allowed to get away with it.

In the 1970s, black militancy faded as the civil rights movement stalled. In many ways "benign neglect," advocated by Daniel Patrick Moynihan in a widely leaked memorandum to President Nixon, became government policy, even though "affirmative action" was institutionalized. As Americans grappled with gasoline lines, Watergate, stagflation, and terrorism, race relations became just another problem, often linked with urban blight and crime or with controversial remedies like busing or quotas. Except in a momentary crisis, blacks were less visible in the seventies in entertainment shows and especially on the network news. In *TV Guide* only Edith Efron expressed irritation that coverage had "slowed to a sluggish trickle." Predictably—and somewhat perversely—Efron blamed liberal journalists, the magazine's perennial target, for jettisoning civil rights in their hasty campaign to make viewers forget their support of "the later, violent, separatist, revolutionary stage" of the movement. The powerful need of these liberals to defend the Welfare State, moreover, compelled them to downplay the persistence of poverty. "Ideological bankruptcy is painful and humiliating," Efron wrote, especially when it sacrificed blacks on the altar of its own image (Nov. 30, 1974).

On this issue, however, Edith Efron did not speak for *TV Guide*. Never hesitant to lambast a liberal, the magazine's editors and writers were not averse, in this case, to a neglect they apparently thought beneficial. Uncomfortable with racial consciousness throughout the sixties, *TV Guide* looked forward to a time when integration made blacks invisible, when race played no role in employment. Thus the magazine applauded when George Stanford Brown played a part that had "nothing much to do with being black" in the comedy "Black Jack": "He was making progress," and so presumably was television (May 4, 1974). *TV Guide* itself reached something of a milestone in 1973 with a profile of Lloyd Haynes that mentioned his work with disadvantaged children but not his race (Nov. 10, 1973). In fact, "As We See It" opposed efforts to ban or edit films (scheduled to appear on television) because they were offensive to minorities. Rather than dwell on the past, "however deplorable it may have been," Merrill Panitt suggested, minority groups should look to a color-blind future (Jan. 5, 1974). Consciousness-raising agitation, the editor implied, was not the best way to root out race prejudice.

Considered even worse were race-conscious remedies. Minority programming, "whatever that is, may be fostering segregation," insisted Frederick Breitenfeld, Jr., executive director of the Maryland Center for Public Broadcasting. The view that people of a particular race or national background should write, produce, perform in, and watch a program before it qualified as a "minority program" was simply mistaken. Blacks, like whites and Asian-Americans, were citizens, surgeons, and city dwellers; their interests overlapped with those of different races on every offering on television. Good programs appealed to people with diverse attitudes, backgrounds, and "skin colors" (Jan. 25, 1975). Similarly, *TV Guide* viewed with skepticism efforts to compel TV stations to hire more blacks, or produce race-conscious programs. "The Fight to Force Alabama Education TV off the Air" was a "pointless" struggle by outside agitators, ignorant of—or uninterested in—the substantial progress that had already been made. Two of the three complainants to the FCC, the magazine pointed out, had left the state. And the lobbyists relied on data from the sixties, when the station had to exclude blacks or have its funds cut off by arch-segregationists appointed by Governor Wallace. It was as if "the NCAA disqualified a university football team in 1975 for having no blacks in 1967." At present, without fanfare, Alabama provided young black men and women "a more equal chance" to develop themselves than many other states (Feb. 8, 1975). In Mississippi as well, the station had a black general manager, black-oriented programs, and a staff that was 40 percent black. Although the FCC had intervened to put this new team in control, *TV Guide* attributed the station's prosperity to the pragmatism of its managers in recognizing that green was more powerful than black and white—and producing programs with mass appeal (Apr. 5, 1975). An invisible hand governed television, as it did all sectors of American capitalism, *TV Guide* implied. As blacks exercised the power of the purse, the industry would continue to respond. Pressure groups and government agencies just got in the way.

In 1970, before it was clear that black power would give way to benign neglect of civil rights, *TV Guide* did try to make some room, in tone and substance, for black protest. Merrill Panitt told us that he recruited black writers as part of his efforts to broaden the spectrum of the magazine, but he was clearly uncomfortable with the point of view many of them expressed. Consequently, their articles were few and far between, never radical, and always confined to the portrayal of blacks in television. Nonetheless they did dissent from *TV Guide* orthodoxy on race relations. During the relative safety of the mid-seventies and eighties, the magazine became somewhat more hospitable to advocates of race-conscious remedies.

In search of a writer who could bring the black idiom to the magazine, the editors commissioned A. S. "Doc" Young to do a story on the white singer Bobby Sherman. Young worked with Dwight Whitney, the Hollywood bureau chief, who "soon devoutly wished otherwise," according to William Marsano, the associate editor of *TV Guide* at the time. The piece Young turned in, Marsano recalled, was a "mix of black English, slang, jive talk . . . part rap, part scat, part jazz lyric." It was impenetrable to "us white middle-class guys lodged out in Main Line suburbia." There seemed no way out. "On our side, we wished we'd never begun our own naive experiment in affirmative action; Young felt that he was being given a bad time." The final version of the article was so far from the original as to be unrecognizable (Feb. 7, 1970). Although *TV Guide* wanted to be authoritative in its coverage of race, it could not bring itself to publish an article unlike any their seventeen million subscribers had seen before in the magazine.

John Oliver Killens was a black writer who delivered a much more controversial piece in eminently acceptable prose. Although he granted that television employed more blacks, Killens bristled at the integrated image of blacks on series television as an "anemic imitation" of actual experience. The United States, he flatly asserted, is "a segregated society." But Killens was not a champion of integration: "Our struggle is not to be White men in Black skin." Because the black experience was unique, moreover, only black writers could capture it: "Only club members can sing the blues because we're the ones who have paid the dues of membership in the Brotherhood of Blackness." Equality was not likely to come, Killens concluded, until "we achieve some Black control" (July 25, 1970).

Killens's call for race-conscious writing was not taken up until 1974, when Eugenia Collier, a teacher of black literature at Baltimore Community College, pleaded for truth as well as visibility in an examination of television adaptations of the *Shaft* films. Although the programs had been lauded for their treatment of race, Collier objected to the portrayal of Shaft, a character whose affluence, language, and associations were "devoid of the black idiom"; even Shaft's Afro was "clipped and firmly disciplined" in an apparent attempt to avoid offending white viewers. Like Killens, Collier was skeptical of integration when it was a whitewash: "I feel that I am being erased" (Jan. 12, 1974).

These sentiments were overwhelmed by traditional *TV Guide* themes, by now embedded in the numerous profiles of black stars that appeared in the seventies. In agreeing with Sammy Davis, Jr., that conditions were a "thousand times better for black actors" (Nov. 10, 1973), the magazines gave credit to those who had humbled themselves during the lean years. In the mid-seventies, when "colored" was a dirty word, Scatman Crothers was often derided for shuffling around. "But his being colored," producer James Komack pointed out, "paved the way for people to be black." Once members of an audience acknowledged that one black man was a decent fellow, "pretty soon it's not only 'that one' but all of them." Even after the turmoil of the sixties, Crothers remained a patient man: "After working 50 years to become an 'overnight success,' Scatman figures he can wait a little longer to become a star" (Mar. 13, 1976). And while Eugenia Collier objected to a domesticated Afro as a concession to whites, Leslie Raddatz defended Theresa Merritt, a large black woman with a gap in her teeth and hair pulled back, from charges that she was perpetuating a stereotype on "That's My Mama." At a church in Los Angeles, Raddatz observed, Merritt was greeted with a standing ovation and an avalanche of audience seekers, who recognized, as the critics did not, that love and affection permeated her character and the show: "If that makes her a stereotype so be it. After all, who wants to hug Redd Foxx?" (Jan. 18, 1975).

Blacks did not need control, *TV Guide* implied, when influential whites were so eager to help. Gladys Knight and the Pips were naive country bumpkins ready to be ripped off when they met Sid Sidenberg, the manager who would march them to stardom (July 12, 1975). Sherman Helmsley's trip "Up from the Ghetto" would not have been possible without producer Norman Lear. Born in the ghetto of South Philadelphia, where "the vibes were so vicious" he almost got shot in a gang fight, Helmsley suppressed his show business aspirations after he was refused entry to a taping of "American Bandstand" because he was black. After a tour of duty in the air force, he pursued his dream at the Philadelphia Academy of Dramatic Arts while earning a living in the postal service. Cast in a Broadway musical, Helmsley was spotted by Lear who hired him for "All in the Family" and then the lead in the spinoff, "The Jeffersons." Thanks to his friend, this former underdog was "now top dog" (June 21, 1975). Finally, blacks needed to understand, as John Amos did, that they were best served when they worked with the white power structure. In detailing Amos's shift from professional football player to the first black writer on a network program, "The Leslie Uggams Show," to star of "Good Times," Ira Berkow gave the actor the last word: "I'm enjoying what I got as long as I got it. I figure it's like I'm on a team and who knows when they'll cut you" (Aug. 17, 1974).

Although it seemed less and less necessary, *TV Guide* continued to lash the not very live horse of black militancy. In a transparent imitation of Tom Wolfe's famous essay "Mau-Mauing the Flak-Catchers," Michael O'Daniel warned readers about the "time-honored technique perfected by street-wise blacks in dealing with white men. If whitey gives you what you ask for don't say thank you and go home, throw him a curve and ask for something else." As soon as they smelled fear and appeasement, black militants escalated their demands, which often amounted to little more than individual aggrandizement. As Redd Foxx's former personal manager, O'Daniel had seen a master at work as the gravel-voiced comedian bluffed his way through negotiations with NBC over his hit show "Sanford and Son." In the mid-seventies, however, whites played poker, too, without folding at the first raise. In ignoring the new realities, Foxx was an anachronism, O'Daniel believed, who was "apparently bent on self-destruction" (Feb. 14, 1976).

Foxx was an anomaly as well, at least in show business, where performers repudiated such tactics. Della Reese of "Chico and the Man" went straight to the point. Proud that her character took guff from no one, Reese made sure Ellen Torgerson Shaw did not mistake her for a militant. "She has no need for it. She's above militancy" (Dec. 4, 1976).

With David Sendler as editorial director in the late seventies and eighties, *TV Guide*'s treatment of race did not change in any fundamental way. Like Merrill Panitt, Sendler strongly supported the employment of minorities throughout the industry, a subject often addressed by "Cheers 'n Jeers," which needled the networks for "turning a blind eye" to Hispanics on soaps and prime time (May 28, 1983) and using a predominantly white cast in "The Blue and the Gray," a saga about the Civil War (Feb. 5, 1983). To cajole but not coerce remained the *TV Guide* philosophy. To reverse past discrimination blacks must try harder, and whites, as individuals and through corporations, must volunteer to help. To this end, for example, Walter Annenberg contributed large sums of money to the United Negro College Fund. This view also constituted the policy of Ronald Reagan, and in the eighties the magazine and the government sounded much the same. One difference, however, began to emerge. If the Reagan administration addressed the inequality of blacks with an inattentive optimism that could be called complacency, *TV Guide* sounded more resigned in its feature articles on blacks in television (though not in its profiles), and occasionally even skeptical. Still committed to voluntarism, it was less convinced that compliance was inevitable.

More than ever, profiles of black performers celebrated the sunny side of American life. On his TV special, Ben Vereen wanted to show viewers what it "means to be black and happy in this country. The joy we have in just living" (Feb. 28, 1978). Similarly, Ernie Thomas of "What's Happening!!" was not at all embarrassed about appearing on a marshmallowy program as a character indistinguishable from a white middle-class youngster—except for his black skin. Although Thomas had been raised by a single parent and had often felt the sting of having to buy groceries with food stamps, he saw no value to placing poverty on prime time: "I think it's bull to tell it like it is. I don't want to be scraping grits out of pans. It won't do anyone any good—black or white— to show the guy on the street with no respect for anything" (Mar. 18, 1978). In a sense, *TV Guide* took Thomas's advice. On the rare occasion that a black faltered in a profile, race disappeared, lest it appear to be a cause of the problem. Thus Gail Buchalter's article on Clifton Davis's dalliance with women, cocaine, and easy money did not mention that the actor was black. As a person, regardless of his race, Davis was his own worst enemy and his only one (Jan. 17, 1987).

Many blacks "are more stubbornly American than even they want to acknowledge," wrote R. C. Smith, managing editor of *TV Guide* in the 1980s, in a preface to his profile of Oprah Winfrey. A man with great sensitivity to and knowledge of racial issues, Smith recognized that chauvinism, especially when uttered by black performers, was always welcome in the magazine. Oprah believed that "in America you are free to create a self that can transcend the grubby world you find yourself in. And that if you have the confidence and energy and courage, your new invented self can pierce reality the way tornadoes drive straws into the utility poles." Smith carefully assessed the costs of Winfrey's willful creation of her own reality—she was unmarried, secretly afraid, perhaps, that she remained "the same unlovely, unlovable, Milwaukee kid"—but readers were left not with an anxious, unhappy woman, but with a megastar quoting Jesse Jackson's assertion that excellence is the best deterrent to racism (Aug. 30, 1986).

Performer after performer played variations on the same theme. Marla Gibbs of "The Jeffersons" complained that black youngsters were repeatedly told what they could not do (Aug. 11, 1979). Seven years later, now star of her own show, "227," Gibbs was thinking positively as a member of "The Science of Mind." Through generations of slavery and oppression, she believed, blacks had become accustomed to passivity and poverty. Albeit unintentionally, Ronald Reagan had helped by forcing them to believe in and do for themselves (May 17, 1986). Robert Guillaume celebrated his success not at Hollywood parties, but at his old neighborhood, to teach a lesson to the guys who said "Better not leave here, cause you never gonna make it any place else" (Sept. 15, 1979). The beloved Ossie Davis and Ruby Dee had once marched with Martin Luther King and worked with the NAACP and their friend Malcolm X. As active as ever in promoting black culture and civil rights, they spoke in *TV Guide* less about America's problems than its promise, which looked greater to them than that of any other nation on earth (Mar. 22, 1980). Twenty years after he participated in the Watts riots of the sixties, Roger E. Mosley of "Magnum, P.I.," with "one foot in the ghetto, one in his Rolls Royce," spread the philosophy of Reverend Ike: the best way to help poor people is to avoid being one of them (Aug. 28, 1982). And Tim Reid of "Frank's Place," having had enough of poverty when he was young, excelled in two careers as an "executroid" with DuPont and an actor/comedian. To remind himself of how far he (and by implication many other blacks) had come, Reid kept on his wall a painting of a slave sale: "Another time, another place," he was pleased to conclude (Apr. 16, 1988).

Even when it became clear that work for blacks in television had tapered off, the same attitudes prevailed. "I am the American Dream," announced Berlinda Tolbert of "The Jeffersons." Refusing to live her life as a victim, Tolbert was determined to be a star despite a scarcity of roles for black actresses in Hollywood (Oct. 16, 1982). Carl Weathers was also undaunted though he too was aware of how few dramatic leads on TV were black. No legislation, after all, mandated that *his* series, "Fortune Dane," could not be a hit (Feb. 8, 1986).

TV Guide writers did not hesitate to chime in when stars did not sing the praises of individual opportunity in the United States. Although the magazine had reported the declining employment of black actors, Elaine Warren treated the problem as essentially psychological in a profile of LeVar Burton. A nineteen-year-old drama student at the University of Southern California when he was tapped for "Roots," Burton became an instant star. Good roles, such as "Looking For Mr. Goodbar" and "The Ron LeFlore Story," came his way, Warren wrote, until money, women, and drugs took control. As his career slowed, Burton told himself that scripts were not sent because he was black. Eventually Burton entered psychotherapy and, a wiser and healthier man, he found himself cast in "Star Trek: The Next Generation." Burton's odyssey allowed Warren to ignore structural forces in the economy and society by locating success and failure in an individual's struggle with discipline and dissipation (Aug. 13, 1988).

This theme also predominated in the articles of Ellen Torgerson, even if the performer had to be corrected or misread. Marla Gibbs's character on "The Jeffersons," Florence the maid, occasionally asked her employers, "How come we overcame and nobody told me?" A bitter line from the mouth of a working-class woman who had not made it, the question was somehow incorporated into Torgerson's celebratory conclusion: "No one told Marla either. But, then, she overcame about 10 years ago" (Aug. 11, 1979). As she wrote about Madge Sinclair of "Trapper John, MD," Torgerson became an advocate, engaged in debate with her subject. Beautiful and talented, Sinclair was not yet famous, a fact she attributed to the return of tokenism in the eighties. "Well, maybe," Torgerson responded; although there were not as many blacks on the small screen as in the seventies, there were more than a few. Despite complaints that blacks were not getting parts, "some blacks did and became superstars." Sinclair made $10,000 a week, not bad by any standard, but more than respectable when compared to the $12,000 a week earned by Gregory Harrison, the hunky star of the show. Torgerson was not impressed with Sinclair's whines or, for that matter, with any attempt to blame personal failure on discrimination: "On occasion blacks, women, short people, freckle-faced people and other groups say 'Hey we didn't make it because we're etceteras.' Maybe it's true. Maybe it isn't." Torgerson's "maybe" sounded like a "no"; her equation of blacks and freckle-faced people was a vote for the individual as the only meaningful unit of social analysis. After all, Madge Sinclair herself knew that if she dwelled on "all the possibilities of racism and sexism, I would never do anything" (Aug. 17, 1982).

To dwell on discrimination was to enhance its impact. Of course every black should fight back against acts of prejudice, as Terry Carter did when a kid in his music appreciation class called him a "darky." But significantly, Carter did not allow the incident to give him a view of the world as a place hostile to blacks (Apr. 26, 1975). At its best, self-reliance, bolstered by benign neglect, would help blacks move quickly through race consciousness to a fuller and more fulfilling individuality. This happened to Tim Reid, who could not fight his "biggest battle"—control of his temper—while confronting the Ku Klux Klan and stereotyped roles (June 23, 1984). Robert Guillaume could address his ambition only after he established ethnic integrity in his character (Sept. 15, 1979). Thus liberated, with a more secure sense of self, every black, as Lorene Carey put it, could "cut through all the racial hooey, the love-hate ties of black and white in America, and love"—and, just maybe, make a bundle doing it (Dec. 6, 1986).

In an essay for *TV Guide*, Richard Reeves came close to articulating the attitude toward race that permeated the profiles. Racism was the nation's biggest problem, Reeves asserted, "But we do try to fight it. American democracy is about trying to be better as a people than we know we are as individuals" (Mar. 26, 1983). Racial progress, according to the magazine, came not through law or government programs, but one person at a time, through self-improvement.

While profiles were single-mindedly sanguine, analytical articles on blacks in television were more critical, although they, too, invariably invoked the progress that had already been made. Race relations were not high on the national agenda in the eighties, but Sendler ran several pieces on the subject. Just as John Oliver Killens and Eugenia Collier had been lonely defenders of race consciousness in the seventies, Mary Helen Washington, teacher of English at the University of Massachusetts, Boston, accepted the assignment in the Reagan era. In "The Blanding of the Jeffersons," she criticized the show for mainstreaming its characters. When George and Louise Jefferson joined "the wine and quiche set," readers received a "political message that race is no longer important because blacks have achieved." Only Florence, Washington claimed, saved the show from mediocrity by insisting that racism still flourished and that "an oppressed people need pride in their roots to survive" (July 30, 1983). Washington praised "The Cosby Show" three years later for its subtle display of race consciousness, in placing paintings by black artists in the Huxtable's home, and in the consideration of black colleges by the children. But, like "The Jeffersons," Cosby did little to deliver Americans "from the pretenses we live by—that racial problems have been solved" (Mar. 22, 1986).

Mary Helen Washington had few allies in *TV Guide*. In a review of a book about television's failure to become the great integrator, Lorene Carey dismissed as "chimerical" the hope that pay and cable TV might provide more than "upbeat and upscale descendants of old Hollywood mammies, pickaninnies and native guides," but she did not make clear whether she was advocating racial consciousness or mainstreaming (May 21, 1983). Novelist David Bradley began his essay with a blast at television for letting whites see blacks as they wanted to see them, but he quickly moved to a thesis that undercut his criticism: most important is whom one watches television with. To the conventional, sometimes "poisonously negative" images of blacks on the TV tube, black people could offer each child "antidotes" through explanation and example. Paradoxically, then, television helped Bradley strengthen his family as the Bradleys watched the tube together, "never minding what [was] on the screen" (Mar. 22, 1986).

More typical were feature articles that, like the profiles, contributed to what Washington might have called "The Blanding of *TV Guide*." Ralph Ellison told an interviewer that he had a "healthy and unsnobbish appreciation" of TV comedy, citing "Barney Miller," for its funny yet realistic stories of social hierarchy in the police station, and Bill Cosby's show, for the way it cut across race and class. Although Ellison made the not very controversial statement that television comedy often ignored the tragedy beneath the laughter and then decried series dramas like "Knight Rider" that trivialized life, he seemed neither critical nor angry as his "rich baritone laughter fill[ed] the room" (Apr. 23, 1988).

Malcolm Jamal-Warner, the young star of "The Cosby Show," was confused about the value of race consciousness. He knew why color was important to many people but didn't understand "why it should matter to a kid what color he is when he sits down to write me a letter." The fact that flight attendants and passengers found it difficult to accept that his mother was traveling first-class suggested to him that racism was alive and well; the fact that nonwhite foreign correspondents often described how dark they were convinced him that whites did not have a monopoly on prejudice. Warner's own ambivalence surfaced in his discussion of his parents' reaction to interracial dating: "On some level they would care, but on another it wouldn't matter at all." Although Warner was proud to be a role model, he worried that producers stamped him a black actor; all the scripts they sent him had a racial theme (Sept. 24, 1988).

A thorny topic, race consciousness surfaced only in this handful of essays. David Sendler, at least as much as Merrill Panitt, used most feature articles to pressure television executives to employ more blacks in all phases of the industry. By publicizing underrepresentation, *TV Guide* could help remedy it. Although the magazine acknowledged that overt, conscious racism had "long since ended," it charged that management remained insensitive, especially when the "affirmative action spot-light was off," as it had been in the eighties ("Black Reporters," July 18, 1981). For *TV Guide,* as we have seen, turning the light back on was, by itself, the only affirmative action program necessary. To do less was to be guilty of neglect that was not benign; to do more was to invert the discrimination. And voluntary compliance often followed an exposure of injustice: the magazine reported that when the NAACP protested that ABC's "Just Our Luck," a comedy about a black genie, had no black writers and threatened a boycott, "presto!"—three blacks appeared on the payroll (Sept. 17, 1983). *TV Guide* feature writers had the same result in mind. As had their predecessors in the sixties and seventies, they revealed a contemporary racial reality much less rosy than that contained in the profiles. But for the first time, a faint scent of resignation clung to the analysis. Although they dutifully invoked the progress that had been made, these writers seemed skeptical that the eighties would be the blacks' decade.

As Richard Levine referred to the "giant step" in employment since the sixties, he revealed that black reporters were "Window Dressing on the Set." Well paid and much praised, they were assigned to black beats, like the Department of Housing and Urban Development, and confined to the "weekend ghetto" when the news was slow and the ratings low. Levine asserted that the network had hired black reporters in more than token numbers only "when the ghettos began to burn," a position rarely taken in a magazine willing to attribute nothing positive—even indirectly—to the militants. Equally important, Levine cited, without much rebuttal, informed sources who despaired that the number of black reporters and their influence had peaked (July 18, 25, 1981).

In "Discrimination in Hollywood," Michael Leahy and Wallis Annenberg drew the same conclusion for entertainment that Levine had made for news: "There is always talk about equality in Hollywood from producers and studio executives. . . . Of course such portrayals have always been largely written, directed and produced by white males." Black actors seemed typecast in the eighties as criminals and misfits; black writers, if they were hired at all, were limited to "black scripts." Seeing "no signs" that they would "gain the kind of power that can effect change," blacks in show business, Leahy and Annenberg concluded, had begun to accept any jobs that came their way (Oct. 13, 1984). Two years later Scott Hays confirmed that racial barriers remained in place by examining the difficulty the stars of "Roots" had in getting roles almost ten years after the blockbuster miniseries had been shown. Insecure and unsuccessful actors, he wrote, were not the only people to blame the industry. Although network executives did try to capitalize on "Roots" with "King," "The Lazarus Syndrome," and "Paris," they hid behind the Nielsen ratings when these programs flopped, blaming the viewers for their refusal to produce black dramas. Whatever the reason, Scott asserted that blacks were underrepresented in television (Nov. 29, 1986).

Joanmarie Kalter agreed, although she was a bit more precise than Hays. She noted that blacks appeared on television in numbers equal to their percentage of the population (10 percent), if not their percentage of the network television audience (17 percent). Significantly, however, they were cast not in dramas but in comedies: "Webster" and "Diff'rent Strokes" featured cute little blacks, with whites clearly in charge; "The Cosby Show" was better, but its upscale, professional setting suggested a reluctance to explore the lives of middle- or working-class blacks. Only on "Frank's Place" did more fully realized characters appear, but Kalter took little solace from this aberration. She concluded her essay with the bottom-line observation of an executive of Batten, Barton, Durstine and Osborne: advertisers don't solve social problems (Aug. 13, 1988).

TV Guide writers of the eighties did not go beyond the bleak picture they painted. If they came closer than their predecessors to asserting that blacks were victims of forces beyond their control, such as racism and the economy, they held back, perhaps because they were convinced that feeling victimized could become an excuse for inaction. The long-standing *TV Guide* antipathy to government intervention in the economy, moreover, intensified in the eighties. With voluntarism the only available alternative, all they could do was keep the pressure on.

Investigations of blacks in television began to disappear soon after Rupert Murdoch purchased *TV Guide* in 1988. Articles on the subject were apparently among those Murdoch considered too cerebral for readers of the magazine. Profiles of black performers continued to appear, but increasingly they failed to address racial issues. When they did, as in a preview by Susan Littwin of a TV movie based on the murder of three civil rights workers in Mississippi, writers employed *TV Guide* formulas. Littwin wrote that although actor Blair Underwood's family was solidly middle class, still it often mattered that he was black. For him, as for other blacks, "sometimes the pain shoots right through the armor of success." Yet Littwin was evidently at a loss for an incident, painful or not, to demonstrate the roots of this pain. The best she could do was to cite the advice of Blair's mother that, unlike whites, he could not afford *not* to do his homework. Although she listened as Underwood insisted that a black with a nice car was invariably stopped by the police, Littwin ended her piece with a "glimpse of the easygoing actor with a taste for thrills," flying upside down with the Blue Angels, the navy's daredevil pilot unit. It was "a long way" from Mississippi and James Chaney, the character he had played in the TV movie (Feb. 3, 1990).

TV Guide editorials, now confined to "Cheers 'n Jeers," also provided less than met the eye. The magazine jeered at "blatant tokenism" on the CBS sitcom "City," then backpedaled quickly lest it seem unenthusiastic about hiring minorities. The ensemble cast of the show starring Valerie Harper was racially and ethnically mixed, with "Harper's Jewish right-hand man, her black secretary, the Hispanic purchasing agent, the Asian mail clerk, and the WASP social worker. We'd be cheering this office melting pot except for one important detail: the supporting cast members are two-dimensional archetypes, not fleshed-out characters." With much fanfare, then, *TV Guide* had unequivocally opposed poorly developed characters on prime time and supported ethnic and racial diversity on TV when it was well done (Mar. 10, 1990).

It is most likely significant that the only article on racial discrimination to surface thus far in the nineties appeared not in the wraparound but in the program listings. In an essay on an impending investigation by the United States Commission on Civil Rights (May 11, 1991), Stephen Galloway and David Lieberman began with chairman Arthur Fletcher's charge—America is a "racist nation"—and then reviewed the depressing statistics of minorities on screen, backstage, and in Hollywood's corporate offices. Galloway and Lieberman drew no conclusions (in an article that many readers may have missed anyway). In the Murdoch era, it is not likely that the breezier magazine will often revisit race in substantive ways or give this subject a prominent place in the national edition.

5

"It's a Man's World": Women in *TV Guide*

Unlike blacks, women were always visible in the pages of *TV Guide*. Aimed at the supermarket shopper, the magazine regularly ran women's features on fashion and food preparation. Every issue carried at least one profile of a female in show business. According to Merrill Panitt, the magazine presented neither a message nor a social agenda in its treatment of women: articles on actresses examined each one as a performer; issues related to gender were addressed only when the star brought them up. And yet, from the outset, one can detect a tension in *TV Guide*'s coverage of women. A mass circulation medium covering a mass circulation medium, *TV Guide* originated in a decade preoccupied with harmony, homogeneity, stability, and the pursuit of affluence—it did not leap ahead of its readers by challenging the adage that a woman's place was in the home. Its subjects, however, were not happy housewives but career women, many of them quite comfortable in corporate chairs. The magazine, therefore, contained a species of feminism in spite of itself. As it aspired to authoritative coverage of an industry that was more business than art, *TV Guide* found itself assessing the role and rights of women as well as endorsing the responsibilities of television and American society to provide equal opportunity to them. At the same time the magazine retained a male chauvinist tone, mocking women's liberation and implying that reform had gone far enough.

The decade of the 1950s was a difficult one for advocates of women's rights. World War II, like its predecessor, had been good in some ways to the women of the United States. By removing men from farms and factories, these wars opened up occupations to women that had traditionally seemed outside the female sphere. World War I, "the war to make the world safe for democracy," provided the ideological and political pressure necessary to pass the nineteenth amendment to the Constitution, which granted the vote to women. Because American troops were in Europe for a relatively short time in World War I, women gained a small and fleeting measure of occupational experience and economic control. Nonetheless, just as it was no longer quite as easy to keep infantry men down on the farm after they'd seen Paris, so was it a bit more difficult to keep women who had earned a paycheck inside the circle of domesticity. The 1920s returned the nation to its prewar normalcy, but some women continued to press for change.

During World War II women entered the work force in unprecedented numbers, often toiling for years on assembly lines and even as managers. Almost twenty million women labored in support of the war effort, nine million more than were employed in 1940. With the defeat of Japan in 1945, questions about the role of women in the postwar economy were widely debated. If women worked, would a labor surplus drive the nation into another depression? Would Rosie the Riveter agree to trade her weekly wages for the apron she had hung up four years earlier? With the establishment of the United Nations Commission on the Status of Women in 1946, would the relatively silenced majority acquire a platform to launch a campaign to secure political, economic, and educational equality?

For many Americans the prospect of career women, especially women drawn from the middle class, threatened not only to disrupt the economy but to destroy the nuclear family. Traditionalists found the idea of separate spheres, supposedly rooted in biological differences between the sexes, as valid in the middle of the twentieth century as it had been in the nineteenth. Again and again in postwar America, they reminded women of their duty and destiny to be wives and mothers, promising them a pedestal in place of a paycheck.

Fortunately for traditionalists, many women discovered that ideology proved more powerful than experience or economic calculations. Work for them was, at best, a temporary expedient, necessary to protect hearth and home. On Mother's Day, 1942, the military ordered officers and enlisted men to write to their moms "as an expression of the love and reverence we owe to the mothers of our country." Perhaps because so many Americans agreed with J. Edgar Hoover that mom was "our only hope," half of the nation's housewives declined to work on machines since blue-collar work, though crucial to the war effort, carried a loss of status. Not surprisingly, women quit their jobs at the end of the war at more than double the rate of men to make room for veterans and to produce a generation of "baby boomers."

Some women, however, did not choose to leave: women were fired at twice the rate of men in the postwar years. Still, by the mid-fifties, 70 percent of the middle-class families in the United States featured two workers—both mom and dad. These developments alarmed traditionalists, who believed that juvenile delinquency was one more consequence of mothers in the work force. In the late forties and fifties, they urged women to forget the independence they experienced during the war and stand by their men. In January 1945 *House Beautiful* explained: "You, to whom the veteran is returning, are entrusted with the biggest morale job in history. . . . Your part in the remaking of this man is to fit his home to *him*, understanding why he wants it this way, forgetting your own preferences. After all, it is the boss who has come home." Self-abnegation did not abate, of course, when the veterans had readjusted to civilian life. There were kids to consider, new standards of cleanliness and dress, and labor-saving devices that seemed to generate more work. More than ever, a woman's place was in the home.

Television played a key role in this campaign. In commercial after commercial women consumed when they didn't clean and cook, always finding fulfillment in a spick-and-span kitchen and lemon-scented furniture, enjoying satisfying companionship in Mr. Clean and Josephine the Plumber. In family comedies that saturated the airwaves, women in two-story suburban houses tended terminally cute kids and always acknowledged, even when evidence was in short supply, that father did indeed know best. The man-hunting Margie and the schoolmarm Miss Brooks, with her eyes on Mr. Boynton, and Hazel, the surrogate mother-maid, were exceptions that proved the rule. Who, after all, wouldn't want to be Harriet Nelson or Jane Wyatt; what woman didn't admire Donna Reed, "corn-fed and wholesome—as welcome as a late summer breeze in an Indiana hay field," and married to a doctor to boot (Feb. 14, 1959)?

Like television, *TV Guide* in the fifties was awash in stereotypes about women. Female readers, it assumed, identified themselves as homemakers eager for tips about how to please their husbands with food or fashions. For women who read the magazine, it was "Hips, Hips Away" (Jan. 9, 1955). "Janis Paige's Year-Round Diet" (Nov. 24, 1956) was a typical advice column "For the Girls": "Nothing puts the crimp in romance or marriage like a diet handled the wrong way." Although she didn't spend her days doing housework, Janet Blair believed that a woman should look just as gorgeous while cleaning as she did for her husband in the evening. Posing as a housewife for *TV Guide*, Blair prescribed colorful outfits for "Blue Housewives" (July 18, 1959). Apparently, *TV Guide* feared that television might keep women from kitchen chores. In all seriousness Merrill Panitt devoted an "As We See It" editorial (Aug. 21, 1954) to a *Los Angeles Times* story about a female TV fan who had been knifed by a hungry husband. The tragedy, according to Panitt, "points up a crying need for the sort of television set that can be installed in the kitchen" so wives could watch TV and cook at the same time. "If not a good meal, at least a cheese sandwich."

In *TV Guide* women were seldom more than pleasant surfaces, better to look at than listen to. When meteorologist Francis K. Davis protested that "Weather Is No Laughing Matter" (July 23, 1955), *TV Guide* presented overleaf the pictures of six pretty weather girls and commented: "It may be that [Davis] carries the scientific approach a bit too far." Merrill Panitt also liked to gaze, but not at pretty girls keeping their mouths wide open in an effort to look like Marilyn Monroe. He noted in "As We See It" (Mar. 23, 1957) that as Lynn Dollar had led a contestant into the isolation booth on "The $64,000 Question," she had seemed to be "preparing to chomp down on a club sandwich. Please girls," he pleaded, "all together now. One, two, three—shut!"

On December 5, 1959, as if to sum up the decade's definition of attractive females, Enid Haupt contributed a piece entitled, "How to Influence the Dobie Gillis Type." Editor and publisher of *Seventeen* magazine, a Triangle publication, Mrs. Haupt seemed an authoritative voice on adolescents. She also happened to be Walter Annenberg's sister. The golden mean—moderation—Haupt asserted, was "the by-word by which a girl can judge her dating rating." The boys "concur that the girl who gets a minus can be summed up by a two-syllable adjective: extreme. This applies to everything—dress, deportment, makeup, morals." Supersophisticated girls who preferred steak to sundaes in soda shops, hypersensitive girls whose feelings were always hurt, superintellectuals who expounded "knowingly all evening on books without plots, point counterpoint, sundry high-flown data," and ultra-possessive girls who forgot "the gentle touch and used a jealous clutch"—found themselves on a boy's black list but not in his black book. Most important, Haupt urged deference as the solution to the riddle of courtship and romance. Her advice, presumably, was as valid for married women as it was for dating daughters. Females should be self-confident but must "always remember to talk about HIM. Don't make suggestions about where to go unless asked. . . . Make him feel appreciated. . . . Don't be obvious in your pursuit. Let him chase you until you catch him." Not surprisingly, Dobie Gillis agreed 100 percent with Enid Haupt's recommendations.

Along with Panitt and Haupt, most *TV Guide* writers treated "the girls" with a benign and amused contempt that assumed definitive truths about women as superficial creatures with superficial concerns. An article on Lugene Sanders's working wardrobe matter-of-factly remarked, "When the average female says she has nothing to wear, it usually means she's down to her last five dresses and can't decide which one to sport to her bridge club" (June 8, 1957). And anti-intellectualism, as American as apple pie, was especially true when applied to women. "Judging from the caliber of some daytime programs," "Why Housewives Holler" reported, female viewers "will tolerate just about anything on a TV screen." Although the article claimed that gripes ranged "from the legitimate to the loony," with the exception of opposition to canned laughter, all examples were drawn from the latter category. Some women, the writer smirked, reached for their towels as they raced from the tub when the phone rang, certain that TV announcers could see them (July 9, 1954).

Hollering housewives, however, were sometimes more shrewish than silly. In "Harry Morgan's Wife Doesn't Scare Him—on TV" (Oct. 6, 1956), *TV Guide* repeated a string of jokes: for example, Morgan's character, Peter Porter, says of his wife, "That mackerel reminds me, Gladys is waiting for me." The fact that the show is "all in fun on TV," said the article, doesn't lessen Peter Porter's "enviable status in the eyes of the millions of censored husbands who watch December Bride." Peter Porter has it made, the writer concluded. "No two ways about it . . . but look at it this way, men. What's he going to do when Gladys gets around to demanding equal time?" In "As We See It" Merrill Panitt adopted a similar stance three years later (Jan. 3, 1959). Arguing that television did not signal the demise of conversation, Panitt pointed out that wives had simply become better listeners: "This is a boon to her husband and saves wear and tear on her vocal chords (although there is no record in medical history of a woman's vocal chords ever wearing out)."

TV Guide's cavalcade of clichés, however, was not the whole story. The magazine, as we have noted, was seeking to improve the quality of television by persuading viewers to practice dialsmanship. Essential to this strategy was an assertion that women, the principal consumers of TV fare, especially in the daytime, preferred informative and aesthetic programming. Articles in the 1950s, to be sure, pressed the point gently. In "Elaine Carrington: Soap Opera Queen" (Dec. 11, 1953), *TV Guide* strained to identify the useful and profound wisdom in daytime dramas, singling out the care of wounded soldiers overseas, relief for mothers, and advice for pregnant women. The audience for these programs, *TV Guide* stated in an effort to elevate quality, was not neurotic women but "young college-educated women, fine American housewives." Viewers of daytime TV were not career women, of course, but the magazine had managed to place the practical securely inside the circle of domesticity.

In "As We See It" a few years later, Merrill Panitt carried the argument a step further. In a slap at the network lineup, the editor compared TV programs to the women's pages of the daily newspaper. The latter treated women as wives, mothers, and citizens; the former condescended to them. Television executives, Panitt argued, should build on the interest women showed in watching the Kefauver racketeering hearings, the Army-McCarthy confrontation, and United Nations sessions. Better television might strengthen the marital bond by giving couples more of substance to talk about: "Can anyone imagine a woman being eager to tell her husband that she saw an amusing quiz while he was slaving over his desk at the office?" (Nov. 22, 1958). In applauding the series "Women" a few months later, Panitt chided networks for overestimating women's power by tailoring commercials to them while underestimating their intelligence (June 6, 1959).

Arguing that women should be treated as intelligent human beings was not a terribly risky thing to do, even in the fifties. Nonetheless, *TV Guide* effectively practiced linguistic ambiguity and added a masculine wink that undercut its own position. In "Ladies Love the Panels" (Oct. 2, 1954), for example, the magazine recognized that being "too bright before the cameras" could be a liability for female panelists. Nina Foch had been fired because she refused to stumble around a bit to "perpetuate the awful lie that women are idiots." The writer of the article, however, did not make clear whether he was stating a fact or decrying injustice. The "awful lie" seemed laden with more irony than indignation.

Sometimes *TV Guide* found intelligent and cultured women in the most unlikely places. "Jayne Mansfield Tells All" (June 23, 1956) juxtaposed a titillating title (associated with a sex symbol known in the euphemistic and Oedipal fifties as a "bombshell") with a story that rubbed against the grain of readers' expectations, a technique increasingly popular in Radnor. The article subverted the sexual promise of its headline by revealing the well-educated, socially conscious, culture-vulture beneath the glamorous facade: "On the afternoon preceding Murrow's visit to her home, Jayne visited an orphanage in the Bronx and the Botanical Gardens in Brooklyn, took a dancing lesson, had lunch with Murrow, read all the gossip columns, had her hair set and attended a speech class. Then she returned to her flat, sat down calmly on the divan and began to practice her violin." In many ways, the listing of Mansfield's activities is comic in its representative diversity, especially given her public persona as the quintessential "dumb blonde." Indeed, as long as her intellect operated in private, but was absent in the performing woman, Jayne Mansfield remained a tame sex kitten.

The article also worked because it was an exception that proved the rule. Connie Francis, to give another example, was deemed "a girl of substance and perspective in a field where such gifts are rather rare" (July 4, 1959). Week after week *TV Guide*'s "Pretty Girl Pages" presented starlets who were as vacuous as they were voluptuous. They were "sitting ducks," staff writers remember, because they mouthed pretentious platitudes about their "craft" and "goals" that came straight out of a press agent's notebook. Staff writers invited readers to laugh at each woman as she struggled in vain to convince someone that she wasn't just another pretty face. In such a context intelligence was simply incongruous.

The ambition and business acumen of women in show business presented a more serious challenge to *TV Guide* editors and writers. How should successful career women be portrayed? The titles of fifties profiles promised a balanced analysis: "She Really Has the Last Word" (June 30, 1956); "Dinah Says It's Tough to Be a Woman" (Dec. 15, 1956); "Eva Wolas Bosses Playhouse 90" (Jan. 19, 1957); "Jane Wyman Is All Business" (Feb. 2, 1957); "Gail Patrick—Business-Like Beauty" (June 21, 1958); "Ann Sothern, Businesswoman" (Mar. 21, 1959); and "How Loretta Young Deals with Businessmen" (May 16, 1959). Each article had essentially the same theme. According to Dinah Shore, show business was "a man's world. So is everything else, for that matter." Jane Wyman was a "female phenomenon" in "what is largely a man's world of television." And yet they had made it, overcoming the resentment of men at "being ordered around by a woman—and a pretty young woman at that" (June 30, 1956). Loretta Young, the magazine observed, approached money matters with "simple, devastating [masculine] logic," not at all shy about negotiating her own salary.

On the difficulty of commanding clout in the television industry, *TV Guide* had a mixed and somewhat contradictory message. Although women will find it "a little harder" to find work at the networks, asserted Herbert Leonard, producer of "Rin Tin Tin" and "Circus Boy," "you'll find no prejudice against women in TV" (Oct. 5, 1957). Thousands "hold down important jobs," from producer to secretary, reported "Women Are Welcome on TV" (May 30, 1959). Even the prejudice against women writers of westerns seemed to be diminishing (June 6, 1959). Just as typical, however, was the claim that for a "mere slip of a woman" like Gail Patrick "to ease past all her masculine television contemporaries and install herself in the driver's seat . . . is comparable to Jayne Mansfield's suddenly becoming vice president of Metro-Gold-wyn-Mayer" (June 21, 1958). The tone of the articles about Dinah Shore, Jane Wyman, Loretta Young, and the others reflected the writers' surprise at the drive and business savvy of these women—and a strong conviction that they were a rare breed.

More unambiguous in the fifties was the formula, articulated by the show-business women themselves and abetted by *TV Guide*, that explained and justified success. In contrast to the male theme of hard work and persistence, "the ladies" downplayed ambition, insisting their careers had been launched by accident. In fact, according to Eva Wolas, who "bossed" "Playhouse 90," the paucity of female producers might well be due to the reluctance of many women "to work that hard" (Jan. 19, 1957). Actress after actress told an implausible story to an easily persuaded writer, whose narrative implied that most stars, unaware of their beauty and talent, had been plucked from oblivion by perceptive male press agents, directors, and friends. Barbara Hale "never wanted to be an actress." "Side-tracked" into modeling while attending art school in Chicago, she was then spotted by a talent scout (July 5, 1958). Similarly, Nancy Gates didn't want to be a star. "I never had that kind of driving ambition" (Nov. 21, 1959). Dorothy Provine was acting at the University of Washington and wound up in Hollywood "through no fault of her own." She spent two weeks there with a friend, met an actor who arranged a screen test, and the "next thing [she] knew," she had been offered a part on "Wagon Train" (Sept. 26, 1959). This conceit, however improbable, has persisted in *TV Guide* for more than three decades, as the following samples, drawn almost at random, suggest: Linda Evans got into acting through "happenstance pure and simple" (Dec. 24, 1975); Kelly Lange got into radio "by accident" (July 22, 1978); and Heather Thomas's acting was "reluctant and accidental" (June 19, 1982).

This theme reflects the desire of women to retain public confidence in their femininity. Without it, Dinah Shore insisted, "a woman star is dead." Indeed, realizing her dependence on the male, Dinah surrounded herself with trusted masculine advisers. Nor would she have it any other way, leading *TV Guide* to exult, "Vive la différence!" "A girl's job is to be a girl," Arlene Francis agreed. "Once she takes over a man's position, she loses her femininity and place in society" (July 9, 1954). Jane Wyman tried to avoid the image of a female executive, "whose whims come clad in iron," because she feared a negative reaction from her fans. Anita Louise, according to *TV Guide*, had the intelligence of a brilliant executive but enough of a female brain to hide it (July 19, 1958). If, as David Susskind said, women were "more sensitive than men, more perceptive and certainly more analytical" (May 30, 1959), they also had to learn not to display those skills and to defer to men, or at least appear to.

Deference also included a ritualistic affirmation that marriage and family were more important than career. Not every star sought to portray herself, as did Arlene Francis, as just an "ordinary housewife" (July 9, 1954), but nearly every one felt the need, with little prodding from *TV Guide* (according to Merrill Panitt), to discuss her priorities. Carmel Quinn had "no axe to grind, no ambitions for stardom, and no driving compulsion to 'get somewhere'—except home every night to her family in Leonia, New Jersey" (Dec. 8, 1956). Cloris Leachman liked her new role on "Lassie" because it did not require her to be a star: "I'm afraid of the demands it would make on me and what it might do to my family life." If she were single, she would act in Broadway plays, but her husband wished to stay in Hollywood (Dec. 28, 1957). If Rosemary Clooney's husband, Jose Ferrer, preferred that she not perform, she would comply, but "he is allowing me to work" (Feb. 22, 1958). Barbara Hale (in a marked contrast to the hard-boiled—and single—Della Street she played) doted on husband and children and was "a booster for the Early American Ranch House and the frilly apron" (July 5, 1958). But the most splendid spouse was undoubtedly "Carolyn—the Belle Who Tolls for Frankenheimer" (Apr. 25, 1959). A former model and a member of Phi Beta Kappa at Cornell University, she worried constantly about how hard her husband John was working. Omnipresent in the studio, ready to deliver hot coffee or a snack of fresh fruit, she massaged the director's neck and facial muscles whenever a "take 15" break was called. "And she did all of this without talking—which may make her a jewel of a wife."

Rarely in the fifties did *TV Guide* think the ladies protested too much. The writer of the Arlene Francis profile could not help noticing the servants who "comfortably staffed" her house as she claimed to enjoy scrubbing bathroom and kitchen floors. And the author of an article on Lucille Ball branded her claim to be a homebody a "non-sequitur" (July 12, 1958). But for the most part the magazine played along with the fiction that the stars preferred housewifery to the glamour and power of their careers. The audience, presumably, would accept an emancipated body, only if assured that the woman's heart and soul remained in the right place.

TV Guide also reminded readers that many career women lived lonely, even desperate lives. Significantly, writers relied little on the testimony of the women they interviewed for this insight, preferring to trust their (usually male) intuition. Thus Jane Wyman's plunge into a man's world was a "compulsion," responsible for three failed marriages. Sadly, it left her even more driven because she had no other outlet for her energies. To say "Jane Wyman Is All Business" was to pity her. Carol Channing was still working on her third husband and made no excuses for making a life as a professional. Nonetheless, *TV Guide* moralized that she maintained no permanent home, didn't know how to cook, and took her four-year-old son with her on tours "whenever possible." The nomadic life, the profile implied, would take its toll on this family as well (Jan. 4, 1958). Jane Harrison, Alfred Hitchcock's producer, was another slave to her work. In "this business," Hitchcock told her, "you don't just leave at 5. You stay until the work is finished." Because she had done just that, Harrison had risen from a $15-a-week job as a secretary to her present position. But she, too, had paid a price: unmarried, she lived alone in a one-bedroom apartment (Mar. 8, 1958). And Ann Sothern provided a perfect object lesson for the magazine's readers. Her father, importer-exporter W. J. Lake, who had wanted a son, tutored Ann instead in the principles of business. President of five corporations, Sothern divorced Robert Sterling in 1948 and led a "lonely life" plagued with illness, weight problems, and fatigue. She would much prefer to run a home than a business, she confessed to *TV Guide* (Mar. 21, 1959).

Amid the puffery of fifties profiles, these cautionary tales warned that women must not stray too far from the domestic circle. A few superwomen like "Diana Lynn, Shrinking Tigress" could balance constant work as an actress "and the good life she has just being Mrs. Mortimer W. Hall" both emotionally and physically (Aug. 22, 1959). Most women should understand, *TV Guide* often asserted, that "You can't work constantly and still be a good wife and mother" (Nov. 21, 1959). Ironically, this message came from women who did not practice what they preached, and it is impossible to gauge its impact on readers. In using career women to defend traditional female roles, *TV Guide* may, unconsciously, have given a bit of encouragement to those who wished to transcend them.

For many women the sixties era began in 1963 with the publication of *The Feminine Mystique*, by Betty Friedan. In essays in *Mademoiselle*, *Ladies Home Journal*, and *McCall's* and in her best-seller, Friedan gave middle-class housewives words to describe "The Problem That Has No Name," the sense of emptiness and lack of fulfillment felt by "happily married," well-educated women, and helped revive the women's rights movement. Friedan was surprised at the warm reception her book received from men as well as women, but, in retrospect, her message was less threatening than she might have thought: after all, Friedan argued that a woman could achieve her own goals and be herself without sacrificing marriage or motherhood. In any case, the book helped create the climate for the insertion of the word "sex" in the Civil Rights Act of 1964 prohibiting discrimination in employment, the establishment of a Presidential Commission on the Status of Women (1965), and the start of the National Organization for Women (1966) and countless other organizations that pressed for equal rights for women.

In many ways Betty Friedan's two-part article "Television and the Feminist Mystique" (Feb. 1, 8, 1964) was a natural for *TV Guide*. By the early 1960s the magazine was soliciting pieces from influential Americans, and the image of women on television was bound to stimulate reader interest. Friedan's indictment of the medium was harsh indeed: on the small screen the American woman was "a stupid, unattractive, insecure little household drudge who spends her martyred, mindless, boring days dreaming of love—and plotting hasty revenge against her husband." On television, as in American society, men created the image of women, "a sophisticated mishmash of obsolete prejudices," forcing them to live vicariously through love, husband, and children. Without men and mechanical devices, Friedan argued, the women in commercials could barely get through the most menial household tasks. With politics, art, and science apparently beyond their comprehension, women on daytime TV had no interest in the world or the ability to understand it—let alone act in it.

If not for the real tedium of the housewife's day, Friedan pointed out, she would not willingly endure the tedium of daytime TV, with its stupid game shows and soap operas, where a woman did anything to hook her man. But the powerful images of television, by perpetuating these stereotypes and encouraging women to evade "the choices, efforts, [and] goals which would enable them to grow to maturity and full human identity" had created a new generation of passive, frustrated, and resentful women. TV's little housewife would become a "self-fulfilling prophecy [writhing] forever in that tedious limbo between the kitchen sink and the television game show," unless television depicted women as heroines, taking control of their own lives, teaching, voting, building libraries, and even going out on strike. And in vanquishing the monster in the kitchen, television might itself become more realistic, dramatic, humorous, and appealing.

While television, the mass medium, had failed women, *TV Guide*, television's mass medium voice, implied it would do better. Throughout the sixties, as we shall see, TV Guide would occasionally raise a feminist voice as it monitored television's progress in depicting women. The

magazine, however, did not enroll itself in the women's rights movement, nor was it really more progressive than television in its treatment
of gender issues. Betty Friedan spoke for herself, but in *TV Guide* other,
older voices could still be heard, as in the two advertisements that
appeared on the pages of Friedan's second article. The first, for "D-
con mouse-prufe," showed a pretty young woman perched on a chair
in a traditional posture of sexy fear, clutching her skirt above shapely
legs and shrieking "Eek! A Mouse!" The second depicted "Deborah,"
head in hand, "Sunk in Periodic Pain" from menstrual distress, then
springy and smiling, free of headache, backache, and jumpy nerves,
"Gay Deborah Saved by Midol." As the American people reassessed sex
roles, *TV Guide* would remain of two minds, with two peacefully co-
existing messages, each seemingly unaware of the presence of the other.

When *TV Guide*'s editors wanted a respectable feminist point of view
in the sixties, they frequently turned to critic Marya Mannes. In occasional reviews of television shows and feature articles, Mannes encouraged housewives to practice dialsmanship and at the same time
derided female stereotypes. In a review of soap operas Mannes acknowledged that relaxation of the brain and suspension of belief were
sometimes healthy but alerted viewers to the inherent social patterns
of the sudsers: "Nothing Exists outside the Family Unit; Women with
Aprons Are Good Women; They Drink Coffee Every Two Minutes; Bad
Women Drink Cocktails and Have Careers" (Apr. 13, 1963). Three years
later, although admitting that standards were subjective, she urged female viewers to exercise their critical intelligence: "If you are happy
with what you see on television we can only envy you" (Mar. 19, 1966).

By 1968 Mannes was even more outspoken. In "Should Women Only
Be Seen and Not Heard?" (Nov. 23, 1968), she bemoaned a hiring of
female news commentators "so token that it is virtually nonexistent."
Objectivity, Mannes observed, was traditionally claimed a masculine
virtue, while opinion was deemed a male prerogative and a female flaw.
Writing in the heyday of the civil rights and black power movements,
Mannes drew a parallel between women and blacks: "We are oddities,
often praised because we are women." "There is still, let's face it, a
deep resistance to the career woman as such," Mannes concluded, although she was careful to qualify her indignation in a refrain that would
soon make its way into *TV Guide* editorials: "This resistance is quite
understandable in the case of militant females who bulldoze their opinions with strident voices, contorted faces and guerilla tactics." In a year
of assassinations, demonstrations, and credibility gaps, Mannes offered
a soothing feminism based on a woman's "special way of looking at
things" and on "centuries of instinct and experience [of] how to pre-

serve a family." Since a woman's job had always been to create and not destroy, she might be best suited to keep the peace. The moderate Mannes message reached for a mass audience.

Women's issues also attracted the attention of Edith Efron, *TV Guide*'s resident iconoclastic individualist in the sixties. As she jabbed at platitudes and poseurs early in the decade, Efron sounded much like Betty Friedan. Lucille Ball's insistence that she could have been happy as a homemaker struck Efron as a "symbolic fantasy": "It was not a passion for being an old-fashioned homemaker that drove the 16-year-old girl to Broadway, and to fight her way to the top of a savagely competitive field. And nothing is keeping her now from retreating to a log cabin, churning her own butter and curing her own meat" (Sept. 29, 1962). Conversely, Efron had nothing but admiration for Shirl Conway of "The Nurses," a refreshingly honest woman, unlike other actresses who "tiresomely" insisted they were normal. Like Liz Thorpe, the character she played, Conway was unconventional, a rebel with a backbone who did not believe "woman is intended just for a biological role. . . . 'It's been evident to me all my life that housewives have been in psychological misery.' " On dates she spurned "the womanly practice of playing dumb." Married four times, Conway had always chosen career over husband, and apparently she did not regret it (July 13, 1963).

Impatient with and skeptical of the "preoccupation" of career women with family, Efron skewered Barbra Streisand, whose marriage "presumably" provided happiness (Efron found it difficult to tell). Streisand's desire for a "normal" woman's life, Efron concluded, blinded her from her own talent and deprived her of pleasure with her fame. In the last analysis, Streisand didn't like herself and thought having a baby was "real creativity" (July 22, 1967).

Efron, however, like Marya Mannes, did not believe that women's rights should be purchased at the cost of femininity. In Aline Saarinen, sometime ambassador to Finland and TV talk-show host, she found the ideal modern woman. Saarinen attributed 25 percent of her success to the fact that she was Mrs. Eero Saarinen. "One might dispute the percentages," Efron wrote, "but it was a sensible answer." More important, Saarinen, who respected orderly, logical people and scorned the self-indulgent "who go endlessly to psychiatrists," was a thoughtful woman who also had traditionally feminine attitudes such as wanting to look up to a man. With one foot in the women's liberation movement (she believed that women workers experienced discrimination), she disliked nonetheless its excesses (children in test tubes). In an age of extremists Saarinen was a militant moderate, the Roy Wilkins of women's rights, in short, Edith Efron's—and *TV Guide*'s—kind of person.

Such women did not appear frequently on the small screen. By the end of the decade Efron, acting as the virtual spokesperson for her magazine, combined indictment, exhortation, and optimistic forecast. In "Is Television Mocking the American Woman?" she quoted feminists who objected to the portrayal of women as helpless, stupid sex objects in commercials and as brainless or passive characters in dramas or comedies and their complete absence from newscasts. The "growing grass roots feminist movement," however, was lobbying hard for a more humanized depiction of women on television, and the men who ran the medium were "listening with at least one ear," especially to their own wives, daughters, and friends, "who have something on their minds besides how white their wash turns out" (Aug. 8, 1970).

If television was listening to reform-minded American women in the sixties, so was *TV Guide*. When Bette Davis filled in on "Perry Mason" for Raymond Burr, who was undergoing surgery, she caused a stir not unlike the startle she once gave Hollywood by placing the following ad in the trade papers: "Situation Wanted, Woman." Now she asked an even wider audience, "Why can't there be a television series about a woman lawyer?" (Jan. 26, 1963). *TV Guide*, which had featured a story a year earlier suggesting that in television the woman's field was dead ("Who Says Women Are Here to Stay?" Dec. 2, 1962), now responded more sympathetically. Writers frequently found that the feminine formulas of the fifties now looked transparent and trite. For one thing, they were learning from some of the women they interviewed. Eve Arden really didn't regret that her career submerged that of her husband, Brooks West, who tended their zucchini farm (Dec. 9, 1967). Suzanne Pleshette really meant it when she decided marriage must wait and told ardent admirers, "Sorry, on Thursday I'm dying of leukemia on Dr. Kildare" (Jan. 6, 1962). And Pauline Frederick was really right when she deemed newsmen "patronizing and downright catty" to female colleagues (June 16, 1962). Deeply involved with her husband and two children, who were used to the idea that she worked, Pat Crowley gave Robert DeRoos a "funny-surprised look" when he asked whether her marriage of eight years was going to last (Jan. 29, 1966).

And when female stars continued to spout clichés, *TV Guide* writers, like political journalists, spotted a credibility gap. Debunking, as we said in chapter 2, became a trademark technique of the magazine in the sixties. Thus, Kathy Nolan, interviewed in "The Unreal McCoy," was tagged by her own line: " 'I want a husband and I want children' is her favorite conversational gambit to anyone who will listen" (Apr. 7, 1962). In a review of "Calendar," Gilbert Seldes resented Mary Fickett's comment that a story on equal voting power for city dwellers was "technically confusing to a female brain like mine" (Sept. 1, 1962). When Dorothy Loudon loudly proclaimed that she really hated show business and wanted a family because it was what a woman does best, Maurice Zolotow was not convinced. Was she "just another home economics poseur?" he asked, citing intimates who claimed they would believe Loudon when they saw a ring on her finger (June 1, 1963). By now *TV Guide* was placing quotation marks around the phrase "just a housewife" when an actress like Annette Funicello announced an intention to trade her career for "a normal life" (Oct. 12, 1963).

The old rules that actresses could do double duty, at home and at work, it seemed, did not apply any more. When Lola Albright married Bill Chadney, husband number three, in 1962, she took no chances that he would get away, refusing acting assignments away from Hollywood and getting up at 2 A.M. to cook him a light meal. According to *TV Guide,* when "Today" chose Barbara Walters, who acted like a reporter rather than "a feather-headed hostess," they challenged a television axiom: "that too great a display of brains and competence in a woman would shrivel the mass audience" (Aug. 5, 1967).

In Doris Day, the Hollywood bureau chief, Dwight Whitney, found the perfect vehicle to chart the changing times and mark *TV Guide*'s awareness of the dawn of a new Day. The quintessential girl next door, like so many women, had come to believe in her own myth: "that she was the wholesome, high-spirited, freckle-faced girl with the zingy figure, [who] insisted that marriage was an unalterable prerequisite of making love." With the death of her husband, Marty Melcher, her buffer against the real world, Day had been forced to go it alone. "It never occurred to her that these values might undergo any alteration." Not surprisingly, however, Doris Day was finding that she could manage quite well on her own (Dec. 28, 1968).

The writers and editors of *TV Guide,* then, capitalized on the aroused consciousness of their female subjects and readers. In their desire to remain authoritative, they could not set their faces against the winds of change. But the magazine was not a feminist organ in the sixties. A national consensus on women's rights, let alone women's liberation, had certainly not been reached. On July 2, 1965—the day the Civil Rights Act of 1964 took effect—the *New York Times* continued to publish its segregated columns of help-wanted ads for men and women, filled with references to "Girl Friday" and "mail boy." As before, the *Times* had no sexually neutral column of ads. In a small box at the top of the section, the editors explained their way of complying with the law: "Qualified job seekers of either sex are invited to consider job opportunities in either the Male or Female help-wanted columns." A month later, the *Times* discovered "the bunny problem," wondering aloud what would happen when a male applied to be a Playboy Bunny or when a woman sought a job as an attendant in a Turkish bathhouse. Congress, the editors snickered, ought to "just abolish sex itself" (Aug. 21, 1965). Fit to print in the *Times*, this viewpoint was even more appropriate to *TV Guide*, ever-mindful of its traditionalist readers. Articles regularly undercut the mild support, implicit and explicit, for expanded opportunities for women. Debunking, moreover, could cut two ways, and *TV Guide* abounded in condescending and snide displays of male chauvinism. Profiles with fifties themes lived on in a *TV Guide* time warp. The magazine told its readers what to think, but they could usually find an opinion they liked, be it emancipation or misogyny.

Marriage remained the sine qua non of female fulfillment for *TV Guide* writers, even when it didn't for their subjects. The "Cluttered Life" of Anita Corsaut, including her devotion to acting (on "The Andy Griffith Show"), was a transparent attempt to compensate for the fact that she was unmarried at the ripe old age of thirty-three. Corsaut, it turned out, was a tomboy who played baseball while going out on dates and who believed she could have been a major league ballplayer but for, "she hints darkly, prejudice in high places against women" (May 20, 1967). This jab at women's liberation reinforced the magazine's view that spinsterhood was an unnatural and often unnecessary act. After citing the opinions of Dorothy Loudon's friends that she was another home economics poseur, Maurice Zolotow reversed himself and confirmed that she could, in fact, cook and sew, and he pronounced her ambivalent about her life in show business, as are "so many other American career women." Marriage for Loudon might be a blow to those who enjoyed sophisticated humor, but Zolotow implied it would clearly be good for the comedienne (June 1, 1963).

Even a sophisticated writer like Dwight Whitney could still find stereotyping quotations within which to sheathe Ida Lupino, the distinguished actress and director. From her husband, Collier Young: "the finest wet nurse in the history of young talent"; from crew members: "She does everything the instinctively feminine way"; from Ida Lupino herself, a sigh of relief that she was not born a "glamorpot" (Oct. 8, 1966). Whitney was fully capable of establishing ironic distance from the people he interviewed, but in this piece he played it straight.

Whitney was not the only writer to hide behind a quotation. A profile of Ann Prentiss concluded with the actress's statement that if she deserved it, a "good whacking" by a husband would do her good (June 17, 1967). Other writers, however, did not hesitate to express themselves, some with a sneer, some with a leer. Cleveland Amory could always be counted on to play male chauvinist in his reviews. Noting the desperate attempts of espionage shows to renew themselves by incorporating "girl" secret agents, he exclaimed: "Imagine! Girls and secrets—the very idea is a contradiction in terms" (Feb. 24, 1968). And an article on how to use television to keep peace on Thanksgiving Day mixed misogyny with its humor. In the modern family, on Thanksgiving Day kids could be kept busy with toys and adolescents sent to the movies, while women "provide their own entertainment cutting up absent friends," but men require attention, particularly bar service, unless diverted by TV. A second set, however, should be set aside for the time when wives, "tired of yelling at their rotten kids and resentful of the fun the men were having" watching football, demanded to go home. Not discussed was the kind of programming that might mollify the moms, since sports substituted for the soaps on Turkey Day (Nov. 18, 1967).

Throughout the sixties, then, *TV Guide* played with the changing consciousness of women, counterpunching feminists as well as traditionalists. To the extent that the women's movement discouraged women from trying to attract men with their looks *TV Guide* would remain unreconstructed in its chauvinism. Readers, it ironized, should "pity poor" Mary Ann Mobley, the former Miss America, who yearned to command respect as an actress "and forget this stuff about the body beautiful. Eight long years and it still hasn't happened" (Dec. 23, 1967). And when Pia Lindstrom told Robert DeRoos that her dimensions were no one's business but her lover's, the rebuff merely roused his phallocentric instincts: "Well, I thought about that. . . . I decided that you and I really are not interested in the span of a girl's waist, even though she is blonde and leggy and lively and about to become rich and famous" (July 29, 1967). Similarly, at the end of the decade, a piece on the miniskirt, ostensibly to give tips on how to remain a "lady" while wearing it, was little more than an excuse to revel in a revealing fashion (May 17, 1969). Much had changed in the sixties—but much remained the same.

Like the civil rights movement, the women's rights coalition contained militants as well as moderates. In the late sixties and early seventies, the radicals, among them Marxist feminists and lesbian feminists, were more vocal and visible. Propelled by the pill, the "new morality," with its sexual promiscuity, which was often displayed in public, seemed to threaten the nuclear family. *TV Guide* blamed the media, especially television, for giving excessive space and air time to extremists. Edith Efron, for example, blasted producers of network news programs for covering peripheral pseudo-events like bra burning. Nonetheless, in these years *TV Guide* succumbed to the trend it condemned. "Women's lib" got under the skin of Merrill Panitt and many of his writers, who did not quite define the movement by its excesses but seemed at times to forget the center in the rush to the periphery.

Between the fall of 1970 and the spring of 1971 Panitt wrote five editorials on women's issues, more than he wrote in any comparable period on civil rights. He began, innocently enough, by asking if the fixation with clean clothes in detergent commercials was normal: "What about women who don't give a damn whether their kid's clothes are whiter than white?" Panitt backed off from this potentially liberating perspective, however, and attacked permissive mothers who greeted dirty clothes with "a smile of appreciation . . . for providing a new enzyme challenge" rather than giving the kid "a sore bottom" (Sept. 5, 1970). It was not yet clear what Merrill Panitt was angry about, beyond a concern that modern mothers were insufficiently concerned with the welfare of their children. But the editor was just warming up.

On September 26, 1970, in "As We See It" he agreed with Betty Friedan and "the women's liberation people" that commercials degrade women by showing them interested only in washing and waxing. From this feminist preface came a confused, barely coherent editorial that seemed to blame women for the hang-ups of men: "It's a bit harder for us to go all the way and treat women as people rather than just sex symbols." Why? "Many of those who appear on television rather enjoy being considered as sex symbols. And then, of course, the roles that many women play on television hardly fit in with women's lib ideals. We might even classify some of them as 'goofy' sex symbols. But nice."

Mercifully, Panitt did not define a goofy sex symbol, at least not for two months, when "As We See It" addressed the reported demise of the swimsuit competition in the Miss America contest. Given the easy availability of pornographic movies, the parade of bathing beauties was an anachronism, but Panitt was sorry to see this "pleasant harmless bit of America" go. It was, he sighed, "a vestige of an age of innocence . . . when a gentleman would look only if a lady seated opposite him inadvertently revealed a knee" (Nov. 28, 1970).

In 1971 Panitt was less nostalgic and more annoyed. What if "The Golddiggers," a variety show hosted by a troupe of scantily clad dancers, did use women as sex objects? "Women's lib or no women's lib, there is such a thing as physical attraction, and lovely, wholesome-looking women have it. It may be blasphemy to say so nowadays, but gazing at beautiful girls is a delightful pastime for men. . . . Greg Garrison seems to be the only television producer who knows it—more's the pity" (May

1, 1971). Two months later the irked editor mocked the complaints of "the women's lib red-hots" about "language discrimination." Some of them, he snickered, wanted to make pronouns unisexual by using *ve* instead of he and she. "Imagine identifying Raquel Welch and Jim Arness with the same word—ve!" There was "good sense and justice in giving women equal opportunity and equal pay," Panitt admitted, almost parenthetically (he did not devote an entire editorial column to this subject). But women's lib activists on television, like "the ladies with the nutty pronouns," often made "wild statements" that did the cause more harm than good (July 17, 1971).

TV Guide was beyond reproach on women's issues, Panitt told us, because the magazine had always given women credit for intelligence and business acumen: "let me assure you that I am not anti–woman's lib. I was, and am, against their excesses . . . silly excuses—bra burning, complaints about bathing suits in beauty contests, concerns about sexy women being treated as sex objects in sitcoms and such that seemed to trivialize a serious subject." Whenever he used the pronoun "he" instead of "he and she," Panitt got mail from some "real red-hots." A man who had to grind out a column every week for more than twenty years was "damned glad to find a subject that lets you be just a little amusing." But, Panitt insisted, *TV Guide* "agreed wholeheartedly" with the demands of women for equal rights and equal pay.

Panitt is concerned that no one read more into his editorials than he intended, but their tone and emphasis, reinforced elsewhere in the magazine, did tend to mock the women's movement without providing much space to discuss or endorse the aspirations and grievances he considered legitimate. As with the rise of black militants, the women's liberation movement seemed to give *TV Guide*'s editors the license to display their traditionalist instincts. Twenty years later, Panitt's tone remains dismissive of elements of mainstream feminism. In addition to references to "the Ms. business" and "the red-hots," Panitt jokingly characterized the publication of Betty Friedan's *The Feminine Mystique* as a day that would live in infamy. There is more than one way, women's rights advocates might say, to trivialize a serious subject.

In the early seventies, *TV Guide* seemed obsessed with women's lib. "Observations of a Newsnut's Wife" mocked the all-American housewife who dried her hands on a dish towel, sat down to watch TV, got one look at Harry Reasoner's tie, and then switched to see what Dan Rather was wearing. Having established that the empty-headed housewife did little more than clean house, cook dinner, and scream at the children, Louise Logan Melton concluded the piece with the woman interrupting her thoughts to cheer a women's liberation demonstration in Boise (Mar.

27, 1971). Anne Tolstoi Foster, vice president of J. Walter Thompson Advertising Agency, was more direct. In an article calling for Ad Lib for Women, in which she chastised the makers of television commercials for ignoring working women, Foster began gratuitously: "You would have to be blind, deaf and very dumb today to be ignorant of women's lib, the noisy movement for equal opportunity for women" (June 19, 1971). Similarly, an article assessing the impact of "Sesame Street" noted that pressure from women's liberation forced the program to make a character who had been a housewife a nurse as well: "Women's lib has a thing about housewives" (July 10, 1971). Finally, endorsing motherhood in a TV editorial was dangerous, Richard Doan reported, because "the Women's Lib movement clobbers" anyone who places women in the home (Nov. 21, 1970).

Even Melvin Durslag, the reliably bland reporter (except for his quick jab at Cassius Clay in the sixties), weighed in with an essay on the crumbling of the walls of male chauvinism in sports. Posing as historian of the revolution, Durslag noted the following developments: the National Organization for Women was monitoring TV to see how many hours were devoted to women's athletics; a woman's sportscaster was bemoaning her failure to crash the dressing room of the New England Patriots; and Billie Jean King was reporting "Indignantly—that's the way many women are reporting these days"—that for every one dollar spent on female team sports, ninety-nine were spent on male teams. Durslag concluded on the same note of wry amusement with which he had begun: "We don't like to throw a damper on any phase of women's liberation, but a lot of women have exclaimed, with equal satisfaction [to those who participate in sports], 'My God, I got my husband to do the dishes!' " (June 29, 1974).

Perhaps the best way to understand *TV Guide*'s evolving treatment of women is to examine its treatment of beauty pageants, a favorite target of moderates and radicals, who deplored the parade of sex objects. In the relative innocence of the fifties, the magazine confined itself to a profile of Miss America, Lee Ann Merriweather, a brainy beauty who read John Synge plays and yet remained wholesome enough to say "golly" at every available opportunity (Sept. 3, 1955). In the mid-sixties, when the women's movement seemed moderate, Panitt in "As We See It" could acknowledge that Miss America contests had little social value, though he skirted the issue of their sexism. The show's huge audiences proved "only that television was then functioning at its most popular level, not necessarily its best. There has to be something better than Bert Parks' singing" (Apr. 16, 1966).

By 1968, when Joan Barthel covered the Miss America, Miss Universe, and Miss Teen America pageants, *TV Guide* was beginning to sound defensive and dyspeptic. Although Barthel admitted the shows were "marshmallow-eclairs," she dubbed them an American institution that was cherished, respected, indispensable, and profitable. The pageants were changing with the times, stressing talent, personality, and scholastic achievement and downgrading the swimsuit competition. Although Barthel stressed the commercial value of the televised competitions, she observed the dignified treatment of the contestants, several of whom won scholarships to college. Pageant organizers, like Miss America president John C. Rowe, believed that the concept of the ideal American girl "was somehow necessary if this Nation is to long endure." And, warming to his topic, "When you see some of the things that go on in America, he said, like hair down to here and guitars, and then see these clean-cut American girls, it gives us hope that we have girls like this to go out and do the job for us."

Debra Dene Barnes, Miss America of 1968, agreed. Americans loved to watch the pageant, she said, because they were curious "to see what kind of girl America is turning out" (Apr. 20, 1968). Joan Barthel never forgot that pageant people took their pride straight to the bank, but she had also portrayed them as "informal and gracious and frank and nice."

By 1970 *TV Guide* was more and more in love with beauty contests for the enemies they made. As we have seen, Panitt bemoaned in an editorial the passing of a pleasant pastime. The magazine also gave the much-maligned Bert Parks his innings. The "disgruntled" women's libbers would return to Miss America, he predicted, to reject "the biggest Cinderella story" in the land. Apparently they now preferred "burning their brassieres in the cool salt air" to partaking in the American dream. Parks concluded with an obligatory swipe at the physical appearance and sexuality of the protesters: "All I know is one of them used to play left end for Notre Dame" (Sept. 5, 1970). Three years later, the New York bureau chief, Neil Hickey, who had written the story about Parks, echoed his sentiments in "I Judged a Beauty Contest." "Oh yes," Hickey began, "I know all about women's libbers and their sorehead hostility toward (what their aviator-spectacled eyes dimly perceive as) exploitative displays of semi-nude female beauty. Well, that's their problem." The contestants, according to Hickey, were intelligent young women who rejected the criticisms directed at beauty contests. Miss Colorado wanted to marry a man who was not a radical; Miss Hawaii enjoyed the things men did for women; and Miss Massachusetts, destined for Yale, did not feel demeaned: "Since I have a body, why not look at it and appreciate it?" *TV Guide* had found the silent female majority (Dec. 29, 1973).

A few feminist pieces could be found in the magazine in these years. Invariably written by guests with established reputations, these articles criticized the stereotyped depictions of women on television. In "What's TV Doing for Women?" Caroline Bird, author of *Born Female,* pointed out that on the small screen, women's liberation "always gets into the script as a gag." Old-fashioned and obsolete, television feminism never challenged "the family system." Independent women were always single and were never head of the firm. Although she acknowledged that the industry was trying to make women characters more fully human, she insisted that prime-time shows had four subliminal messages: "You're really not interested in work," "What you really want is a man," "Women can't boss men," and "You are powerful and smart—only on your own feminine turf." Such themes, as we have seen, characterized *TV Guide* as much as television, but Bird made no mention of the magazine for which she wrote. All over the nation, she announced approvingly, "women's lib groups are monitoring their television sets to prove that women simply don't get their fair share of the tube." Even Lassie, though supposedly a female, was played by a male because the director believed that males "were easier to train and don't shed all over the studio." "Now what do you suppose made him think of that?" Bird concluded in the first unambiguous defense of women's liberation in *TV Guide* since Betty Friedan's essay (Feb. 27, 1971).

In "TV and the Single Girl," Diane Rosen was a bit more equivocal. Insulted by the inanity of "The Dating Game" and the theme of "That Girl" ("There is Nothing as Endearing in a Young Woman as Incompetence"), Rosen showered praise on "The Mary Tyler Moore Show." To be sure, Mary Richards was little more than a glorified secretary, and her sexual life was handled a bit immaturely. But Rhoda Morgenstern, with her "interest in men, her messy apartment, her general crankiness [and her admission] that the mere mention of her mother's name sets her back 15 years," was a more interesting woman (Nov. 6, 1971). Faint feminism though it was, Rosen's piece did question the stereotyping of women, although Rhoda, as she described her, hardly seems liberated.

Even in 1973, when the "threat" of women's lib began to fade, *TV Guide*'s feminist critique of the depiction of women on television seemed fainthearted. In comedies, argued Leonard Gross in "Why Can't a Woman Be More Like a Man," women appeared "at best professional auxiliaries, at worst as self-denigrating, if amusing idiots in the tradition of Lucille Ball." Wasn't Maude, "for all her riotous sass," little more than a wasted romance languages major whose hobbies were marriage and divorce? Drama, moreover, presented few opportunities for women, perhaps because there was something threatening about them in lead roles. Doctors, lawyers, and detectives might have to be women in real life before viewers would accept them on television. Gross, however, was optimistic about the networks' earnest commitment to change. Blithely conceding that "militant feminists will find scarce comfort" in the prime-time lineup, he singled out Blythe Danner's role as a strong-willed lawyer in "Adam's Rib" and a Norman Lear project about a career woman whose business interests conflict with her love life. Significantly, the liberal Lear, according to Gross, was impatient with the impatience of "militant feminists," who seemed to forget that the women's movement was in its childhood, as was television in its efforts to represent it (Aug. 11, 1973).

The most aggressively feminist writer in *TV Guide* during Merrill Panitt's tenure was Letty Cottin Pogrebin, a magazine editor and author of *Getting Yours: How to Make the System Work for the Working Woman*. In a background article on ABC's "A Woman's Place," Pogrebin revealed how she hid her intelligence while growing up, learning in half a lifetime to unlearn the lie for herself. Only recently, Pogrebin observed, had women begun "teaching the truth to our daughters so that growing up female can mean growing up free" (Sept. 1, 1973).

Far tougher, indeed militantly feminist by *TV Guide* standards, was Pogrebin's "News Watch" column, "Ten Cogent Reasons Why TV News Fails Women." Coverage of International Women's Day, she observed, had been minimal and mocking. ABC seemed most interested in the all-woman band marching down Fifth Avenue, while on NBC Tom Brokaw "smirked" about a demonstrator who came dressed as a male chauvinist pig. All three networks, in fact, routinely devoted more time to sports and weather than women's issues. They reported stories on poverty, education, and employment as if only men were affected. They kept women in their place by using sexist labeling, informing viewers, for instance, that Alice Rivlin, director of the Congressional Budget Office, was a mother. They lightened the news with gratuitous jokes at women's expense. Concluding with indignation rather than optimism, Pogrebin lobbied for more women producers and newscasters and exhorted her readers to "blitz the networks with letters demanding more news coverage of substance and dignity" (Oct. 4, 1975). Letty Pogrebin's tone and her byline marked her as an alien in *TV Guide*, due a single column and a polite reception, but not much more. Nonetheless, her essay showed that the times were changing—as were the editors of America's most popular magazine.

With the installation of David Sendler as editor in 1976, the *TV Guide* recipe for covering women's issues changed, although the ingredients remained much the same. Sendler "had strong feelings" about equal rights for women, he told us. He hired more women in responsible positions on the magazine, including Helen Newton, the first female editor in Radnor. Sendler's penchant for articles examining the values embedded in network programs combined with his own support of women's rights and the acceptance of mainstream feminism in American society to produce pieces sympathetic to the aspirations of women and critical of those unwilling to respond to them. If some profiles still sounded traditionalist or even reactionary, the balance had shifted. Staff writers and editors, as well as guest columnists, made little attempt to hide their impatience with television's cultural lag on gender issues.

"Even Edith Bunker Has a Paying Job," by Ellen Torgerson, was an early indication of the matter-of-fact feminism that had come to *TV Guide*. As more women's scriptwriters were hired, Torgerson pointed out, female characters became more realistic, if not more liberated. Television, of course, had a long way to go. Feminist stereotypes remained "as popular as jelly doughnuts" because "out there in the real world are more domesticated cats than there are jungle cats fighting for corporate territory. Therefore television is more likely to continue to present next-door-neighbor-type ladies, not women rejecting mom and apple pandowdy and going out and getting jobs as steelworkers." Torgerson did not attempt to hide her dismay that cultural conditioning had not caught up with the literature of liberation. Noting that Edith Bunker had recently become a paid Sunshine Lady, Torgerson concluded, "Now that's not exactly radical feminism. Nonetheless, each minute victory represents one small step for womankind" (Sept. 17, 1977).

In an article on women who combined acting with motherhood by bringing babies to the set, Elaine Woo applauded the "matchless" personal rewards that came to those who "have it all—marriage, family, and a rewarding professional life." In contemporary America, pregnancy and motherhood exacted a high price for career women, who should not have to carry the burden alone, according to Woo: "Until more men begin to buck the traditional role and institutions adjust to families' changing needs," women "will continue to play a delicate balancing act" (Sept. 19, 1981). In the sixties, babies bawling backstage would have provided a moment of merriment in *TV Guide;* now it was a welcome sign of progress.

More and more, *TV Guide* was reporting that the portrait of women on prime time was shallow and inaccurate. "Torn and guilt-ridden as they juggle motherhood and careers, many women in TV would agree that the mother on Cosby is too good to be true," staff writer Mary Murphy reported. Television actresses, she added, bemoaned the fact that they perpetuated a myth on the screen as they experienced the reality. Indeed Murphy, herself a mother, often cursed or cried as she juggled (June 21, 1986). A month later Kathleen Fury agreed that it was "Still a Man's World." Glad that marriage was no longer ridiculed, Fury nonetheless made the plea, radical for *TV Guide,* that television help women achieve equal pay for equal work, maternity/paternity leaves, day care, and flexible work schedules (July 26, 1986). In "TV Mothers: Myth vs. Reality," Joyce Maynard exposed the new and dangerous stereotype of the eighties: television moms who had no childcare problems, dressed well, and had interesting jobs, which they managed effortlessly along with domestic work. Always calm, they never really suffered with their children (May 9, 1987).

TV Guide even informed women that some of their sisters saw through the stereotypes on the small screen. Although the "picture of cozily domestic mom, with Donna Reed waving warmly from the doorway [had] faded to that of the wise working professional," working women remained critical. They sensed what the magazine reported as fact: on TV, 64 percent of women worked outside the home; of that number, 61 percent were professionals; in real life, only 23 percent of working women wore white collars. Career women, according to the *TV Guide* poll, thought sitcoms "too neat, too superficial," preferring shows like "LA Law" that left problems unresolved. Working-class women, "lacking, perhaps, a sense of real power," sought not to identify, but to escape by watching "Wheel of Fortune." Both groups believed that television did not deal with the difficulty of working and running a home (Jan. 30, 1988). In this article, as it reported, *TV Guide* was raising consciousness.

With writers like Mary Murphy, Susan Littwin, Elaine Warren, and Joanmarie Kalter on the staff, *TV Guide* profiles were also permeated with a feminist sensitivity. Betty Ford, Littwin reminded readers, had grown up at a "time when talented young women routinely disappeared into the Bermuda Triangle of their husband's ambitions" (Feb. 28, 1987). Even more than Littwin, Mary Murphy delivered didactic stories of women who had eluded the dead hand of the traditionalist past, as if to remind her female audience that they, too, could overcome. Until her demanding role in "Extremities," for example, Farrah Fawcett had been "somebody's daughter, somebody's wife, somebody's protégée, a sweet girl from Texas who had been as passive as a house pet for three decades"—devoted, dutiful, domestic, and Catholic. Her divorce from

Lee Majors, in Murphy's view, marked her liberation. No longer willing to play the game when the man was the boss, Fawcett fired her agent and her lawyer. Murphy gave old friend Ryan O'Neal the last word: "Those TV guys are never going to be able to push her around again. Isn't she great?" (Dec. 31, 1983). Angie Dickinson was another woman "who has learned." She put up with an alcoholic father, then became the wife and emotional pillar of Burt Bacharach. Although she was a major star, Dickinson prepared to let her career go to run "the moviola while he worked feverishly night and day." Her reward, Murphy believed, was a philandering husband and, ultimately, a divorce. Although it was tough going to pick up the pieces of her career, Dickinson had returned to stardom and a more secure sense of self with "Police Story" (May 2, 1987).

The old verities no longer seemed relevant, or even true. Once certain that gazing at girls was a delightful and harmless pastime for men, *TV Guide* was now aware of the painful price it exacted on women. The magazine told "In Harrowing Detail How Hollywood Almost Crushed Kim Novak," who seemed to be "an artifact of an era when producers sought to give breathlessly sexy starlets new names that would evoke images of hot and pliable sex kittens, and then the sex kittens themselves checked into hospitals for treatment of exhaustion and despair." Women like Novak who lived "in a dime-store snowball . . . that the owner could turn upside down at will" should learn that "sometimes it is best to run" rather than risk the fate of Marilyn Monroe (Oct. 25, 1986).

The image of women as sex objects became evidence for cultural criticism, a theme used repeatedly by Michael Leahy, the staff writer responsible for the Novak profile. Like Mary Murphy, Leahy saw Farrah Fawcett as a symbol, this time of the danger of forcing a woman to rely on her beauty. "The problem with a fantasy is that we need someone to live it, someone who can survive under the pressure of being what we want her to be, who will not crack when she can no longer play the part" (Nov. 22, 1986).

Farrah was a survivor. Of another sort was Vanna White, a new kind of pop star "in a Spaghetti-O kind of America enamored with designer trademarks and minor celebrities." White's very vacuousness, Leahy implied, resonated with a nation that had lost its defining essence: "She talked in a breezy monotone, with one eye on the seamstress beneath her, of the innocuous and the devastating, of crocheting and cats, and life and death, asking periodically if the visitor was hearing what he needed, looking at a watch, flowing from topic to topic with such alacrity that the total effect was less banal than mesmerizing, a glimpse at the burdens we place upon those who live off their persons" (Nov. 19, 1988)

The American obsession with beautiful women could be banal, but it was certainly not benign. "Sexual Harassment in Hollywood" originated in what Mary Murphy saw as a pervasive problem: the "exploitation of women." Because "there is vengeance in their business," actresses insisted on anonymity, but they reported with depressing unanimity that the casting couch was anything but an industry myth. "To succeed Hollywood starlets must first survive—beat back those who want to exploit them—and then find a way to outsmart the system." Tragically, only those who had been there understood that Hollywood was "a business, not a dream factory." Thousands more arrived each year, compelled "by their innocence and capacity for wonder, by their hunger for fame . . . This is precisely why they come—and precisely why they fail" (Mar. 29, 1986).

In this light, beauty contests also looked less harmless, especially when women wrote about them. At the end of the seventies Roger Simon did mount a halfhearted defense of the Miss America pageant. Although he acknowledged that for most contest winners it was more fun to run than to serve, Simon cast doubt on the myth that they suffered tragically. In documenting the successful lives of several Miss Americas, Simon sought, albeit indirectly, to answer critics who charged that the pageant "used" them (Sept. 1, 1979). Four years later Jane O'Reilly was ready to admit that the 1968 demonstrations against the Miss America pageant had taught a valuable lesson. Although the protesters burned no bras because they could not secure a fire permit, they started women "wondering about the then widely accepted idea that 35-24-35 offers an adequate base-line definition of ideal womanhood." Millions watched the pageant, O'Reilly knew, but perhaps only because they took "deep delight in bad taste displayed on a truly lavish scale" (Sept. 17, 1983). Near the end of the decade, however, kitsch no longer sufficed. If the newly appointed chairman of the Miss America contest could get it by the sponsors, Lisa DePaulo reported with evident approval, he would eliminate the swimsuit competition altogether so that a contestant like Kaye Rafko could promote more effectively her profession, nursing, and her cause, AIDS education. Apparently, DePaulo felt neither inclined nor compelled to give the sponsors equal time, summarily concluding: "Let's hope Leonard Horn can carry out his threats. Because by last year's standards, Kaye Lani Rae Rafko was just the dumb chick in the hula skirt" (Sept. 10, 1988).

Famous feminists found it easier to be published in *TV Guide* in the eighties as well. In an essay on TV "hunks," Ellen Goodman blasted the "idea that consciousness has raised the pectorals." In hard times, Goodman guessed, people often returned to the old mythology that men are "essentially loners"; hence, the attraction of hunks who did not lust, smolder, or love. But at bottom, women were turned on less by muscles than by character and commitment—and "hunks don't interact, they pose" (July 16, 1983). More important, perhaps, were articles by Barbara Ehrenreich (author of *Hearts of Men: American Dreams and the Flight from Commitment*) and Jane O'Reilly (author of *The Girls I Left Behind*) on the sitcom "Kate and Allie," about two divorced mothers living together with their children. Ehrenreich and O'Reilly applauded the show for not being about what "two women making do until the real thing—be it love or a single-family dwelling in the suburbs—comes along," and for showing women as friends, alone together, sharing a household. Ehrenreich and O'Reilly even took time, in the pages of *TV Guide,* to scoff at the clumsy efforts of the producers to assure viewers that Kate and Allie were not lesbians. The conclusion suggested, moreover, that adults and children, living outside the nuclear family, were "capable of having a dynamite good time doing it" (Nov. 24, 1984). Even more than "Kate and Allie," "Cagney and Lacey" was a realistic exploration of the relationship between working women, and Sendler persuaded Gloria Steinem, the bête noire of *TV Guide* in the seventies, to analyze the controversial dramatic series (Jan. 16, 1988).

Now editorials addressed sexism in the plots, characters, and even language of network television, as well as discrimination in the industry. At the end of the seventies Panitt in "As We See It" began to recoil at the sight of "jiggly bosoms" because shows attempting to cash in on the sight were sad and cynical efforts to increase ratings that would ultimately enrage or bore viewers: "There are other ways to hook viewers without turning into a hooker" (Dec. 15, 1979). By the eighties, "Cheers 'n Jeers" and The Annual J. Fred Muggs Award (bestowed by *TV Guide* on people who made monkeys of themselves) were the vehicles in which the editors campaigned for a more enlightened attitude from the networks. When CBS dropped Meg Foster from "Cagney and Lacey" because she and Tyne Daly "seemed like a pair of dykes," *TV Guide* waxed indignant (Jan. 1, 1983), as it did three months later when CBS introduced an episode of "Nine to Five" as the story of "three girls" (Apr. 23, 1983), and again at the end of the year when a media consultant asked a focus group if newscaster Christine Craft was "a mutt" (Dec. 31, 1983). A "loathsome episode" of "Mr. Belvedere," featuring a "Bowser Ball" to which "only the ugliest coeds were invited" also earned a jeer: "It's high time TV laid to rest the shallow beauty-queen ideal once and for all" (Oct. 22, 1988).

Equally important was the magazine's pressure on the industry to hire women as writers, producers, and newscasters—and to cast them as professionals. In a feature article, Joan Barthel admitted that women had made progress as network reporters but pointed out that 82.8 percent of the correspondents were white males (Aug. 6, 1983). "Cheers 'n Jeers" informed viewers that only 20 percent of prime-time characters from 1955 to 1986 were females; although 36 percent of corporate executives in the United States were women, a mere 14 percent of TV brass were (Oct. 11, 1986). The medium, *TV Guide* insisted, must not remain a male preserve.

In some circles it was as fashionable to be a feminist in the eighties as it had been to snigger in the fifties. In fact, polls indicated overwhelming support for equal pay for equal work and access to employment opportunities shorn of discrimination based on sex. David Sendler's domesticated brand of feminism was shared by most of his readers, as well as members of the television industry, who were already doing what *TV Guide* was urging them to do. At the same time, however, the 1980s was the decade of Phyllis Schlafly, anti-ERA lobbyists, and antiabortion activists. Traditionalists and even male chauvinists could find sympathy and some support in the pages of *TV Guide,* but theirs was now a minority report, alternately nostalgic and nasty, a hostile witness to change. Articles on sports, not surprisingly, remained bastions of male chauvinism. In an assessment of "Monday Night Football," for example, Dick Friedman insisted: "Whether you like this kind of shtick or loathe it, you must admit that the sight of a Dallas Cowboy cheerleader shimmying in the Texas moonlight is one of the great byproducts of the Industrial Age" (Dec. 10, 1983). Profiles, moreover, revealed that some women were retreating from feminism. Although she spent weekends grouting her sink, Stephanie Zimbalist refused to commit herself on the ERA while volunteering her distaste for "Ms.": "It means manuscript and that's all it means." Staff writer Michael Leahy beamed: "She is fast making old-fashionedness captivating" (Nov. 20, 1982). Anne Murray was "Dorothy come home from Oz [who has] spent too many years on the road, a yellow brick road but too littered with loneliness." Now married with children, spending five to six months a year as a housewife in a Toronto suburb, Murray had achieved a better balance, according to Don Kowet (Jan. 15, 1983). And Susan Scammel of "Search For Tomorrow" wanted to have a career for five years, Clark DeLeon found, before retiring to produce five kids and fulfillment (July 9, 1983).

More militantly traditional was "TV's Grave New World," in which Benjamin Stein chronicled the decline of man and the ascendancy of woman, desperate, angry, and alone. On "Lou Grant," Billie is attractive and successful but convinced that she is under "permanent male chauvinist siege." Always ready for an assault, she has exercised her moral muscles to the point of hypertrophy. "In her never-ending diatribes about the female condition," this quintessentially modern woman was a "nightmarish reversal of the contented coos of 1950s TV women" (May 18, 1982). Nor was Stein the only writer to vent his spleen in *TV Guide* at a feminism that had lurched beyond the pale. A May 8, 1982, "As We See It," for example, seemed plunked from the files of the sixties. In the event of a football strike a man would lose his excuse for refusing Sunday dinner "at your mother-in-law's. Worst: actually having to talk to your spouse on a fall Sunday. That alone could mean the end of marriage as we know it." Although by this time "As We See It" appeared only occasionally, Merrill Panitt had weighed in once again.

More difficult to explain is the J. Fred Muggs award given earlier in the year to Betty Friedan for acknowledging to Phil Donahue that feminist extremists existed but so did male chauvinist pigs. "Later in the program, however, Friedan softened her stance; 'Sometimes you do want to be treated as a sex object and a cutie-pie.' 'But,' she quickly added, 'not all the time.' " The title chosen for the piece revealed the sentiments behind its selection: "Aw, Shut Up and Give Me a Kiss, Cutie-Pie" (Jan. 9, 1982). This piece, Sendler acknowledged, "certainly does not seem sensitive to the kind of things we were doing." Nonetheless, like Panitt before him, Sendler did not want to align *TV Guide* with "a movement in and of itself." Women's liberation, unlike the civil rights of blacks, remained open to humor and even mockery, and to a policy of hearing "all sides of the question." Nonetheless, Sendler's assertion that *TV Guide* articles were "moving in the same direction" while he was editor is by and large true. On women's issues, male chauvinists—and maybe even Merrill Panitt—seemed out of place.

Under Rupert Murdoch, *TV Guide* retreated a step or two from feminism. The magazine cheered both Maria Shriver and Mary Alice Williams for "their courage in choosing what's right for them." Shriver's decision to leave "Sunday Today" to be with her new daughter Eunice, the editors implied, was just as courageous as Williams's effort to balance caring for her baby and performing her job as a news anchor. "In the '70s sacrificing a new career to raise children was anathema. Conversely, by the '80s wags were warning women they couldn't have it all." *TV Guide* reserved its "ultimate cheer" for the day when every woman—not only TV superstars—would have the freedom to choose, but it seemed that with the wags, the magazine was sliding to the right (May 19, 1990).

With this change of emphasis came reminders that *TV Guide*, no less than television, was a business with a bottom line. The age-old wisdom that sex sells was reasserted, though it was sometimes hidden within see-through disguises. The words might still be mildly feminist, but the tune was voyeuristic. "Cheers 'n Jeers" lambasted "Entertainment Tonight" for gratuitously training its spotlight on Mary Hart's legs—as it trained its own spotlight in the some direction. The "flimsiest excuse" has her sashay across the set "so the camera can admire her outfit and figure" (Jan. 14, 1989). Similarly, "Actresses Who Pose Nude," its eye-catching title having fulfilled its purpose, piously concluded: "It's a maneuver that is based on miscalculation and desperation and a large amount of pure, unadulterated naivete" (Aug. 26, 1989).

Even more often, piety disappeared. "How Good Are TV's News Queens?" had much more to do with contemporary fashions than with current events. (The writer, Murdochian Joanna Elm, came to *TV Guide* from a tabloid and the sensationalist show "A Current Affair.") Of the newscasters, Elm reported, two were blondes, two dark-haired. Three would not see forty again. None had children, although two were pregnant. The panel of "experts" commissioned by the magazine worried about Connie Chung: "She's a little uptight in the way she dresses—yet she has such a friendly personality. She doesn't need to dress quite so conservatively and traditionally" (Aug. 19, 1989). But the worst was yet to come. "Fashion milestone: Miss USA decides to allow padding," trumpeted Ivan Chubbock. The pageant now provided equal opportunity "regardless of race, creed or bra size." Chubbock asked on behalf of his readers what the best bra size was. One veteran thought it a "nice rounded B," another a 34C. Women's consciousness may or may not have been rising in the United States, but in the nineties *TV Guide* was too concerned with sagging sales to care.

6

"That's Not Fair, But It's Television": News and Politics in *TV Guide*

In its first decade, 1953 to 1963, *TV Guide* covered a medium that paid little attention to public affairs. Given prosperity at home and the United States' superior military power abroad, most viewers stretched out in front of the tube expecting to be entertained rather than enlightened. This, after all, was only the middle of the American Century, and already the United States accounted for a third of the world's goods and services. As yet unconcerned with nuclear waste, foreign competition, and the strength of the dollar, many Americans looked to their leaders to combat communism and keep the economy robust. Although discrimination and poverty persisted, viewers did not want to hear about social problems or see the suffering they produced.

Network executives, by and large, were willing to oblige. Until 1963 the network news was fifteen minutes long, with a talking head providing little more than headlines. Documentaries were infrequent and at best uneven. In the fifties, television could not compete with the newspapers, which had correspondents stationed around the world and saved space, it seemed, for all the news that was fit to print.

From the outset, however, *TV Guide*'s editors recognized the enormous potential of television as a source of information. The magazine, as we shall see, lobbied the networks to recognize their responsibility, in a democracy, to equip citizens to make intelligent choices. As it covered the news, *TV Guide* demonstrated that it was a serious, analytical publication rather than a fan magazine. More important, from our point of view, *TV Guide* developed a discernible perspective on the political issues of the times. The magazine tried to be objective and neutral (and succeeded, according to Merrill Panitt and David Sendler). Nevertheless,

even treating news coverage impartially involved making political judgments: in teaching readers how to watch the news, especially in the
turbulent sixties and seventies, *TV Guide* often structured the issues for
them as well. For a brief time the magazine was also explicitly partisan.
For almost forty years *TV Guide* has had a political voice.

Because television brought the viewer instantly to the site of the
action, *TV Guide* argued in the fifties, television could be better than
newspapers. John Cameron Swayze, for example, switched from city to
city for eye-witness news reports and used film flown in by jet from
places inaccessible to live broadcasts (May 15, 1953). If, in 1953, Americans eager to see the coronation of Queen Elizabeth had to settle for
live voice pick-ups, backgrounded by "movies, wire photos and other
graphic arts displays to simulate the actual events in London" (May 29,
1953), technology was racing to the rescue. With transistors boosting
the power along the way, the magazine reported, cables under the Atlantic would soon make possible live telecasts from Europe (May 22,
1953). Inside the United States, only the politicians stood in the way
of televised coverage of congressional sessions and committee meetings.
"As We See It" pointed out again and again that in a democracy it was
"senseless to bar television, the one medium that cannot be inaccurate
in its reporting of current events" (Sept. 18, 1954).

As this editorial suggests, in its first decade *TV Guide* often claimed
that television was an objective medium and that TV news was nakedly
empirical, uninterpreted and self-evident. With it, Merrill Panitt proclaimed, "we are close to achieving the founding fathers' dream of a
completely informed public. It is difficult for the average citizen NOT
to know what sort of men are running for office; what measures they
propose to improve the lot of all of us" (Aug. 11, 1956). And according
to Panitt, Democratic party warhorse James Farley agreed that the camera did not lie. Because television presented a "true picture" of politicians, demagogues could no longer "get away with their old spiels"
(Aug. 11, 1956). And Cleveland Amory boasted that TV news could not
only "give you everything except perhaps the comics and the crossword
puzzle," but, more important, it allowed each viewer to "actually *see*
between the lines" (Sept. 28, 1963).

Recognizing the importance of television in a democracy, *TV Guide*
demanded the expansion of the evening network news from its fifteen-
minute format to a half-hour program. Panitt, in "As We See It," refused to believe that public affairs shows could not attract an audience:
some television industry executives underestimate TV viewers, he insisted (Oct. 10, 1959). *TV Guide* also held newscasters to traditional
journalistic standards, praising Douglas Edwards for emphasizing the

news, not the newscaster. "Sold on straight reporting," Edwards "seldom, if ever" imposed a conclusion, interpreted the news, or played up sensationalist "bits of scandal, divorce or ledge jumpers" (Dec. 11, 1953). Walter Winchell ensured objectivity by making his studio off limits to network executives and sponsors who might try to influence program content (Apr. 3, 1953).

If *TV Guide,* like Sgt. Joe Friday, was looking for "just the facts," it also recognized that a visual medium demanded dramatic images. Professionalism was essential to television journalism, Panitt acknowledged in "As We See It," and he wondered whether "the boys overlooked the importance of dramatic ability and sartorial elegance. . . . The ideal newscaster should be a good reporter AND be acceptable to the public" (Apr. 10, 1953). Panitt's negative example was "Look Here," where host Martin Agronsky, according to *TV Guide*'s reviewer, conducted in-depth interviews with people from politics, show business, and sports. Although the content was interesting, visually the program was static, with Agronsky and guest nailed to their chairs and "tennis-ball wordage between them." Appropriate for radio, the show might more accurately be called "Listen Here" (Apr. 5, 1958). Even the best public affairs programs could not compete with entertainment shows and were sold to sponsors at a discount. If they sank deeper into the ratings basement, *TV Guide* implied, these shows might diminish in number as they proved that they were intrinsically unappealing, except to "eggheads."

Fortunately, most network news programs came in handsome packages. "As We See It" applauded William Paley of CBS for a televised report on the president's Materials Policy Commission, spiffily entitled "Resources for Freedom." The commission's findings, "hardly palatable in the form of thick volumes filled with small type, complicated charts, and masses of figures," were presented to the public in a pungent, comprehensible way (Jan. 29, 1954). More important, producers and newscasters recognized that they must capture the drama of the news. Television gave Walter Winchell, with his expressive face and gestures, "maximum impact" (Apr. 3, 1953). Edward R. Murrow "assumed almost a glamor boy status . . . with his handsome mien, suave dress and smooth voice. Above all, he hasn't let humor escape the show" (Apr. 17, 1953).

Of course, looking and listening were fraught with consequences, as *TV Guide* began to discern in the fifties, albeit dimly and intermittently. Television might well be anything but an unmediated medium, drama might get in the way of accuracy, and the gist of the news might be in the hands of the cameraman. In Mike Wallace's "sensational and controversial" interview show, *TV Guide* found the tendencies of television to substitute showmanship and "self-conscious attempts to be provocative" for "straight, objective news reporting." A combination of Edward R. Murrow and Senator Joseph McCarthy, as Panitt perceived it in "As We See It," Wallace was an inexperienced reporter who hooked viewers by asking provocative and personal questions. Argumentative, but not well prepared, he allowed Gloria Swanson to push an alleged cancer cure, a Ku Klux Klan member to make a pitch for segregation, and gangster Mickey Cohen to criticize Los Angeles city officials (June 29, 1957, Aug. 10, 1957). Perhaps James Farley was wrong: demagogues and dupes might find a home on the small screen.

TV Guide also focused on the camera's role in influencing viewers. Before the presidential nominating conventions of 1956, *TV Guide* ran a "Handy Handbook for Delegates," which showed that television took a position every time it selected a shot or adjusted an angle. Use makeup, *TV Guide* advised: "If you're bald, ask the attendant for a semi-gloss finish. Pancake makeup is tricky stuff. A hasty once-over to conceal 5 o'clock shadow can show up on the screen like lather in a shaving soap commercial." Sometimes there was no defense: a good speech may fail to reach a television audience or seem to be ineffective because "the party Big Shot sitting behind you may yawn in the middle of your best lines." No doubt, he'll get the camera: "That's not fair, but it's television" (Aug. 18, 1956). The actor Robert Montgomery, who advised President Eisenhower, agreed that when the camera lingered on delegates asleep during a speech, viewers concluded that the speech was a bore (June 23, 1956). Nothing appeared to stand between the image on the screen and the audience, yet how persistent and powerful that nothing turned out to be.

In the fifties, however, awareness rarely led to analysis. *TV Guide* articles on the news appeared infrequently, usually in the form of profiles of newscasters. Distortion and subjectivity were rarely analyzed in "As We See It," and in articles with more upbeat themes they were only discussed as asides. "Is TV Keeping America Informed?" acknowledged that television was a recent arrival on the news scene but celebrated its "super job" of covering the Army-McCarthy and Kefauver hearings and the professionalism of its newscasters. Yet Ed Murrow asserted that television was inherently limited because "most news consists of ideas, not happenings. It's tough enough to translate an idea into words. It's almost impossible to translate it into pictures" (Feb. 9, 1957). Similarly, the writer of "Do Newscasters Have Freedom of Speech?" did not pick up on the suggestion of Quincy Howe, president of the Association of Radio-TV News Analysts, that all newscasters editorialized through emphasis, inflection, and omission (Aug. 3, 1957). *TV Guide* clearly supported a separation between "straight news reporting" and opinion but was not sure how television news could achieve it. In an age of consensus, the issue seemed remote and theoretical, and the magazine joined Eric Sevareid as a prophet of bloom in hailing the capacity of TV news to promote "the mutuality, the togetherness" of a nation sharing tension and triumph in events like John Glenn's flight into space, "which transcended all sectional, religious, economic and racial groupings" (Apr. 6, 1963).

Beneath the surface in the 1950s, the United States was a nation divided, but *TV Guide,* like many of its readers, was not inclined to dig. As we have seen, when racial tensions erupted in the South, the magazine looked the other way. One issue, however, was not ignored. Perhaps because it so dominated the decade and was embedded in the past and present of Hollywood, the specter of communism found its way into many articles. Anticommunism performed several functions in the magazine: through a ritual of affirmation, denunciation, and derision, it united Radnor with its readers in a community of shared ideas and interests; it was also a useful tool in *TV Guide*'s campaign to expand television's news coverage. Nonetheless, *TV Guide* did not red-bait: the magazine's editors and writers were well aware of the destructiveness of blacklists and witch-hunts.

Of course, *TV Guide* was capable of treating communism with a solemnity that looks like irony only from the vantage point of the nineties. In 1953 two articles reported on the fulminations of Bishop Fulton J. Sheen, who attacked communism in twelve of his twenty-six shows. "Be not deceived," the popular priest proclaimed. "Remember when Russia talks peace it is a tactic and a preparation for war." In March, Sheen had recited "with almost hypnotic forcefulness," a parody of the death scene from Shakespeare's *Julius Caesar,* substituting the names of Malenkov and Molotov and intoning, "Stalin must one day meet his judgment." Nine days later the Soviet dictator was dead. According to *TV Guide,* when Sheen was asked about his prophecy, he remained uncharacteristically silent (May 29, Oct. 9, 1953).

The magazine also provided space to retired Rear Admiral Ellis Zacharias, consultant to "Behind Closed Doors," a program about the intelligence services of the United States. In discussing the three methods of addressing the world's problems, Admiral Zacharias left no doubt where his sympathies lay. Appeasement, of course, "gets us nowhere,"

he insisted, and law and order were "words not in the communist vo-
cabulary." What was left? "Power politics, and that's what we've got to
play with whether we like it or not" (Dec. 27, 1958).

In *TV Guide* the evil empire was also the butt of jokes, primarily
from the pen of Ollie Crawford in a weekly column of one-liners called
"Fine Tuning." In the fall of 1953 Crawford imagined what Soviet
television might be like: "Russians try television 'give-away' programs.
The one safe answer is 'Hooray for Malenkov.' " One program on Rus-
sian TV was like "Strike It Rich." "If you win you get shot for being a
capitalist." The communists can't have soap operas, Crawford cracked,
"because they still don't have anything like soap" (Oct. 23, 1953).

Early the next year Crawford wrote copy for communist advertising
agents: "Buy liquid kumquats by the gallon, or you'll be dead as Marshal
Stalin"; "Collective housing's cold and damp, but it's better than a labor
camp" (Jan. 22, 1954). Jokes about the brutal and bureaucratic communists may well have had the paradoxical effect of reducing the perceived threat by portraying the Soviets as inefficient buffoons.
Nonetheless, Crawford, like his more serious colleagues, was tapping
into an anticommunist consensus that was not challenged even by those
who censured Joseph McCarthy.

TV Guide became most exercised by the red menace when righteous
indignation advanced their agenda for improving the quality of television. In striking out at "Strike It Rich," Merrill Panitt asked readers
in "As We See It": "Can't you just hear the Red propagandists citing
that as proof that the poor in America must bear their misery on television shows in the hope of winning medical treatment?" (Jan. 8, 1954).
Similarly, at the end of the decade Panitt found a novel argument against
the proliferation of cowboy and private-eye television series. Since these
programs were sold abroad, they validated Soviet charges that Americans were naturally violent and warlike. Better television programs
strengthened the image of the United States abroad (Sept. 5, 1959).

More frequently *TV Guide* used communism as a club to expand
network news coverage, much as the Pentagon saw Red at budget time,
and the educational establishment cited Sputnik as the reason to support
the sciences. In this respect, the magazine wholeheartedly agreed with
Edward R. Murrow. In a six-page article, then an unprecedented
amount of space for the magazine, Murrow bemoaned the constant
concern for ratings and called on the networks to produce "itching
pills" as well as tranquilizers. Because the United States was in competition with "malignant forces of evil who [were] using every instru-
ment at their command to empty the minds of their subjects" and fill
them with slogans, it was imperative that television provide information
to every citizen (Dec. 13, 1958).

"As We See It" had sung this song for two years before Murrow's refrain reached readers. In blasting Congress for refusing to allow cameras in its chambers, Panitt pointed out that Soviet TV routinely covered parliamentary sessions (Mar. 24, 1956). The failure of the networks to preempt commercial programs to cover the Hungarian uprisings and the Suez crisis brought charges of an "almost cynical neglect" of responsibility to the public (Nov. 24, 1956). A similar sermon followed two years later when "The Price Is Right" and a Paul Muni movie did not give way to a speech by President Eisenhower on the communist threat. As long as the network news departments were content to record and play later (in snippets or not at all) a far-reaching policy pronouncement on communist Chinese aggression against the tiny islands of Quemoy and Matsu, "Complacent Americans, their senses dulled by crisis after crisis, and thinking wishfully that Communists won't dare to challenge our strength," could not evaluate the seriousness of the challenge they faced (Oct. 4, 1958).

Although sincerely held, then, *TV Guide*'s anticommunist convictions were at least as pragmatic as they were passionate. The magazine was cautiously cool, moreover, to anything that smacked of red-baiting. In its first year *TV Guide* dismissed the probe of Lucille Ball's brief affiliation with the Communist party as much ado about nothing (Oct. 2, 1953). No discussion of blacklists appeared in the fifties, nor did Panitt use "As We See It" to comment on Murrow's attack on Joseph McCarthy or the latter's response. Outside the editorial column, however, the magazine hinted through humor at where its sympathies lay. The writer of "Teletype Hollywood" thought Murrow "the most courageous man in the country" for taking on Senator McCarthy and Groucho Marx in the same week (Apr. 2, 1954). Ollie Crawford used the same approach as the Army-McCarthy hearings wound down, suggesting a summer replacement entitled "The Best of Grouchy" (July 9, 1954). Moreover, *TV Guide*'s praise for "See It Now" after the McCarthy program was, in a sense, a quiet vote for the embattled Murrow (Apr. 16, 1954). And six months after the hearings Panitt bestowed "high praise" on the journalist, while a feature article hugged the middle of the road: Murrow was neither the greatest American since Patrick Henry nor a communist, "although he certainly is on the side of freedom"; his show on McCarthy was a "conscience piece," perceived differently by people on either "side of the political fence" (Feb. 5, 1955).

TV Guide's moderation was most apparent in its treatment of "I Led Three Lives," the adventure series based on the story of double agent Herbert Philbrick. In a feature article on "A New TV Program Which Fights Communism," the magazine noted that sponsors bought the show because they wanted to be associated with its political point of view, "figuring it is good public service material and thus a natural for their institutional kind of advertising." Spokesmen for the show, however, stressed that it was entertainment, and Richard Carlson, who played Philbrick, distanced himself from the charge of red-baiting that was likely to be made, "the temper of the times being what it is." Carlson made a point of saying that he led three lives because it paid well and that he rarely watched his own show (Dec. 1, 1953).

A review of "I Led Three Lives," published at the height of McCarthy's power, suggested that *TV Guide* agreed with Carlson. Although the show was a natural for a nation preoccupied with "the communist problem," the reviewer thought it was "beginning to show signs of wear. While there are many industries in the country into which communists can infiltrate, 'Three Lives' ran through the list and then bogged down into another cops and robbers series" (May 7, 1954). Something less than a ringing endorsement of the imminent danger of Soviet subversion, this review was followed two years later by a profile of actress Virginia Stefan, who was "amazed" by the seriousness with which viewers approached "I Led Three Lives." "It's hard to believe, but people actually write us and ask us to investigate communists in their neighborhood" (June 30, 1956).

The anticommunist credentials of *TV Guide* were impeccable. "As We See It" frequently supported the government's efforts to combat communism by tripling the United State Information Agency's television budget (May 23, 1959), then doubling it (Feb. 27, 1963), and its policy of offering free information and public affairs programs to Asian and African countries, thus using the technological advantage of the United States "in the battle for men's minds" (Aug. 4, 1962). As a mass circulation magazine skeptical of extremists from the left or right, *TV Guide* was not tempted to join the band of McCarthyite zealots, especially while covering an industry badly divided by investigations and blacklists. Patriotic to the core, finally, the editors of *TV Guide* were too complacent in the fifties to be crusaders.

In the sixties the complacency of many Americans turned to concern over racial injustice and the war in Vietnam. There seemed to be so much more news during the decade, as assassinations, urban riots, and casualty lists invaded American living rooms, shattering the illusion of consensus and replacing it with polarization. "Which side are you on?" Americans asked one another, and some shouted that anyone who was not part of the solution was part of the problem. In this charged political atmosphere, network news coverage expanded and its influence grew.

Inevitably *TV Guide* covered the coverage. Surprisingly, given the conservative political convictions of Walter Annenberg, the magazine remained rather balanced throughout most of the decade, even as its
latent concerns about distorted coverage became manifest. However,
with Richard Nixon in the White House and domestic disturbances
endangering American values, the magazine became more explicitly
partisan. It was difficult to be objective about subjectivity in the news,
especially when one detected systematic liberal bias. As it watched newscasters in the late sixties and seventies, the magazine gradually revealed
which side it was on.

The politicization of *TV Guide* began in 1962 with an ABC documentary, "The Political Obituary of Richard Nixon," that enraged Walter Annenberg. Upset that his friend was being pilloried after his defeat
in the gubernatorial race in California, Annenberg was angered when
he learned that Alger Hiss had been a witness for the prosecution. He
inserted a story in *The Philadelphia Inquirer* explaining that WFIL, the
ABC affiliate he owned, would not run a program that permitted "a
convicted treasonable spy to comment about a distinguished American."
Actually, Hiss had been convicted of perjury, not spying, but no one
at the *Inquirer* was brave enough to correct the boss. In any event,
censoring the show caused a furor in Philadelphia; WFIL and the *Inquirer* were inundated with protests. In a "Letter from the Editor,"
Annenberg responded that the use of a spy who had been convicted of
perjury to assess a former U.S. vice president, was, he assumed, "re-
pugnant to most viewers," the more so because the documentary was
scheduled to appear on Veteran's Day.

Not surprisingly, the controversy found its way into *TV Guide*. Without referring to Walter Annenberg or WFIL, "As We See It" announced
that some stations would not show "The Political Obituary of Richard
M. Nixon" because it included comments by Alger Hiss, a man "convicted of perjury in denying he gave secrets to the communists." With
a "peculiar sense of timing," ABC had scheduled the documentary for
Veteran's Day: "This is journalism of a sort, we suppose." The editorial
included a perfunctory defense of ABC's right to air "even what some
of us believe is in bad taste," but it also defended the right and responsibility of individual stations not to broadcast an offensive program.
No station, Panitt insisted in "As We See It," should supply airtime
"just because [a program] happened to be on the network" (Dec. 8,
1962).

This episode was not the opening salvo in *TV Guide*'s campaign
against liberal bias in the network news establishment. Walter Annenberg's passions cooled quickly, and the documentary, hosted by Howard

K. Smith, who was hardly a radical, did not really list to the left. With its fifteen-minute format, moreover, the network news remained a headline service in 1962, short on analysis and documentaries. With Murrow gone, the news seemed more timid. To be sure, when John F. Kennedy was assassinated, television demonstrated its power to command the nation's attention in three and a half mesmerizing days of continuous coverage. But its impact was, by all accounts, benevolent. According to the editors of *TV Guide,* "television became a pure information medium," a glass through which events unfolded as they happened (Dec. 7, 1963). Could network news deliver the same service in its everyday coverage? Should it do more? Was there a place for analysis and editorials? *TV Guide* was not yet certain, even when the nightly news expanded to thirty minutes in 1963.

A consistent advocate of more network news, *TV Guide* wavered between a desire for objectivity and a recognition that it could not be reached. Objectivity, moreover, might be a synonym for sterility or superficiality. Acknowledging that television had become the major source of news in the United States, Panitt worried in "As We See It" that only a few stories were on the screen for more than a minute or two, and even these were presented more "in length than depth" (Feb. 29, 1964). Two years later "As We See It" branded most news reports "surfacy and, more often than not, so sterilely objective as to make truth indistinguishable from falsehood" (Sept. 24, 1966). As late as 1968 this theme surfaced again, when Neil Hickey analyzed "The Headline Syndrome" in a two-part article arguing that television news, preoccupied with pictures, "frequently at the expense of fine, tight, explicatory news writing," provided only "a skeletal version" of current events. This was a problem for the nation since 64 percent of Americans got their news from the small screen, while politicians held opinion polls "close to their hearts." Reporters, Hickey charged, were neither adequately prepared nor inclined to ask probing questions and often handed the microphone to public figures and special pleaders, whose half-baked opinions were thereby disseminated. "More in sorrow than anger," Hickey concluded that TV news could not "contain the letter and spirit of our world" but called on the medium "to lead public taste, not follow it," by making programs "rich enough and spacious enough to engage the public imagination" (Mar. 9, 16, 1968).

To do so required investigative journalism, controversy—and subjectivity. Edith Efron, for one, welcomed just such an approach. "TV Speech Is Not Really Free," she insisted, because in 1949 the FCC required broadcasters to air all sides of controversial issues, or none. To avoid complaints broadcasters ran all views through a blender, from

which they emerged bland and inoffensive. The Fairness Doctrine prevented Americans from being exposed to the full spectrum of opinion
(Apr. 11, 1964). Along with Efron, "As We See It" clamored for its
repeal. A similar editorial appeared at least once a year until the FCC
responded in 1987.

In Efron's view, TV news was a "Timid Giant." Despite freedom
from censorship, the networks' "floating political anxiety" resulted in
a reluctance to criticize business, industry, government, and labor. Television ignored "titanic struggles" in the stock market and unions and
contented itself with the stories it was fed by politicians. Efron doubted
that government agencies were seeking a pretext to regulate the industry
and urged that the issue be aired publicly "once and for all, and solved"
(May 18, Aug. 10, 1963). When it was, she was ready for more "idealistic
and exciting" documentaries. That most viewers disliked documentaries
was "The Great Television Myth." People did not watch "social problem" documentaries on subjects like inflation, pollution, and racial
oppression, she argued, because they were abstract, ignored the individual, substituted talk for action, and focused on misery and evil without offering a resolution. The public—and Efron—were "holding out
for drama," for "reality films" that took a stand (May 6, 1967). A year
earlier, an article on "CBS Reports" had made much the same point,
lamenting that controversy had been "conspicuously absent" from recent programs, and noting with approval producer Fred Friendly's
promise to stimulate thought with "Homosexuality and the Law" (Feb.
19, 1966).

At the same time *TV Guide* recoiled from some of the consequences
of a more freewheeling news style. In the "reality films" advocated by
Edith Efron (or, for that matter, "The Political Obituary of Richard M.
Nixon") how could readers distinguish fact from fiction from opinion?
Wasn't television news already succumbing to the temptation to substitute surfaces for substance? Does TV news "have to be show biz?"
Samuel Grafton asked in an article on the transformation of national
nominating conventions. "Apparently it has been so decided" (Sept. 5,
1964). More and more "pseudo news" events dominated public affairs
programs and even the nightly news. Politicians chose the setting, the
time, and did everything but point the camera. The phrase "photo op"
had not been invented yet, but *TV Guide* could recognize the phenomenon. And on interview shows, heretofore polite panelists assaulted
politicians, manufacturing conflict to hold their audience.

Most important, once the opinion-spouting genie was out of the
bottle, no one could control what was said on television. It was becoming
easy, Neil Hickey insisted, for extremists with a tiny following to get

the attention of millions of people by buying airtime. Right-wing self-proclaimed patriots, whom Hickey carefully distinguished from responsible conservatives like William F. Buckley and the Young Americans for Freedom, clothed themselves in religiosity and the flag, creating "for their opponents the laborious task of sorting out the untruths, innuendo and cant which an imperfect democratic process guarantees them the right to purvey on the air." At stake, according to Hickey, was not freedom of speech "but the fair use of a natural resource—the broadcast spectrum" (Apr. 15, 1967). Viewers often did not distinguish between a paid political commercial and a public affairs program. Thus television executives could confer legitimacy on a fringe group simply by selling time. Hickey presented no plan for keeping fanatics off television, nor did he investigate what would become a major concern of *TV Guide* within a year: how could extremists, predominantly from the left, be kept off the network news when their rhetoric and their actions were so photogenic?

On the nightly news, where correspondents increasingly injected assessments into their reports, Samuel Grafton argued that the danger was greater because it was more difficult to detect. Dan Farmer of ABC News, for example, asserted that the United States was not neutral in the Dominican Republic, it was assisting the government. Bill Lawrence stated that the nation was getting embroiled in Vietnam in a war experts "doubt we can win" (Oct. 2, 1965). Perhaps Chet Huntley was right: "Whether we like it or not," the NBC anchor told Edith Efron, "we're engaged in personal journalism—we're giving the individual's view of events" (June 19, 1965). Nonetheless, *TV Guide* clung to the CBS solution: maintain Walter Cronkite's "quality of believability" by handing over interpretation to Eric Sevareid (July 2, 1966). Although helpful, this division of labor hardly solved the problem, something "As We See It" recognized ruefully toward the end of the decade, falling back on its perennial plea for self-restraint. To maintain credibility in an election year broadcasters must avoid any appearance of bias. "And in the case of newscasters whose political leanings are well known it is especially important that they clearly label editorial opinion as such" (Aug. 3, 1968).

It was clear to *TV Guide,* and virtually everyone else, that much was at stake because by the mid-sixties television news had enormous power, not only to shape public opinion but news events themselves. The network news, as Grafton put it, "lives a curiously enveloping life, in which it absorbs the event being covered, and influences it, and is part of it." In the forties the Democratic party would not have hesitated to remove the Mississippi Freedom party delegation from the convention floor.

But in 1964, with the cameras present, the Democrats compromised (Oct. 17, 1964). Televising the hearings of the Senate Foreign Relations Committee on Vietnam, Arthur Schlesinger, Jr., acknowledged, "for better or worse," gave a boost to the critics of American policy (Oct. 22, 1966). Quite possibly, in fact, television might elect the next president of the United States because more and more voters were swayed by how candidates looked on TV. Thus, despite apprehension that "one-minute political plugs threaten to reduce the electoral process to jingoism," every candidate, Richard Doan predicted, will be "packaged and peddled like soap" (Feb. 10 1968). The newspapers had been elbowed aside by an upstart medium that could exploit or alter a story by its presence, that commanded the attention of leaders and followers alike (July 15, 1967).

As they recognized the power of TV news, the editors of *TV Guide* took more seriously their self-proclaimed responsibility to monitor the medium. The Vietnam conflict, the "living room war," became a test case of the thoroughness and accuracy of the network news. That television helped end the war became a commonplace of the seventies and eighties, when baby boomers recalled graphic scenes of brutality and assassination, followed by Walter Cronkite, who asserted his avuncular authority after the Tet offensive and announced that the war could not be won. Actually, television journalists were cautious in covering Vietnam in the sixties, although they gave voice to a disquiet about a most unconventional conflict. Similarly, *TV Guide* could not locate the center of gravity in the nation, and the editors and writers hesitated to take a stand—or to find much to criticize in the network news. Nevertheless, in subtle ways the magazine gave some credence to the charge that there was no light at the end of the tunnel. *TV Guide* was to fight the battles of the sixties, and of bias on the networks, in the seventies. Before then, the magazine, like many Americans, unenthusiastically supported a war about which it had doubts and endorsed TV coverage of the war as sincere and, on the whole, accurate.

In 1966 as antiwar activity increased almost in proportion to the growing presence of American troops in Vietnam, *TV Guide* began in earnest to report on the war, focusing at first on the travails of newspeople on the scene. Aline Saarinen was sent to Saigon by NBC News to assess the social revolution that "the communists falsely promise and without whose achievement the war would have no purpose." Suspended between "hope and hopelessness," Saarinen seemed anything but optimistic about the outcome of the conflict. As she contrasted the beauty of a Saigon restaurant with its frequent transformation into a balcony seat for combat, Saarinen noted that the Vietcong controlled almost all the roads outside the city. Like her male colleagues, Saarinen "knew we couldn't abandon the Vietnamese," but "the problems were monumental and it would take a long, long time to win this war" (Jan. 29, 1966).

"It Ain't My Kind of War," by Jesse Zousmer, vice president at ABC and director of its TV News, described the oppressive heat, the inedible food, and the endless whir of the helicopters in a war zone where every soldier (and journalist) had to be constantly ready to react. "The horrible thing is that one sniper in the nearby hills can annoy the whole complex" (Apr. 16, 1966).

Although these articles described uncomfortable conditions rather than ideology, they were, of course, full of political implications. Despite hundreds of thousands of American troops and millions of dollars in aid, no place was secure, not even downtown Saigon. Yet *TV Guide*, like television, passed the analysis along to readers without labeling it as such. Only once in 1966 did the magazine pause to call attention to the line between fact and opinion. In a profile of Frank McGee, readers learned that in December 1965 the newsman had asked for "more candor" from public officials and fewer "doubtful arguments" about the American presence in Vietnam. If "a compelling argument cannot be made," McGee had said, the United States might, as had Britain and France, "retire with honor from untenable positions." Official spokesmen for NBC had tried to gloss over the fact that McGee had delivered an opinion, *TV Guide* reported, and the newscaster had steadfastly refused to alter or retract anything he had said (June 25, 1966).

Significantly, "As We See It" was silent on this episode and all Vietnam reporting throughout the decade. Neither Merrill Panitt nor Walter Annenberg, we suppose, disagreed with Frank McGee. One did not have to be on the left to have grave doubts about the war. In a faltering way, the actor Fred MacMurray expressed the sentiment that may have animated—and restrained—the *TV Guide* staff. Not "a dove necessarily," MacMurray never thought Vietnam "would turn into what it turned into." Because General Westmoreland could not go all the way, he had to "make all those statements. You can understand kids feeling the way they do, I'm afraid, because so many intelligent men feel the same way and are not in favor of this whole thing" (Oct. 25, 1968).

Of course *TV Guide*'s restraint was not without limits. It was permissible, in an article that was "encouraged for the future of America," to refer to a sixth-grader's assertion that protesting against the war in Vietnam was not un-American because democracies encourage freedom of expression (Nov. 6, 1966). Not to be tolerated, however, were people who denied the good intentions of American policymakers, praised the

Vietcong, or supported peace at any price. *TV Guide* found the radicalism of some show business personalities anathema. David Carradine characterized his own antiestablishment stance as "heroic naivete," but writer Robert DeRoos thought him more pathetic than profound: "Peace," Carradine said with a "sweeping motion of his right hand that looked very much as though he were putting thumb to nose at me and anyone else within range. He denies that is his intent." And DeRoos left the actor with an ironic "Peace, David Carradine, Peace" (Dec. 17, 1966). Even less appealing was Pernell Roberts, whose view of Vietnam "as a tragic farce" propelled by a nation mulishly "saving face" was set in a relentlessly negative profile of a tactless, self-righteous actor who had departed "Bonanza" with blasts at cast and crew, convinced that "there's no altruism in the world" (Aug. 6, 1966).

TV Guide did not detect these attitudes in the ranks of the network news. A four-part series in the fall of 1966, "The Vietnam War: Is Television Giving Us the Picture?" was a sympathetic recitation of the difficulties faced by TV journalists. "Exorbitantly . . . demanding, both mentally and physically," the war—and the heat and the workload "and the general impenetrability" and waywardness of Vietnam politics— eroded the professional resources of many. In this environment, not surprisingly, coverage was less than perfect, especially when the "competitive bind" compelled many correspondents to seek out graphic scenes of combat and to opt for battles over background. By following a platoon or squad, a TV network correspondent might win the ratings war but lose the big strategic picture. The problem, then, was to balance "the seductive and the significant," to find "substance behind the shadow." Network news coverage, *TV Guide* concluded, was honest but not adequate, and assessments of the outcome perilous because "total objectivity in Vietnam reporting is as elusive a quality as total candor."

If anything, the Vietnam series in *TV Guide* gave credence to those who thought American involvement an exercise in futility. In the first installment, ABC's Roger Peterson revealed he was "revolted and angered by the senseless bloodshed all around him." The only sane thing Peterson saw in Vietnam was a dog chasing a cat. In the concluding article, *TV Guide* attributed the "credibility gap" uncovered by the media to a lingering and justified reaction to the lies of the Diem regime and the efforts of public information officers to put the American military in the best possible light. Television correspondents resented having their patriotism impugned because of their impressions of United States policies in Southeast Asia. Noting, parenthetically, that many reporters approved of the war effort, the magazine acknowledged that others had "over-reacted" to demonstrate their independence. In essence, *TV Guide* put a qualified seal of approval on television coverage of a war it worried about (Oct. 1, 8, 15, 22, 1966).

A year later little had changed, although TV's power to shape the perceptions of Americans led Martin Maloney to dub the war TVietnam. Although reporters were "professional and conscientious," Maloney observed that on the tube the war "approaches simultaneity [and] the fight goes on forever, seemingly in the same terms." As it reduced the experience of the conflict to "doll terms," television detached the viewer from it. Without a geographic logic, the Vietnam War was an unconventional, confusing phenomenon: "it is hard to tell whether We are at war or not, or with Whom." Understandably, the American officials reduced the war to numbers of people on each side killed and wounded, but as viewers watched the same scenes every night, who could "seriously believe," Maloney asked, "that the war will actually end?" Maloney stopped short of endorsing dissent, but he was not surprised (nor apparently upset) that Americans exposed to the war on the little box "protest, complain, demonstrate, cry out" (Dec. 2, 1967).

After the Tet offensive of January-February 1968, television's top newsmen, Richard K. Doan noted, showed "less and less inclination to hide their bitterness" toward American involvement in Vietnam and the policies of President Johnson. Only Chet Huntley and Howard K. Smith continued to support the administration. Each newsman noted that his views were his own, and not necessarily those of the network, Doan added (Mar. 9, 1968). That Doan was relatively untroubled by this outpouring of opinion is suggested by his report on the PBS airing of a two-hour North Vietnam documentary despite the protests of thirty-three members of Congress that it was communist propaganda. Doan did not assess the program, but he informed *TV Guide* readers that the telecast produced the largest outpouring of favorable comment on any public education program since 1965 (Mar. 16, 1968). On the eve of the presidential nominating conventions of 1968, then, *TV Guide* detected a guarded view of the Vietnam War at most network news desks and a willingness to express it on the air. No sense of alarm or outrage accompanied these observations, however, nor was the magazine ready to level a charge of bias.

During the spring and summer of 1968 Martin Luther King and Robert Kennedy were gunned down, race riots rocked dozens of cities, and huge antiwar demonstrations filled the campuses and the streets. The remarkably stable United States seemed, for a moment, to teeter on the brink of revolution. *TV Guide*, taking its cues from Richard Nixon, who appealed to the "silent majority" throughout his presidential campaign (although he did not use the phrase until November 1969), began to search for the other America, the land that was proud, patriotic, hard-working, and fundamentally sound. Implicitly, the magazine was criticizing TV news for eliminating the positive as it accentuated the negative. *TV Guide* did not often feature a singing group, but in "The Young Americans, Happies Not Hippies," Judith Jobin found entertainers reaching out to the "vast American public, increasingly discomfited and unnerved by rampant 'naysaying' among the country's youth." The Young Americans earned no salary; the money they received went to college scholarships. With a "sprinkling of Negroes and Orientals in the group," the Young Americans helped dispel racial misunderstanding. Jobin distanced herself from the group, whose members were, she thought, limited intellectually, conversationally, and musically and more "complacent than they have a right to be" in a year of ferment. Nonetheless, she had identified a cultural tendency in the nation and an important theme for *TV Guide* (Apr. 13, 1968).

In "The Rise and Fall of the Hippies," the magazine brought together its celebration of middle America and its growing sense that television bore some responsibility for the perception that the nation was divided and decaying. TV had blown the hippie movement "out of all proportion to its importance, and it altered an isolated social and artistic phenomenon into a grotesque street carnival." Coverage lured dropouts and runaways to hippie havens like Haight-Ashbury in San Francisco, and the street scene "degenerated from the beatific 'seekers' to kids lured in looking for kicks." To a great extent, then, television in its quest for the unusual ignored the real America and provided free publicity for those who contributed least to the nation's well-being (May 18, 1968).

Not surprisingly, *TV Guide* tapped Edith Efron to express its commitment to listen to the silent majority, even as the radicals tried to shout them down. "Everything, of course, is not dying," Efron wrote in an appeal to the networks for more programs about middle Americans: "Beneath the weirdly potent illusion of the omnipresent evil, and the nation's very real problems, Home Country USA is still there. The Forgotten American, of every race and creed, is still living quietly, and working productively, from Maine to California. . . . The soothing balm was the sight of American goodness. It is a vital necessity, in this troubled period of our history, to show it on the screen" (July 20, 1968). Efron's essay, it is important to remember, was about a documentary that did discover real America. Sensitive to cultural moods and tendencies, both television and *TV Guide* showcased the "silent majority" shortly after the politicians proved its popularity with the public. More than television, however, *TV Guide* applauded as the electorate slowly swung to the right. Forced to be more explicitly political to counter the distortions of the radicals, *TV Guide* added to the pressure on the networks to balance their coverage, to alter the "strangely distorted picture" of American ideas, values, and home life—to help guide the nation back to the principles that made it great ("As We See It," Oct. 19, 1968).

The Democratic Convention in Chicago in August 1968 shook the nation and called into question the credibility of television news. Thousands of protesters descended on the city to demonstrate their opposition to the war. Mayor Richard Daley, determined to preserve law and order, sent the police into the streets. As a huge television audience watched, the police beat bystanders as well as the demonstrators, who chanted, "The whole world is watching." The apparent anarchy in the streets reinforced the perception that the Democrats could not control their party, their partisans, their policies, or the country. In the wake of the debacle at Chicago, attacks on television news increased dramatically. Did the cameras film the response of the police but not the provocative behavior of the protesters, thus suggesting to viewers that innocent people had suffered? Did the networks, by their presence, encourage the demonstrators to act? Was TV news biased, a mouthpiece for the liberals?

TV Guide responded cautiously to assaults on the news. Since its inception, the magazine had been a booster for television coverage of public affairs, and the editors, apparently, were reluctant to undercut an indispensable source of information to American citizens. As we have seen, *TV Guide* took the high road in the spring of 1968 when it was relatively silent on bias and exuberant about the silent majority. Following the debacle in Chicago, the magazine defended its natural allies, the networks. In "TV Violence in 'Stalag Daley,' " Doan gave network officials an opportunity to mount a counteroffensive. Reporters, they insisted, had been "harassed, hounded, mauled and even punched by . . . Gestapo types on the very floor of the convention" on the orders of a "local political tyrant" (Sept. 7, 1968).

As late as April 1969, Robert Higgins concluded that a regular commentary feature on ABC News demonstrated the paucity of "hard, abrasive ideological opinions." Of the 150 editorials Higgins studied, only one—a blast on civil rights by actor Ossie Davis—came from the left; only two clearly belonged on the conservative right. If most of the guests came from the liberal side of the aisle, it was while hewing to the murky, common-denominator middle. There seemed little to fear from networks who were frightened of the full spectrum of American political thought (Apr. 5, 1969).

In two editorials, moreover, Merrill Panitt entered the fray. On September 28, 1968, in "As We See It," Panitt praised the "superb" work of the network journalists who filed stories while the Chicago police, "their nerves shattered by the confrontation and provocation tactics of demonstrators," struck out at them. If the coverage was not perfect, the circumstances, and not the intentions of the reporters, were at fault: "tear gas and nightsticks . . . usually do not make for objective, unemotional reporting of facts." A month later the performance had dropped from "superb" to "good," and the emphasis had shifted to the loss of "credibility" of TV news. Panitt refuted the charge that the "vicious actions of the Yippies" were ignored by television and branded as unwarranted the outpouring of abuse from viewers and government officials. But he sounded defensive, acknowledging that mistakes had been made and warning the networks that on election night broadcasters must "by all means avoid jumping to conclusions [or giving] the slightest hint of anything but absolute objectivity" (Nov. 2, 1968).

Clearly Panitt worried that too much criticism might have a chilling effect on the networks, or worse, usher in government controls. When Congress scheduled hearings on violence on TV news, in part to investigate accusations that "broadcasters maligned the Chicago police," "As We See It" found an issue on which it could be unambiguous: "We cannot tolerate a broadcasting system so harassed by government that it must plan its coverage of current affairs not on the basis of newsworthiness of stories but on how this government may react. Let the government . . . abide by the First Amendment" (Dec. 28, 1968). Actually, the danger of government repression was not terribly great, and Panitt may have been seeking to avoid tougher issues by picking on a straw man. Late in the year *TV Guide* did run a vigorous defense of TV news, but it was under the byline of Reuven Frank, the president of NBC News. In "Chicago—a Post-Mortem," Frank denied that the networks devoted disproportionate attention to demonstrations and police suppression. Only 3 percent of TV time went to these topics. Although Frank did not deny that demonstrators provoked the cops, he asked readers to be wary of Mayor Daley's testimony about who started the trouble. Most important, Frank cautioned against what psychologists called "transference": blaming the messengers for the news they bring (Dec. 14, 1968).

Behind the brave words, network executives were beginning to buckle, but not quite fast enough for a *TV Guide* more and more convinced that news coverage was not only distorted but biased, perhaps consciously, by an industry loaded with liberals. Reuven Frank's position was no longer *TV Guide*'s. Early in 1969 coverage of the disorders in

Chicago, which had been "superb," then "good," was now deemed skimpy and "conscientious but fallible" by Neil Hickey. The New York bureau chief dismissed charges that the networks failed to show the provocative acts of the demonstrators, but he left a strong impression that the lengthy indictment of TV news was based on fact. The house liberal, Hickey, did not attack the intentions of network reporters, but he, too, was edging closer to TV's critics (Mar. 1, 1969). Later in the year the magazine called attention to the conversion of TV to the silent majority. Heralded on the front cover was Edith Efron's article, "New TV Theme: What's RIGHT with America." Although a moderate-liberal orientation remained, Efron noticed a "distinct deflation of the coverage of the radical left and of radical left causes," quoting a number of repentant network officials, one acknowledging, "the world doesn't end at the Hudson," while another admitted to ignoring many blue- and white-collar people: "It's bad to pretend they don't exist. We did this because we tend to be upper-middle-class liberals." Liberal network news was in retreat, and the view of America "as one vast abscess" was being corrected, Efron thought. *TV Guide* rolled up its sleeves to make sure the job was finished (Sept. 27, 1969).

In conjunction with Richard Nixon's appeal to the silent majority, Vice President Spiro Agnew, playing bad cop to the president's good cop, tried to end the sixties ferment by attacking the news media. As he traveled throughout the country in 1969 and 1970, assailing students ("parasites of passion"), Democrats ("sniveling hand-wringers"), and intellectuals ("an effete corps of impudent snobs"), Agnew turned to television in a speech in Des Moines bent on discrediting the administration and its policies, network executives, whom he termed "a tiny and closed fraternity of privileged men," hired as newscasters "curled-lip boys in eastern ivory towers." According to the vice president, these eastern establishment liberals, "nattering nabobs of negativism," conspired to undermine traditional values by providing a platform to dissenters and hectoring the duly elected representatives of the people. The networks had established themselves as a fourth branch of government, with the power to shape policies by manipulating public opinion.

Agnew's tirade had a profound impact on the network news, already reeling from criticism of its coverage of the Chicago Democratic Convention. Spokespersons for the industry fought back as Reuven Frank had before: Eric Sevareid lashed out at the vice president as a demagogue who, without evidence, spread the charge that there was a conspiracy by an unelected elite to control the flow of information to the people (Mar. 14, 1970). But Agnew had scored a home run. A Gallup poll rated him the third most admired man in the United States, behind Richard Nixon and Billy Graham. News directors of local stations reported a growing tendency among viewers to blame television, with unspecified charges of bias, for causing the news it broadcast. "The writer just says we're biased," one news director complained, "strolls away and leaves me wondering what he's talking about." More and more viewers detected significance in a smile or a shake of the head (Apr. 11, 1970). *TV Guide*'s first national opinion poll revealed that fully 34 percent of Americans now thought that television news was biased (Apr. 8, 1972).

With their honesty, integrity, and intelligence under attack, news executives made greater efforts to "balance their coverage," the code phrase for more conservative themes and commentators. "What's Right with America" stories became a staple of the nightly news and, under intense pressure, the networks dropped "the instant analysis" of presidential speeches, even as executives denied that it was attack masquerading as assessment. We will never know what documentaries were changed or never made, but there is some evidence that the networks pulled their punches or flinched in the early seventies. After beating back an attempt by Representative Harley Staggers to subpoena outtakes of "The Selling of the Pentagon," for example, CBS agreed to allow all persons interviewed for a documentary the right to receive a full transcript of their remarks. From now on, Richard Doan predicted, "TV's newsmen will be treading warily" (July 24, 1971).

TV Guide did not disagree with the thrust of Spiro Agnew's critique, but its editors reacted cautiously at first. The vice president's indictment of bias, Merrill Panitt was now prepared to say in "As We See It," "may have been true," but, coming from a powerful official of the government, the blast carried "a threat of censorship" (Jan. 3, 1970). Always hypersensitive to the threat of outside interference, Panitt was afraid that the pendulum might swing too far and that the government might succumb to the temptation to regulate. He did not deny that CBS selected quotes out of context for "The Selling of the Pentagon," but he thought the danger "minuscule" compared to "the right of a broadcaster to speak as he sees fit" (May 22, 1971). And when congressional flak began to hit public television after the documentary "The Banks and the Poor," the editor called for permanent funding to insulate PBS from political pressure. "Otherwise it must inevitably face the prospect of becoming the network of garden tours, chamber music and ancient history" (May 29, 1971). Panitt even included a "TV Jibe" in the magazine that took aim at Agnew and government censorship of the news:

"It's a proclamation from King George. He says we're not delivering a true account of the news. He wants us to cut down on Ben Franklin, Nathan Hale, Ethan Allen, and report more on The Silent Majority" (Apr. 4, 1970).

With these caveats in place, *TV Guide*'s sympathy with Agnew's position began to manifest itself in articles and editorials. Walter Annenberg was a close friend of Richard Nixon, under whom he served as the nation's ambassador to England from 1969 to 1974. He shared the exasperation and anger of the president and vice president at the apparent ease with which dissenters gained access to the media. It is no coincidence, we believe, that *TV Guide*'s political passions were aroused when a Republican was in the White House. Merrill Panitt also looked at the demonstrators across a cultural, political, and generational gulf. In "As We See It" he was brought to a "state of nausea" by the groovy phrases of sixties radicals: "Do you turn off when the militants do their own thing, y'know, in search of a meaningful, viable relationship with the Establishment?" No such language would ever appear in *TV Guide*, the editor vowed (Apr. 12, 1969). Neither Annenberg nor Panitt believed that the critics were constructive or that they were always motivated by patriotism. In many ways Chet Huntley spoke for them when he complained: "We've listened to the extremists long enough—and rather politely: they are arrogant, ill-mannered boors [who] have no program—only a tantrum" (Aug. 1, 1970). Panitt acknowledged that television did not cause troubled times, but he was as pleased as Huntley that the "shouters" were getting less airtime, "not necessarily because they're not news anymore, but because they've become a bore" ("As We See It," July 25, 1970).

It is not surprising, then, that the vice president himself issued "Another Challenge to the Television Industry" in the pages of *TV Guide*. Agnew called on the medium to help educate youngsters to be good citizens, but along the way he connected the impatience of youth "evident in the virulence of their protests" to the "disparity between the real world and the Epicurean world inside the television set." Because TV conditioned young people to act and emote rather than think, he argued, they often got caught in events and "carried away by mob psychology." TV, then, was the permissive parent indulging the spoiled child by making a home video of every temper tantrum/demonstration (May 16, 1970).

Thus encouraged, the *TV Guide* of the seventies became a self-proclaimed truth squad, exposing bias and endorsing "balance." In reducing the emphasis on personality on the nightly news, "As We See It" welcomed the replacement of Chet Huntley with Frank McGee and

John Chancellor. "Unfortunately," Chancellor appeared to be an "extremely liberal man," most noticeably in his criticism of the pro-Humphrey forces in Chicago and the Nixon team in Miami in 1968. *TV Guide*'s warning came as a wish that Chancellor would be "able to keep his politics from showing" (Apr. 25, 1970). Panitt now asked, quite rhetorically: is it blasphemy to suggest that newsmen make errors "and display personal bias that betrays their vaunted objectivity?" (Jan. 23, 1971).

PBS became a target as well. Merrill Panitt questioned the wisdom of hiring Sander Vanocur and Robert MacNeil, reporters "generally understood to be somewhat to the left," at the same time that Congress was debating an appropriation for public television ("As We See It," Feb. 19, 1972). Throughout the seventies *TV Guide* took for granted the left-wing slant of PBS. Richard Doan concluded that by encouraging a "pro-liberal bias" in programming, producer Fred Friendly contributed to the decline of public television as a national force. Exaggerated, but not untrue, was the assessment of an admirer of Friendly that "by dabbling in Establishment-baiting causes and far-out theatrics," the producer scared off friends of PBS (Sept. 15, 1973). A similar assessment was made by Benjamin Stein in "PBS under Fire." Because public television was tax-supported, bias was particularly troublesome to the network—and Stein found many examples of "liberal or radical left-wing bias," including "vicious swipes at American whites" in a documentary on civil rights, Shirley MacLaine's superlatives in "A China Memoir," and a refusal to run programming critical of the Soviet Union. Stein linked bias and low ratings by guessing that no one watched Bill Moyers and Peter Lisagore because they were so predictable in analyzing current events. Although Stein believed that PBS producers were sincerely committed to balance, he thought liberalism would dominate unless the monopoly over television held by Washington and New York was broken (Dec. 13, 20, 27, 1975). Like Stein, *TV Guide* continued to believe that PBS was badly needed. But it also helped fix in the public mind the idea that the network sometimes produced pinkish propaganda.

TV Guide's assumption of bias, or at the very least, a marriage of convenience between America-bashing demonstrators and liberal journalists, was evident as well in articles on major network news stories. Usually written by Neil Hickey, the New York bureau chief—and "lefty" to Edith Efron's "righty"—these pieces assessed coverage of an incident or controversy. Hickey wrote informative, balanced essays, but he too bowed to *TV Guide*'s tendencies. "Has the press—many of whom are liberals—been hostile to you in recent years?" he asked Bob Hope (Jan. 19, 1974). He began a four-part series on the occupation of Wounded

Knee by American Indians with a reference to the collusion "witting or unwitting," between network news and "minority groups, special pleaders, publicity seekers and kooks who have mastered the art of . . . grasping public attention by proffering to television an offer of blood and pageantry it can't refuse." Actually, although he believed that some reporters crossed the line between news and commentary, Hickey concluded that television journalists, on the whole, acquitted themselves rather well. But the titles chosen at Radnor for each article in the series belied this assessment: Part 2 announced "Only the Sensational Stuff Got on the Air," and Part 3 sneered "Cameras Over Here! And Be Sure to Shoot My Good Side" (Dec. 1, 8, 15, 22, 1973).

A four-part series on television coverage of unrest on the nation's campuses reveals the same tension. Hickey did discover that television reporters were often reluctant to criticize protesters for fear of appearing illiberal, even though many of them had been "beaten up, threatened and reviled by youthful activities." But he also pointed out that the journalists, blasted by conservatives as well, struggled for balanced coverage of the campus. The plaintive plea of a news director in Columbus, Ohio, clearly elicited Hickey's sympathy: "We don't know what the hell the truth is." Again, however, Radnor's titles for a series, ostensibly critical of sensationalism, succumbed to it after all: "Television Opens Its Eyes Only to Violence. So say campus leaders, who wonder where the cameras are when all is quiet" (Part 1); "It's Show Biz All the Way. Some students feel that TV often reduces their problems to the level of a shoot-out on Gunsmoke" (Jan. 30, Feb. 6, 13, 20, 1971).

In essence, *TV Guide* provided evidence of the tendency of television to distort reality—by emphasizing the visual and the dramatic—and implied that this constituted evidence of bias because the left attracted the cameras and the liberals worked at the networks. Whether the collusion was "witting or unwitting" made a significant difference in theory but not in fact, and the magazine did not directly confront the intentions of network news personnel. It was bad enough to conclude, as *TV Guide* had, that television often reflected and reinforced the polarizing, radical tendencies of the sixties.

In its determination to destroy the unholy alliance between TV and the left, *TV Guide* lost sight of the relationship between the magazine's own political perspective and its critique of the news. Like Spiro Agnew, *TV Guide* believed that America was out of focus because the TV generation was spoiled, passive, and cynical. Liberal modernists did not provide a diet adequate to the national "appetite for affirmation," as Edith Efron put it (Apr. 18, 1970); on the nightly news, viewers saw dissatisfied, sometimes violent people and rarely the splendid "squares" who made America great at blood banks or American Legion halls (Oct. 23, 1971). The result was a loss of political will.

The war in Vietnam, *TV Guide* now implied, was being lost because American liberals were easily disillusioned. With Richard Nixon in the White House, moreover, Walter Annenberg's support of the war became personal and partisan, as well as principled. In the magazine *Extra!* (Sept./Oct. 1988) Robert Ranftel claimed to have uncovered a White House document revealing that Annenberg indicated to the president that he was willing to use his magazine to help swing public opinion behind the policies of the administration. If it happened at all, however, it came in the form of disdain for antiwar protesters and their weak-kneed liberal fellow travelers. Distortion and bias were conflated in the magazine, we believe, because television seemed to Annenberg and Panitt a quintessentially liberal medium, substituting artificial pain for real hardship and habituating viewers to inertia and a short attention span. Thus, according to Joyce Maynard, those who grew up with TV quickly lost interest in the Vietnam conflict; the antiwar movement was little more than a collective cry to change the channel (July 5, 1975). This impatience, Edward Jay Epstein agreed, conditioned Americans to react to the apparent chaos of the Tet offensive by wishing to cut and run. If in the fifties and early sixties Americans swallowed the government's projections of national progress and power, more recently they jumped to the equally hyperbolic conclusion that the foreign policy of the United States was not only disastrous but deplorable (Sept. 29, Oct. 5, 13, 1973).

"If Network News Had Covered the Revolution," *TV Guide* speculated in a thinly disguised epitaph for the war in Vietnam, correspondents would have deplored the savage campaign against the loyalists, scorned the sell-out of freedom in an alliance with the French, and pounced on the performance of the army. As television uncovered the consternation of colonial citizens with congressional opposition to British overtures of peace, an interview with Benedict Arnold, a true patriot, might tip the scales in favor of negotiations, leading to the creation of the United American Provinces with dominion status (June 28, 1975). Unnerved by the rampant nay-saying in the nation, *TV Guide* lashed out against the network news, the magazine's stand-in for the decadent tendencies of liberalism in the modern age. The United States could survive the loss of Vietnam, but with the Soviet Union ready to exploit the slightest sign of weakness, the nation must recover its will, or the American Century would end three decades ahead of schedule.

So clear and present was the danger that "As We See It" abandoned its anxiety that criticism by politicians might presage regulation or discourage free and unfettered speech. At one time convinced that Spiro Agnew was not the right man to take on the networks, Panitt now concluded, in the summer of 1971, that a refusal by the FCC to renew the license of a station criticized by the vice president was "certainly not very likely" (June 26, 1971). The editor found a perverse reason to be pleased that the refusal of the president of CBS, Frank Stanton, to reveal the sources of "The Selling of the Pentagon" did not reach the Supreme Court. When the House of Representatives decided not to cite Stanton for contempt, television retained its freedom, yet Congress "still [had] its club." (Aug. 14, 1971). Presumably, but for vigilant and vocal news watchers, the news everyone watched would be one-sided and hypercritical of the United States.

In 1974 Walter Annenberg directed Merrill Panitt to launch a weekly column called "News Watch," to combat the liberal bias of the networks. For *TV Guide*, which advertised itself as authoritative but not authoritarian, "News Watch" was an unprecedented undertaking, a partisan, polemical voice certain to cause controversy. Nonetheless, the publisher insisted on going ahead with the project. His friend Richard Nixon, deeply implicated in the cover-up of the Watergate break-in, was battling for his political life against, as he saw it, a hostile liberal press corps. The administration and the media, wrote speech writer Patrick Buchanan (the author of Agnew's attack on TV news) to the president late in 1972, are "like cobra and mongoose." The future of the nation depended on the end of the monopoly control over communication of this "small ideological clique. . . . This is not a question of free speech, or free press—it is a basic question of power." A year later, of course, the situation was even more urgent, and Annenberg acted. Since he had sold *The Philadelphia Inquirer,* his only remaining editorial platform was *TV Guide,* but because the magazine was so close to the source of the problem, electronic journalism, it must have seemed oddly appropriate.

The columnists selected by Annenberg and Panitt left no doubt about the political perspective of "News Watch": Patrick Buchanan, speech writer for the Nixon administration, who was among the most unremitting foes of television journalism in the United States; John D. Lofton, Jr., former editor of the Republican magazine *Monday* (Lofton disappeared from *TV Guide* after a few months when someone spotted his "News Watch" column reprinted in another publication without permission from Radnor); Edith Efron, who had left *TV Guide* in the early seventies and was the author of *The News Twisters,* a polemical account of the monopoly power of the "elitist-liberal-left" in network news operations; Kevin Phillips, author of *The Emerging Republican Majority,* a treatise urging Republican candidates to woo white, suburban, middle-class voters and ignore minorities and unions; and John P. Roche, a one-time liberal who had worked in the Johnson White House and was well on his way in a political odyssey that would carry him to William F. Buckley's *National Review.* Although Roche found the notion that he would provide "balance to anything . . . delightful," everyone else we talked to thought it clear he had been tapped as the token liberal of the group to provide the illusion that "News Watch" did not stack the political deck. Merrill Panitt set no ideological guidelines, insisting only on good writing on a pressing issue, but he didn't have to: "News Watch" was a manifesto of the right.

On February 23, 1974, "News Watch" made its debut in *TV Guide* with Patrick Buchanan's assault on the "tiny clique of like-minded men" who had a monopoly over the flow of information. By their own admission, he charged, network newsmen "accelerated the civil rights revolution and turned the American home front against a war in which half a million American troops were engaged. That is power." During the sixties they abandoned all pretense to neutrality and donned the more stylish robes of "pleader, partisan and advocate," thereby, Buchanan concluded, forfeiting any claim of the public respect their predecessors enjoyed (Feb. 23, 1974).

John Roche followed with the same theme in a different wrapper. Conservatives "should cheer," he wrote, because "in creating the myth that the United States was tottering on the abyss of Revolution" and showing "hairy slobs . . . burning the American flag, and shrieking obscene imprecations at police," TV news had helped destroy the Democrats. At Chicago in 1968 electronic journalists had sympathized with protesters as "our children," conveniently forgetting that "the police, too, had parents," and voters deserted Humphrey because they thought "he was going to take this zoo with him wherever he went" (Mar. 9, 1974).

Staff members at *TV Guide* told us that they were embarrassed by the polemical pieces in "News Watch," which seemed out of place in the magazine, but they knew that Walter Annenberg could not be dissuaded. Assertions in *Time* and the *New Yorker* that the column lacked balance met with a sharp rejoinder in "As We See It." For these publications "to waggle an admonishing finger" amused Panitt, who wondered whether *TV Guide* would have been admonished had "News Watch" been "packed with liberals." No one who wrote for the column, the editor assured critics, would be "required to take an oath of allegiance to the White House" (Apr. 20, 1974).

To demonstrate this freedom of opinion Panitt did occasionally invite a guest columnist to attack the attackers. Thus Lesley Hall, a reporter from Scotland, praised network news in the United States as "bright, bold and occasionally brash, holding a mirror to society," blemishes, warts, and all (June 29, 1974), and John Chancellor pleaded "Don't Beat the Messenger" (Mar. 8, 1975). To this window dressing Panitt added several editorials taking mild issue with his columnists. When Kevin Phillips opposed an hour-long format for the nightly news because it would give liberals the power "to destroy politicians, parties and even entire industries" (May 18, 1974), Panitt agreed in "As We See It" that bias must be guarded against, but he endorsed the increased length, given television's "unique" ability to inform (May 18, 1974). And when Buchanan suggested that the American Security Council should have punished CBS for violating the FCC Fairness Doctrine in reporting national security issues by forcing the network to surrender the broadcasting license of one of its stations, Panitt gently admonished him: "We are certain Buchanan would have seen the unfairness of that suggestion, the overkill, if we had brought it to his attention" (Nov. 27, 1976). Of course, Panitt was making distinctions without much difference, for in essence the columnists and the editor agreed about bias in the news. On this subject, none of them needed to take an oath of allegiance to the White House, and the columnists themselves were even less inclined to backtrack. John Roche bristled at the suggestion that he had been told what to say in his column (June 15, 1974), and Kevin Phillips explained that his essays were always negative because few people had grappled with the "self-righteous monopoly" over the news. Only *TV Guide* and *Reader's Digest,* "another mass periodical with roots in Middle America," had the courage to be tough-minded: "So I think I'll leave the encomiums to the house organs of the Liberal Establishment" (Mar. 30, 1974).

Documenting liberal bias, it turned out, meant advancing a right-wing analysis of the promise and problems of the United States. "News Watch" columns covered a wide range of contemporary issues. A brief sample suggests the content and the tone of the articles: (1) Networks propagate the myth that "a bloated Pentagon gorges itself at the public trough." If a military crisis occurs, the American people will remember "who lulled them to sleep" (Buchanan, May 25, 1974). (2) Newsmen "orchestrate" doubts about whether the oil shortage is real. Why don't they expose "the war led by the Save-the-Fishies groups against the building of nuclear energy plants," our only hope for energy independence, as a witch-hunt conducted by "Doomsday and Dead Planet hysterics?" (Efron, Mar. 23, 1974). (3) Where are the documentaries explaining that we hung "weak instead of tough in Vietnam" because politicians paid more attention to the Harvard faculty and the *New York Times* than "to the reports of soldiers up to their hips in the mud and leeches of Asian War?" When will the small screen show "the sleek crowd" at the Academy Awards applauding the Vietcong "and then flash to a shot of bloody refugee bodies?" (Phillips, May 3, 1975).

In 1975 Edith Efron conducted a "little experiment," inducing herself into a state of temporary ignorance of current events by ceasing to read newspapers and relying totally on the tube for information about American political life. Her list of the ideas that left the strongest impact (ideas that constituted the leftist agenda of TV journalism) was a veritable platform on which "News Watch" could stand.

1. America is an invisible police state.

2. American industry is a lethal institution . . . poisoning our air, our water, our soil.

3. Big businessmen are cheats, liars and bribers. . . . Their profits are gigantic, their greed not less.

4. Americans in huge numbers are starving to death . . . The President and his top advisers want to take food stamps away from the poor and hungry, and to prevent little children from eating lunches.

5. American race prejudice keeps growing worse. . . .

6. Prisoners are atrociously treated. . . . They just need therapy and freedom to become good citizens.

7. New York City has been so enlightened and so compassionate to its poor that it has overspent its budget and has gone broke.

8. America and the Pentagon are major threats to world peace. Most other countries in the world hate America.

9. The world today is full of newly formed "socialist republics." That, by definition, is progress.

10. Communist China is a magnificent country. Its political system works well and its people are fully employed, dedicated and happy.

11. Communist Cuba is a magnificent country. Its political system works well and its people are fully employed, dedicated and happy.

12. Communist Russia is eager for detente and America is spoiling detente.

13. For years—possibly always—the Cold War has been a phony, invented by America.

14. A lot of the South Vietnamese who ran from the Hanoi communists are now running away from the United States. They will be far happier under the communists.

Efron acknowledged that her survey was subjective and that the sources of these ideas were "mainly not reporters," but Hollywood stars, panel show guests, politicians, and intellectuals. Her hyperbole, if indeed she saw it as hyperbole, was actually directed at television and American culture in general, even though her conclusion warned readers of the "real danger that they will end up hating either their own country or the broadcasters who are presenting this image of America and the world" (Nov. 8, 1975).

Watergate presented a challenge to "News Watch." With the exception of John Roche, the columnists thought congressional investigations of the break-in and the aftermath part of a vendetta against Richard Nixon orchestrated by the liberal establishment. Indeed, at first they made the charges against the president a test case of news bias. As the evidence against Nixon mounted, however, they began to denounce the networks for implying that his misdeeds were a unique, unprecedented evil in American politics. Many reporters were Democratic "shills," Edith Efron fumed. They were self-appointed "moral cleansing agents of the Republic," who, in a stroke, sought to wipe out the results of the presidential election of 1972 by endorsing calls for the president's resignation while failing to inform viewers that previous administrations had been no more pure than Nixon's (May 11, 1974).

Still, "News Watch" feared that the case for media bias might rise or fall, for most people, on the basic veracity of the Watergate allegations. When the scandal "turned out to be more or less as charged," Kevin Phillips sighed, criticism of bias died down. In an attempt to rekindle the fires of public passion, Phillips claimed that "by harping— and harping—and harping" on Watergate, electronic journalists proved how partisan they were. He took solace in the fact that fewer people watched the nightly news and switched his attention to the "vicious antibusiness distortion" of TV journalists and their advocacy of welfare and busing. But he sensed that the "Lords of the Screen" had won after all. In focusing on Ford's folksiness and exchanging "their vials of sulfuric acid for cool pitchers of cream," they satisfied the public demand for quieter times. When Phillips asked "What will Dan Rather do without a popular President to belittle?" he might well have wondered what a News Watcher would do when the press was lying low (July 13, Aug. 24, 1974).

Sounding equally defensive, Edith Efron called the celebration over the death of bias premature. The Watergate "facts," she admitted, did not demonstrate network bias, but the nightly news did not provide "contextual interpretations that were generous" to the president. Although Efron continued to complain about how "unbridled Nixon hatred dominated" news coverage, she sounded a bit more resigned:

bias "has always been with us and it will continue to be with us" (Sept. 21, Dec. 21, 1974).

Characteristically, Patrick Buchanan barely skipped a beat when Richard Nixon resigned. He blamed the press's "thirst for vengeance" for the dramatic drop in Gerald Ford's popularity after he pardoned the former president. At President Ford's press conference, Buchanan pointed out, sixteen questioners addressed his decision, while two concerned themselves with the rest of the world. Although at present the networks dictated "almost unilaterally which issues dominated the public agenda" and the timid new president "sued for peace with the press," the unreconstructed Buchanan defiantly predicted that some day history would judge the pardon "courageous, magnanimous and wise" (Oct. 12, 1974; Jan. 11, 1975).

Nonetheless, "News Watch" had lost its reason for being. By 1975 the sixties era was over, American troops were out of Vietnam, black militants had been muffled, and the press concerned itself with Gerry Ford's breakfast food. "News Watch" soldiered on for three more years, but more and more the column strained and stretched in the search for damning evidence. Jimmy Carter led the "new left," Edith Efron told her readers (Oct. 8, 1977). Eric Sevareid, the dovish supporter of Hubert Humphrey and civil rights, was called a conservative, she explained, because the "whole spectrum of reporting today is so violently anti-Establishment that anyone who attempts to set the facts out becomes [known as] an apologist" (Jan. 7, 1978).

When topics failed to suggest themselves, the columnists attacked each other. John Roche went after Patrick Buchanan for "overkill" in his excoriation of CBS newsman Daniel Schorr (Apr. 3, 1976), and Buchanan lobbed a gratuitous grenade at all of his colleagues: "Now, I have yet to figure out Sister Efron's ideology; it lies somewhere between Ayn Rand and La Passionara. As for Brother Roche, he ran for a time a generally subversive outfit called Americans for Democratic Action, which should have graced the Attorney General's list, even it if never earned the honor. Brother Phillips is less right-wing ideologue than radical populist. When the Revolution comes, you will probably find him putting the torch to the Burning Tree Country Club" (Sept. 4, 1976).

Perhaps in desperation, Walter Annenberg raced to the rescue by writing several columns himself, though he often forgot that he was supposed to monitor the media, not preach about politics. In the fall of 1976 he listed the major issues of the campaign in what sounded like a summary of the Republican party platform: inflationary government spending, alarming intrusions of government into private enterprise that raised prices and discouraged initiative, and "the shocking conduct of municipal employees, many of them affiliated with national labor unions" (Oct. 23, 1976). Annenberg stopped short of saying Ford was a better idea, but his sympathies were clear. The next year he warned that the United States should not make itself vulnerable by placing its oil pipeline in Canada "under what amounts to foreign control" (May 14, 1977).

It may have been a guest column by Marvin Kitman that finally persuaded Annenberg to pull the plug on "News Watch," in what seemed to *TV Guide* staffers as a mercy killing. "Why Do They Keep Asking the Man in the Street?" Kitman asked, not hilariously. "If he had any brains he wouldn't be in the street, walking. He'd be in a limousine, being driven home" (Mar. 25, 1978). Less than three months later, "As We See It" delivered the eulogy: "News Watch" had been dropped, Merrill Panitt explained, because television news programs had not changed noticeably since the feature had been inaugurated four years earlier. Because news documentaries had declined in number, moreover, writers had been forced to stray from the original purpose of the column: "Frequently 'News Watch' became political commentary with, at best, only a tenuous connection to television news" (June 10, 1978).

It is probably true that "News Watch" did not change the network news. By 1974 the campaign against the media that had been spearheaded by Spiro Agnew had already achieved substantial success, and throughout the seventies and eighties electronic journalists moved to the right, along with much of the rest of the country. That they would have done so without the prodding of *TV Guide* is undeniable, but clearly the assault against them, in which "News Watch" had played a bit part, had hurried them along. This time, Panitt may have been too modest in "As We See It": electronic journalists *were* more defensive, more apt to pull their punches, than they had been a few years earlier.

Although "News Watch" was dead, the politicization of *TV Guide* continued in the form of "Commentary" essays, often written by Walter Annenberg or his friend, Robert Strausz-Hupé, former ambassador to Ceylon, Belgium, and Sweden, who had once been the permanent representative of the United States at NATO. In the seventies Annenberg worried about the political and social costs of the "me decade" mentality when members of Congress proved more interested in reelection than energy policy, labor leaders broke wage-price guidelines, and nuclear demonstrators closed down plants without offering alternative fuel sources. "Freedom always carries the seeds of its own destruction," he fretted (June 16, 1979). With the election of Ronald Reagan, Annenberg bounced back, celebrating Disney's Epcot Center as a "reaffirmation of our faith in ourselves and our country" (Nov. 13, 1983), and endorsing the president's bid for reelection, the only election recommendation ever made in *TV Guide:* "I cannot refrain from speaking up when the result of this election is so critical to the future of the nation" (Oct. 6, 1984).

Strausz-Hupé became the magazine's resident anticommunist in the late seventies. Throughout the sixties, of course, *TV Guide* had remained vigilant about the military threat of the Soviet Union, especially when a Democrat was in the White House. When Soviet-American relations began to thaw in 1968 and Lyndon Johnson met Alexei Kosygin at Glassboro State College in New Jersey, for example, Edith Efron showed how the Russians manufactured "a paranoid hatred of the U.S." among its people by focusing on "belly-bloated Negro babies and tin shanties" and imperialism in Vietnam. Among Soviet leaders, she concluded, "there's nothing very mutual" in the talk of understanding. "In the USSR we are the Enemy" (Jan. 13, 1968). With Republicans Nixon and Ford in the White House discussing detente, such militant rhetoric disappeared from *TV Guide,* only to return when Jimmy Carter became president.

Convinced that "the cancer of deceit has eaten into the very marrow of the Soviet body politic," Strausz-Hupé saw himself as a modern Paul Revere, warning his countrymen that the Russians might soon be coming. In articles touching only tangentially on television, he fought against the SALT agreements negotiated by the Carter administration, with redbaiting rhetoric reminiscent of the fifties. In three essays in the fall of 1978, for example, he deemed the Soviet military build-up the greatest threat to Western democracies in history; cast doubt on the wit and nerve of the United States and its allies to fight "wars of liberation"; denounced pro-SALT arguments as "simplistic," made in a political vacuum, oblivious to the fact that the internal political system of the Soviet Union made on-sight verification impossible; and advocated a cessation of trade with the Soviets. Strausz-Hupé supported a strong American defense no matter what the cost. Most important, given Leonid Brezhnev's attempt to condition the collective psychology of the NATO countries, he sought to awaken "that universal indignation that Soviet behavior should arouse in all moral men and women. Indignation that merely sputters is a confession of impotence" (Sept. 16, Oct. 28, Nov. 11, 1978).

"Commentary" articles continued until Walter Annenberg no longer owned *TV Guide.* But, in a sense, the screeds of Robert Strausz-Hupé allowed "News Watch" to go out not with a whimper but a bang.

In many ways, *TV Guide*'s emphasis on bias between 1969 ad 1975 was an aberration, a response to the political polarization of the period and the assaults of Nixon and Agnew. Although "News Watch" staggered on into 1978, the magazine had long since returned in its coverage of the news to a concern with distortion and superficiality, the twin dangers of a visual mass medium. In a two-part series, "How Networks Choose the News," for example, Eric Levin did not even examine the possibility that political bias played a role (July 2, 9, 1977). *TV Guide* had returned to normalcy.

Like Merrill Panitt, David Sendler was interested in how news stories were selected and edited and in what viewers of the nightly news actually saw. To monitor the news Sendler often called on Professor Edwin Diamond of the Massachusetts Institute of Technology, and later New York University. Diamond's already-assembled research team provided an inexpensive source of labor, and his academic appointments lent authority to his articles. Sendler sought to make readers more "skeptical" of news broadcasts, he told us, and Diamond helped by showing how the complexity of stories, superficiality of coverage, limits of time, and dependence on official sources contributed to the Rashomon Effect of television news. More often than not, viewers found on the screen confirmation of their own existing interpretation of events (Feb. 27, 1982).

In more than a dozen articles Diamond's News Study Group identified the biggest obstacle to in-depth news as the propensity of the networks to provide dramatic pictures and stick to familiar themes. For example, when TV news covered a visit by Andrei Gromyko to the United States, ceremonial images rather than the negotiations themselves dominated the news coverage (Jan. 12, 1985). When crack was a hot topic, the study group observed, black tar was not, because the former affected middle-class neighborhoods, while the latter remained a scourge only in the ghetto (Feb. 7, 1987). Worst of all, according to Diamond, was the network decision to leave serious documentaries to PBS and offer, instead, a "grubby new form," exemplified by "Scared Sexless," an NBC "News Report on America," featuring as "experts" Alan Alda and Goldie Hawn, both with movies to plug. With a 17.5 rating and a 30 share, "Scared Sexless" would no doubt spawn many successors, while the dwindling number of serious documentaries produced by the networks would continue to be scheduled opposite the Oscars and the Emmys (Aug. 27, 1988). But when they went in search of "Where the Bias Is" in network reporting, the Diamond Group failed to get very exercised about subjective tendencies that they believed were inherent in all journalism (July 7, 1984).

Along with Diamond, John Weisman, the head of *TV Guide's* Washington bureau, kept his eye on the news. While pointing out that 67 percent of Americans got most of their information about current events from television, Weisman hammered away at the superficiality of the medium: the networks committed more money to photographing the story than investigating it (Mar. 1, 1980); personality was paramount in accounts of political campaigns (July 5, 1980); few local anchors did well on the current affairs test administered by *TV Guide* (Nov. 22, 1986); and the switch to "infotainment" on the news revealed that the networks cared more about profit than journalism (Oct. 25, 1985).

Bias was no longer *TV Guide's* red flag: although Weisman often showed how television "missed the picture," he did not blame bias at the networks. In an examination of coverage of the energy crisis, for example, Weisman alerted readers to the excessive reliance of television journalists on government officials. Reporters accepted the view that conservation and rationing, not increasing domestic oil production, were likely solutions. In Weisman's opinion, the price controls imposed by President Nixon were "largely responsible" for the energy crisis because they preempted the market as a means to regulate demand. Whether one agreed with this analysis or not, he concluded, was not the point: TV had missed an important element of one of the major stories of the decade (Mar. 6, 1982). An article on the thin coverage of South America two years later indicted the networks for ignoring upheaval on the continent until there were bodies to photograph (Sept. 15, 1984). (Joanmarie Kalter made the same point about coverage of Africa. No network had a bureau on this continent, which never received coverage on the nightly news until famine and drought threatened hundreds of thousands of lives; May 24, 1986.)

Even when bias appeared to be a plausible explanation, Weisman avoided or repudiated it. Bias was not the reason the networks failed to inform viewers that Genady Gerasimov and Vladimer Posner were employees of the Soviet government, providing official points of view in their "commentaries" on television (Apr. 26, 1986). Nor was it the reason CBS News cast the Reagan administration in a negative light in a proportion of more than seven to one. Although White House officials branded the network and Dan Rather as implacable enemies, Weisman thought they confused the aggressiveness of adversarial journalism with ideological or even personal bias (Aug. 27, 1983).

Often very critical of television news, John Weisman nevertheless concluded in 1983 that the networks were "honest brokers," performing a public service while buffeted by criticism from the left and the right (Nov. 26, 1983). Such praise was rare in *TV Guide* in the eighties.

More often, writers in the magazine deplored the "abuse of the (melo)dramatic potential" of television through the "ambush interview," the "scam of the week" (Oct. 10, 1981), the anchor as "omnipresent truth teller" (Apr. 16, 1988), and the search for "soft" news stories (Mar. 5, 1988). But they emphasized that behind these changes was, as Liz Trotta put it, "an unspoken but pervasive contempt for the public" at the networks (Feb. 27, 1988). *TV Guide's* tradition of dialsmanship made it reluctant to agree that most viewers favored fluff, although the editors did run a piece by humorist Mark Russell, "News in the Year 2000," which foresaw as staples of the nightly news chili cooking, quilting bees, and national pickled okra, while only a few senior citizens remained to watch MacNeil/Lehrer (Sept. 6, 1986). But the magazine often implied that electronic journalists were simply giving people what they wanted. In 1988 staff writer Rod Townley began an analysis of Sunday interview shows by revealing that *TV Guide's* editors had asked him to look for bias. He didn't find it. Panelists on these programs were ready to "shoot anything that moves," and "a dab of blood may occasionally be drawn, a fang bared," but Townley could not find anyone promoting a political agenda (Jan. 2, 1988). In the eighties, then, the magazine looked critically at the news but had found more neutral political ground on which to stand.

Indeed, one could even find in *TV Guide* encomiums for leading members of the "News Watch" hit list. Although David Shaw found television news "infuriatingly superficial, relentlessly shallow, childishly theatrical, and utterly predictable," he thought that Dan Rather was doing "pretty damn well" as CBS anchor. Under his direction the nightly news carried more stories of longer length, offered more coverage of social issues, and featured more investigative reporting (Feb. 19, 1983). Larry L. King attributed the sameness of the news not to leftist bias, but to pack journalistic instincts, and he singled out Bill Moyers and John Chancellor, along with George Will, as noteworthy exceptions (Jan. 25, 1986). Norman Ornstein and Michael Robinson concluded that as it covered Congress, television slighted Democrats, not Republicans. To them, the documentaries of Bill Moyers looked "more like old-fashioned watchdog journalism than liberal bias" (Jan. 11, 1986).

Of course the conservatism of *TV Guide* did not disappear during the eighties, though it was mostly ghettoized in occasional "Commentary" pieces, many of them written by Walter Annenberg himself. The owner still fulminated against the networks for naively believing that communists could be "contained by words, by diplomacy, by sweet reason" (Apr. 16, 1983). He still disliked a press with power but no responsibility, making it difficult for President Reagan to govern by airing "gratuitously pessimistic reports" on the economy. As long as TV reporters questioned the motives of American leaders, the president had to support disastrous policies: "increase welfare rather than emphasize private sector job programs, continue to increase taxes, continue to permit the Soviets to maintain nuclear superiority in Europe and extend their influence in our hemisphere" (May 15, 1982). And Annenberg condemned "Political Bias in the Name of High-Sounding Goals" in a blast at PBS's presentation of Ali Mazrui's controversial "The Africans" (Dec. 13, 1986).

Merrill Panitt contributed a piece or two in this vein as well. In a "Commentary" he cited studies showing TV's antiestablishment bias and its tendency to leave viewers "confused and cynical" (Nov. 26, 1983). And in "As We See It" he concluded that ABC "went through the motions of being objective" in a special on J. Edgar Hoover, then charged the former director of the FBI with authorizing illegal counterintelligence, wire-tapping Martin Luther King, and failing to hire minorities in the FBI. Citing Hoover's service to eight presidents, Panitt remembered him as a man with honesty and integrity who "deserved better than to have his name besmirched 10 years after his death" (Oct. 23, 1982). The size of *TV Guide*'s audience, as well as Walter Annenberg's connections, enabled the editors to assemble a distinguished conservative "Commentary" cast in the eighties, including Alexander Haig, Arkady Schevchenko, and Charles Wick. The magazine even publicized the plan of two recent Harvard M.B.A.'s to enhance the prestige of businessmen through TV shows like "That's Deductible" and "Wall Street Blues" (Jan. 15, 1983). But, it is important to add, alongside these articles were essays by liberals like David Halberstam and Philip Caputo on the Vietnam War. If the magazine was guiding TV and its readers to the right, as some critics have charged, it was far more subtle in the eighties. The times were no longer conducive to less.

David Sendler also pushed his staff toward investigative journalism. He hoped *TV Guide* could break a story or two, rather than simply analyze the news on the small screen. In 1982 the magazine attracted national attention for the first time by publishing its most influential article, an indictment of CBS News that provided evidence of liberal bias at the network. "Anatomy of a Smear: How CBS 'Got' General Westmoreland" (May 29, 1982), originated with a phone call from a CBS employee to staff writer Don Kowet, who eventually obtained transcripts of all the interviews conducted for the documentary "The Uncounted Enemy: A Vietnam Deception." Written by George Crile and narrated by Mike Wallace, the documentary charged that General William Westmoreland had intentionally underestimated Vietcong troop strength in the months before the Tet offensive. Crile and his colleagues, Kowet and coauthor Sally Bedell noted, entered the project with a preconceived notion of what their conclusion would be. Contradictory testimony found its way to the cutting-room floor. Crile set up screenings for sympathetic witnesses so they could evaluate the testimony of others and perhaps alter their own. Kowet and Bedell leveled eighteen indictments at CBS, including hiring former CIA analyst Sam Adams as a "consultant" when he was the key witness in the documentary, yanking quotations out of context, and editing out General Westmoreland's explanation. Taking care to explain that they were taking no position on the alleged conspiracy to suppress troop estimates, the authors claimed that Crile and Company had been arbitrary and unfair in their "documentary" presentation.

"Anatomy of a Smear" stunned CBS. The president of CBS News, Van Gordon Sauter, immediately announced an investigation, to be directed by producer Burton Benjamin. A summary of Benjamin's report, issued on July 8, 1982, acknowledged serious violations of the network's guidelines for documentaries and recommended that henceforth a new vice president be appointed to check all broadcasts and enforce new rules adopted as a result of the investigation. The print media, finding it hard to swallow that *TV Guide* had broken so important a story, cautiously supported CBS and cast doubt on the magazine's methods and motives. *Time* snickered at *TV Guide*'s attempt to "introduce a brand of muckraking" to a weekly that had long been "known as something of a cheerleader for the industry" (Feb. 21, 1983). In *Newsweek* Charles Kaiser suggested that with the transcripts in front of them, Kowet and Bedell had merely second-guessed every editing decision Crile had made. Kaiser took issue with *TV Guide*'s use of the word "smear" and gratuitously added that the magazine had little experience with investigative journalism. Finally, pointing to Walter Annenberg's conservative politics, Kaiser asserted that *TV Guide* was "not an entirely neutral forum" (June 14, 1982).

But the fire was not so easy to put out. As Marvin Kitman quipped in *The New Leader:* "CBS found itself innocent of the charges—and pledged not to do it again" (Aug. 9–23, 1982). Eventually William Westmoreland filed a $120 million suit against CBS for libel that was settled years later out of court. But clearly the CBS eye had been blackened by "Anatomy of a Smear," which stood up well to scrutiny. It may well be that the the informant at CBS approached *TV Guide* calculating that Walter Annenberg's politics and antipathy to the network would guarantee a sympathetic hearing. But the article, as we have seen, did not lead to a renewal of partisanship in *TV Guide,* nor did "Anatomy of a

Smear" breathe new life into the theme of bias that had preoccupied the magazine in the early seventies. The prestige that came with the piece (which won the Distinguished Service Award for magazine reporting from Sigma Delta Chi, the society of professional journalists) may well have had a moderating effect on the magazine. To renew the crusade against liberal bias without convincing new evidence would confirm allegations that "Anatomy of a Smear" was politically motivated. And no one, we suppose, wanted to suffer again the ridicule that had come with "News Watch." Sendler tried to break more stories in *TV Guide,* assigning a staff member to investigate terrorism, for example, but investigative reporting required enormous staff time and money, as well as a quicker publication turn-around than *TV Guide* could provide. Merrill Panitt and David Sendler were justifiably proud of "Anatomy of a Smear" but recognized it was unlikely to be repeated for a long time.

When Rupert Murdoch told the editors of *TV Guide* that the magazine was "too cerebral," he almost certainly meant to include in-depth analysis of the news. Shortly after his 1988 takeover, R. C. Smith told the *Columbia Journalism Review,* the Murdochians began "slowly squeezing out the kind of story we would make our lead—media-monitoring stories. Murdoch thinks that's boring, sleepy journalism" (Nov./Dec., 1989). Gone was the News Study Group of Edwin Diamond. Gone by July 1989 was John Weisman, with a blast at the Murdoch love affair with froth. *TV Guide,* significantly, did not cover ABC News's use of a simulation of an alleged spy giving a briefcase to a Soviet agent without informing viewers. Asked why, editor David Sendler explained (not very convincingly) that the magazine's deadlines made it difficult to deliver a piece while the controversy was in the headlines: "We would have had to find a second-day angle and we didn't have one" (*Columbia Journalism Review,* Nov./Dec. 1989). It was undeniable, however, that the number and length of stories on news and public affairs had slowed to a trickle. In the 1990s *TV Guide* covered the news as it covered entertainment, with articles like "Can NBC Break Its News Magazine Hex?" by Monica Collins, the resident Hollywood columnist (some might say gossip columnist) (June 23, 1990), and cover stories like "Sam Donaldson: 'Why I couldn't bring myself to slap Diane [Sawyer] across the chops' " (Aug. 18, 1990).

Coverage of the war in the Persian Gulf is a case in point. Slow to address a story that was changing while the magazine went to press, *TV Guide* entertained readers with "Tales from the Front: The Glitches and Hitches in Bringing the War to Your Living Room" (February 16, 1991).

The situation in Saudi Arabia was so chaotic, Lisa Stein reported, that shopping was almost out of the question for ABC producer Kathy O'Hearn, while CNN cameraman Mark Biello had to live on tuna fish, mayonnaise, and sweet-pickle relish. Only in the last paragraph of the article did Stein mention the tight Pentagon rein on television reporters. In the same vein, *TV Guide*'s cover story a week later was "TV's War Stars," which revealed that since he filed his first reports from the Gulf, "women have been going wild" over Arthur Kent of NBC, dubbed by newspapers, magazines, and Johnny Carson, the "Scud Stud."

There were, to be sure, a few more serious pieces on the war. In "America Rallies Round the TV Set" (February 16, 1991), Jeff Greenfield worried that in a crisis, the editorial function often collapses, and rumors reach the air. TV reporters and anchors, Greenfield advised, must learn to say "I don't know." And after the shooting stopped Neil Hickey mulled over the "Lessons from the Gulf War" in a typicallly intelligent, cautious piece. Any solution to the controversy over media pools and access to the front, he concluded, "will need to reflect the ancient, antithetical instincts of the media and the military" (April 6, 1991).

It took a war and a national obsession, we believe, to get the Hickey piece in a publication far more hospitable to scud studs. Even the failed coup in the Soviet Union in August 1991, where television played a vital role, received virtually no coverage in the magazine. In a sense, *TV Guide* was giving up on dialsmanship. It gave readers the "infotainment" in "grubby new forms" that it had complained about through much of the eighties. "Do You Give Viewers Good Journalism—or the Sensationalism They Prefer?" the magazine had asked the networks in 1988 (Dec. 17). By the 1990s, armed with an answer, they had surrendered to the superficial.

A Note on Sources

This book strongly relies on a careful reading of every article in *TV Guide* from its first issue, April 3, 1953, through the September 7, 1991, issue. In addition, we made an effort to contact men and women who had edited or written for the magazine. We conducted interviews with Edith Efron (July 24, 1989), William Marsano (June 19, 1989), Robert MacKenzie (May 30, 1989), Merrill Panitt (Dec. 21–22, 1989), Carolyn See (Nov. 11, 1988), David Sendler (Nov. 3, 1989), Robert Smith (Nov. 3, 1989), Dwight Whitney (May 31, June 1–2, 1989), and Roger Wood (Feb. 3, 1989). These conversations proved invaluable to an understanding of how *TV Guide* worked. When we have used quotations from these interviews, we have received permission to do so. Notes and tapes of the conversations are in our possession.

Also vital was correspondence with people connected to the magazine. We received letters from Richard Cook (July 28, 1989), Edith Efron (June 15, Aug. 7, Sept. 5, 12, 1989; Jan. 10, 27, Feb. 21, 1990), Larry Fritz (Aug. 13, 1988), Max Gunther (Aug. 8, 23, 1988), Arnold Hano (July 26, Aug. 15, 29, 1988), Dick Hobson (July 3, 13, 16, 17, Sept. 24, 1989; Feb. 15, 1990), Dan Jenkins (Aug. 30, Sept. 21, Oct. 3, 1989; Feb. 6, 1990), Martin Lewis (Sept. 27, 1989), William Marsano (Aug. 7, 29, Sept. 20, Oct. 1, 1989; Feb. 19, 1990), Tom McMorrow (July 29, 1988), Merrill Panitt (Mar. 24, 1990), Leslie Raddatz (July 26, Aug. 9, Oct. 12, 23, 1989; Mar. 5, 1990), John Roche (Aug. 4, 15, 1988), David Shaw (Aug. 17, 1988), William J. Slattery (Aug. 1, 1988), Roger Wood (Apr. 18, 1989), and Maurice Zolotow (Aug. 15, 1988). When we have used quotations from these letters, we have received permission to do so. All correspondence is in our possession.

Although the executives of *TV Guide* declined to allow us access to the editorial correspondence of the magazine, several of the people we contacted provided us with material from their own files. This correspondence helped us understand how articles originated and how they were shaped and changed.

Secondary sources for *TV Guide* are hard to find. We have examined the *New York Times, Time,* and *Business Week* for references to the magazine. To better understand Walter Annenberg we turned to John Cooney's book, *The Annenbergs* (New York, 1982). For information on *TV Guide*'s self-assessment we consulted a book commissioned by Triangle Publications, *TV Guide: A Study In Depth* (Radnor, Penn., 1960). Indispensable to us for comprehending the Murdoch era was Katharine Seelye's article on *TV Guide* in *Columbia Journalism Review* (Nov./Dec. 1989).

Our research was also made easier by two collections of *TV Guide* articles: *TV Guide Round-Up* (New York, 1960) and *TV Guide: The First 25 Years,* compiled and edited by Jay S. Harris (New York, 1978). Both volumes feature an introduction by Merrill Panitt.

Index